I'D GO BACK TOMORROW

First impression 2001
by Wayzgoose
Tatenhill Common
Staffordshire
Tel: 01283 713674
www.jmpearson.co.uk

Casebound ISBN 0 907864 88 0
Paperback ISBN 0 907864 89 9

A CIP catalogue entry for this book is available from the Britsh Library

Originated by Waterways World Ltd, Burton-on-Trent, Staffordshire
Printed by Information Press, Oxford

To John, Carol

Mike Lucas

best wishes

Mike Lucas

I'D GO BACK TOMORROW

Thirty Years of the
Mikron Theatre Company

Wayzgoose

This book is dedicated to the memory of Sarah (1943–1997)

Acknowledgements

I must thank all the people who have worked for Mikron and all our loyal supporters. Without them, we would not be entering our 30th year.

My thanks to my partner, Lynne, for helping to edit the text and checking my grammar and spelling, and for supporting me during the last period of the writing and in my search for a publisher. Thanks to Michael Pearson for being that publisher. Thanks also to Andrea for her computer skills.

CONTENTS

CONTENTS

1

THE IDEA

It's a hot summer's day in July 1997. I'm sitting at my desk in the upstairs room of my house in Marsden. The desk is by a window which looks down on to the Huddersfield Narrow Canal (this section restored and full of water; the whole canal, thanks to Lottery money, is due to re-open in 2001). On the other side of the canal stand the disused coal chutes which, in the heady days of railways (and coal-mines), would be busy every day discharging coal from railway wagons into Co-op lorries for distribution in the area. Now they are crumbling, dangerous and covered in graffiti.

And behind the chutes rise the hills – steep, irregularly-shaped stone-walled fields and perched on what appears to be the top of the hill is a farmhouse with splendid views down into the Colne Valley. But the top is an illusion, for, out of sight, are the moors rising to 1,700 feet before dropping down towards the Calder Valley and the towns of Todmorden and Halifax; the lonely moors populated by a few sheep, with just the occasional sound of curlew and grouse.

So different from the cosy comfort of canals – ribbons of water meandering their way round the countryside, with the differing delights of locks and lock-cottages, bridges, aqueducts, small towns and villages, and fields full of corn, barley and rape, and grazing cows and sheep.

The 1997 National Waterways Tour is underway. I can't help thinking about Richard, Ed, Vashti and Janet, making their way along the Coventry Canal for tonight's performance in Fazeley on the Birmingham & Fazeley Canal. I'm not with them at the moment. I shall be visiting them again shortly. But they are perfectly capable of running *Tyseley* and the performances on their own. Richard is in his fifth year with Mikron and is now tour co-ordinator. He runs a good "ship" and morale is high.

That is good. It has given me time to reflect on Mikron's past and also, more urgently, to endeavour to work out a scheme whereby Mikron can survive into the next millennium. Mikron is in financial crisis: our reserves are now virtually nil, funding is at rock-bottom and business sponsorship is almost impossible to find. These are hard times; Sarah, Mikron's co-founder, my wife, best friend and lover, has

1

died of breast cancer and I have to face these problems, not on my own, because I do have great friends and colleagues, but with the knowledge that, when "push comes to shove", the final responsibility of saving the Company rests with me.

So it would be very difficult for a 22-year-old Mike Lucas to imagine himself sitting here today in Marsden ("Where?" he would have said), facing all these problems and all as a result of a few friends deciding to take a show to the Edinburgh Festival in 1963.

I was at drama school (Webber Douglas); Danny (or Ron as he was called then) was at RADA; Sarah had given up her law degree course at LSE and was working for the social psychology research unit there. We asked Arnold Wesker if he had a play we could take to the Edinburgh Festival. He hadn't, but he recommended Charles Lewsen. Charles had a play called *The Bubonic Plague Show* – a satire about the danger of germ warfare. We liked it. We decided to take it to the Edinburgh Festival or rather the newish and growing Festival Fringe. We gathered together some like-minded actors who were doing their time at various drama schools and rehearsed the show in London before setting off for the glamour and excitement of Edinburgh. We even performed the show *en route* at John Arden and Margaretta D'Arcy's house at Kirbymoorside in North Yorkshire as part of their little arts festival. John was not convinced that the good people of Kirbymoorside would turn out for a play with such a bizarre title, so for the two performances in the village (yes, we had to do a second show as the house was crammed for the World Première) the show was known as *Love Among the Bugs*. I remember only two incidents from this play: one was where a character says to another, while negotiating about germ warfare: "I'll give you syphilis if you give me gonorrhoea"; the other was a great moment of theatre – Sarah's attempt and failure to sneeze while being drilled by me as a sort of sergeant-major on the right way to sneeze in order to spread disease. It may have been her last appearance on the world stage but what a piece of timing. Administration's gain was the performing arts' loss.

And what was that about the glamour of Edinburgh – we were all broke and we stayed in an empty house with a park bench for furniture – oh, and a cooker. We found a café that served a three course meal for 3/6d; so that suited our purses and meant we were able to afford to go to see some of the other and varied shows at the Festival. I remember a stunning production of Ionesco's *Exit the King* and the direst possible rendition of Lorca's *Blood Wedding* by Sheffield University Drama Society.

The name of this little company we took to Edinburgh was the Mikron Theatre Company – so-called because it was founded by *Mike* and *Ron* and Sarah Came*ron* and the word is Greek for small, and small we were and small, in the good sense of the word, we still are.

THE IDEA

So from this tiny but successful beginning (we were well reviewed in the *Scotsman*), we decided to keep the Company going on an ad-hoc basis. I graduated from drama school in 1964 and went straight into jobs in "rep" (repertory theatre), firstly at the end of the pier at Brighton performing a different play every week and then to the positive sophistication of the Manchester Library Theatre, where I spent nearly a year working underground (the theatre is in the basement) for £9 a week (above the Equity minimum, I may add) as an acting ASM (that is someone who does all the dirty work and occasionally is allowed to say a few lines). Some of my more exciting roles were the back-legs of a pantomime horse, a pirate, a sailor and a pterodactyl!

From there I went straight into *Crossroads* and *Dr Who*, followed by appearances in such BBC favourites as *The Dick Emery Show*, *The Frankie Howerd Show* and *The Liver Birds* – so, fortunately, I was kept busy enough forwarding my acting career that Mikron remained in the shadows for the time being.

In 1968, we put on a couple of productions at the Little Theatre in St Martin's Lane in London, one of which I had written myself, called *Dream Monster*. This theatre was innovative in that shows were put on at lunch-time, quite common nowadays but then unheard of. So much so that, when Sarah tried to get newspapers like the *Times* and the *Guardian* to review our productions, she was told that the critics did not review things at lunch-time. A little bit of pioneering on our part, but nothing to what was to come in 1972.

In 1969, I became the first Director Manager of a new theatre on the campus of the University of Kent – the Gulbenkian. I had to organise the completion of the building (it was still a shell when I started there), the programme of events, well really everything, down to the ordering of the ice-cream (do you know how much profit is made from ice-cream? Well...). All very useful experience when Mikron took off again. I left Canterbury after a year, not certain exactly what I wanted to do but knowing that I wanted to make theatre accessible to a lot more folk – not just students or the London theatre-going audiences, and not just panto or large musicals or very esoteric, intellectual, "important" plays.

I went to work as an actor with the Theatre-in-Education team at the Belgrade Theatre in Coventry. This was one of the first theatres to offer theatre-in-education and was an exciting place to work, particularly as we were performing a theatre documentary about Coventry's car industry, *The Car Makers*. I began to see the great potential of this form of theatre.

It was at about this time that two events conjoined to influence the course of the lives of Sarah and myself irrevocably. Sarah became pregnant and, as if not wanting to be outdone by this potential birth in

3

under nine months time, I came up with THE IDEA – the *once-in-a-lifetime I think I've had a good idea or am I just fooling myself* idea. Can it be done? Are we now going to be poor for the rest of our lives? So it was that, whilst shaving one morning, the thought came to me in a flash: you want to take theatre to the people, you like travelling by boat on the canals (we had had several canal holidays and absolutely loved it), why not combine the two – travel around the waterways by boat as a theatre company? Eureka. This had to be it.

2

THE BEGINNINGS

To turn an idea into reality, aye that's the rub. Many a brilliant notion has fallen foul at the first hurdle of practicality.

There was no problem with the first birth. Sarah really enjoyed being pregnant and, afterwards, vowed that she would like to be pregnant all the time – it was a good, positive feeling – but without the responsibility of looking after all the little sprogs that would come into the world. She gave birth to 7lb Sam at the old Charing Cross Hospital (believe it or not this was actually in Charing Cross) without the aid of any drugs or even gas and air. I was there throughout helping with her breathing, massaging and practising effleurage, and keeping us both sane by reading from Spike Milligan's hilarious book *Puckoon*. The doctor said it was a perfect birth and should have been filmed. Interestingly, Sam's ambition now at the age of 28 is to become a film director.

The birth of the waterborne Mikron Theatre Company was not to be so naturally achieved. I contacted the Inland Waterways Association which I discovered (at this stage, remember, I knew very little about waterways and the various bodies that were actually responsible for or felt responsible for their survival) was founded in 1946 by a small group of people determined to see our canal system saved and developed for both pleasure and commerce. They put me in touch with Robert Aickman and Charles Hadfield, two of the doyens of the waterways movement. Robert had many years before fallen out with Charles over the future of the IWA and, in fact, both Charles and LTC Rolt had been thrown out of the organisation for wanting to concentrate on a small number of special waterways thus leaving the rest of the system to become derelict. I knew nothing about all this political intrigue at the time. That was all to be learnt.

Robert Aickman replied to my letter in what at first appeared to be a dismissive manner. He had introduced the arts to the waterways as part of the first National Waterways Rally at Market Harborough in 1950 but didn't think taking theatre around the waterways would work. However, Sarah read between the lines and realised he was challenging us to try. I went to see him. He was charming and very incisive and helpful. He was later to become one of our patrons and came to several of our performances. Charles Hadfield invited me to his White House at Little Venice. Although he had never met me before, he lent me a number of precious waterways books from his collection and gave me every encouragement to get cracking. He also later became a patron of Mikron and we benefited from a bequest in his will.

Sarah, myself and Danny Schiller (Ron Legge as was from the Edinburgh days who had now changed his name for acting purposes) had many discussions as to what we would offer the public on our waterways tour. Our original idea was that we would produce a drama documentary about the history of the canals, a couple of Harold Pinter one-act plays, a revue and a Shakespeare. I even spent many hours editing *As You Like It* so it could be performed, by six actors, all playing several parts of course! An ambitious but varied programme. However...

Although we had no boat, no money, no real contacts we madly decided to go ahead. A new pub-theatre had recently opened called the King's Head in Islington. We would put on two shows there – one, a potted history of the canals in an hour; the other, a play called *Sitting Pretty* about sitting tenants in London written by a friend of ours, Tim Dartington.

In May 1972, we opened our short season with a week of performances at lunch-time of Still Waters, the history of Britain's waterways. We invited the press and some waterways people and waited for the audiences to flood in. Fortunately, it was a very small theatre at the back of the pub and so it didn't look too bad when there were only 12 in the audience. The *Daily Telegraph* gave us a good review: "A group of attractive young people have put together *Still Waters*...it is a cheerful somewhat hobbledehoy piece of work but it chronicles interestingly enough the story of the canal boom in the late 18th century and the inevitable decline as railways took over"; the actor's newspaper, *Stage*, didn't: "*Still Waters* never moves above a rather tepid and sluggish pace...on the level of a simple revue it has a simple, slightly amateur charm. As a professional piece it has little to offer – either by way of documentary material or entertainment." But, more importantly, we got our first bookings – to a festival in Little Venice, to the National Waterways Rally to be held at Lymm on the Bridgewater Canal in August and to Hemel Hempstead to give some performances in schools.

Our performance at Little Venice was quite successful, particularly as the organisers plonked us on the island in the middle with our audience on the bank and a lot of water and passing boats in-between.

Lymm was the first of many National Rallies we have attended over the years (sorry, we all have to call them National Waterways Festivals these days). It was in the proper tradition of Nationals of yesteryear – it was a campaigning rally to put pressure on the Manchester Ship

THE BEGINNINGS

Canal Company, which owns the Bridgewater Canal, to repair the large breach just outside Lymm. Nowadays it is hard to work out what National Waterways Festivals are for – they sometimes raise money, they provide a social get-together for boat-owners and waterways enthusiasts, but is any message getting across to the public at large? Sometimes I am cynical enough to think that all a Festival does is clog up a particular section of waterway with hundreds of boats and waste a lot of water – but, back in Lymm in 1972, it was all tremendously new and exciting. It rained, the mud got on to everything and into everything. We were staying on an unconverted narrowboat, *Clematis*, sleeping in the hold along with members of an organisation I was to get to know well, Waterway Recovery Group. The shows went a storm, we made lots of contacts, Sam at six months old survived the rigours of primitive boatlife, and we were grabbed by that total commitment to the welfare of the waterways that everyone at the rally seemed to possess. It was very catching and once caught you are, of course, hooked for ever.

What we needed now was to find a boat so that we could build a small waterways tour around our school performances. With our few canal contacts, we were able to tune in to the canal "tom-tom" system where messages are mysteriously and rapidly spread around the world of the waterways. The message came back that there might be a boat or boats available. We were put in touch with Roderick Atkin and Jocelyn Thompson who had a pair of narrowboats, *Hood* and *Fazeley*. They were looking for something useful to do with their boats and were really after carrying cargo on their unconverted butty. Coal not actors was their romantic ideal. However, we managed to persuade them that it would be very uplifting for their souls if they agreed to carry the Mikron Theatre Company on its very first canal tour.

Sarah worked hard on booking some venues for our month-long October tour on the Grand Union, mainly village halls with a few pubs thrown in. I re-rehearsed *Still Waters* with some changes in the original cast. I was to act in the show as well as direct it. Danny was still in, along with Roger Oakley (who was from New Zealand) and Karena Mond who was very "posh" and was the daughter of Lord Melchett, boss of ICI. Anne Wells, our stage manager at the King's Head, acted in the stead of Corinthia West, a long-legged elegant daughter of an ex-NATO general, who had left the Company to do greater things. For this first tour we were working on a profit share basis of which there was to be very little; so it was sometimes necessary to take actors who had "means" or generous parents.

Our first short tour along the Grand Union was a modest success marred by the fact that, for virtually the first time, British Waterways' lock-keepers and maintenance men struck for a wage increase. We had every sympathy for them – they were asking for a £3 increase to take

7

their earnings up to £20 a week. But locks were locked, pounds emptied and we were trapped between two locks in the middle of Berkhamsted. There was a little community of boats forced to be together for two weeks and that was our first real contact with people who lived on the canals, and we met such well-known waterways personalities as Jim and Mig McDonald and Bill Young. Our "knight in shining armour" was Tom Park, a local garage owner and boat-owner, who offered his services and drove us to the shows in his van.

3

THE REALITY

We decided to go for bust and plan a six-month tour for 1973 using the same boats. We became a registered charity (essential for applying for money from trusts and grant-giving bodies), received a few donations from well-wishers (including Lord Montagu, Yehudi Menuhin and Margaret Rawlings) and some small grants from Regional Arts Associations. We were a proper theatre company and Sarah was determined that we should pay wages of at least the Equity minimum. So it was that, from thenceforth, Mikron has always paid a fair wage (in actor's terms) for the job – in 1973, this was to be £20 per week. But it was many years before Sarah received a wage of her own; very similar to the boat people, there was just my wage for the whole family.

Apart from Anne Wells, a whole new team had to be assembled for this tour. Danny had decided that a waterways' life was not for him and he ceased being involved with Mikron. There was no disagreement – it was simply that Danny was not physically fit enough for the rigours of touring by boat. He has gone on to appear in films and television, notably in *Personal Services* and *The Beiderbecke Affair* and was for several years part of the BBC's Radio Repertory team.

So, from an advertisement in the *Stage*, we recruited Leonora Keogh, Steve Whittaker and Antony Heaton. Steve only survived for a short time – he gave his notice in before we started performing but did appear in the first four shows while we rehearsed in Stephen Churchett who was to be Steve's replacement. Steve said the show (*Still Waters* again) was "crap" and that Mikron was a totally amateur set-up. Self-delusion was high on the agenda here; perhaps he failed to notice that he was virtually incapable of learning lines. Steve is now a well-known television director!

A theatre company travelling by water – this was fascinating to the media and we had no problems attracting publicity in these early days. We were featured in the *Daily Telegraph*'s colour supplement, and even more significantly on London Weekend's arts programme *Aquarius*. This used to be featured on a Sunday afternoon and followed on from the very popular *Golden Shot* with Bob Monkhouse. So, many viewers found themselves watching pretty pictures of canals and boats and were fascinated enough to carry on watching *Narrowboat in Still Waters*. Hence, Mikron's largest-ever audience and a great boost to our "image". One footnote to this story is that, when we were making our third full-length television documentary in 1983, *Still Carrying On*, the man operating the smoke-machine, giving the early morning mist effect over the canal, was "Bernie the Bolt" who had become famous as the loader of the golden shot in that programme back in 1973. We were also seen or heard on *Omnibus*, the *Today Programme* and *Pm at 5pm*.

Many of our performances on this tour were in village halls. We believed these to be ideal venues, the focal point of a community near to the canal with reasonable facilities. It was always a great surprise to us when we drew between six and twenty-five people to our shows. Where are all the people? Down to the pub to drown our sorrows. Ah, here are all the people – hundreds of 'em. It soon became Mikron's policy to concentrate on canal and riverside pubs as our main venues. We would go to the people if they couldn't be bothered to come to us.

The first half of the 1973 Tour remains for me as a hazy blur – what I think I'm trying to do is forget that it was pretty hellish for a lot of the time. Sam was eighteen months old, going through that difficult transition from babyhood to childhood, and a real handful. He spent much of the daytime with me; Sarah had administration to do which sometimes involved taking a stool and sitting in an unpleasantly sweaty phone-box and phoning newspapers and venues. She would take over when it was time to get ready for the show.

Then there was the rest of the Company to deal with. There were six of us plus Sam. Anne was always fine, good-tempered and hard working. After this tour she went off to help form the Women's Theatre Company. Tony was drunk a great deal – he often slept the night on the top of the boat with a bottle of brandy by his side. He would sober up in the morning by diving into the canal whatever the condition of the water. His favourite tipple was a pint of bitter "spiced up" with a barley wine. Leonora was stoned most of the time and did very little indeed. Stephen was bitchy and ganged up with Tony in constantly niggling at Anne.

But we struggled through somehow. There must have been good moments – Rod and Joss swimming naked together in the canal at midnight. They were usually arguing, particularly when tying up the boats. So, I suppose, it came as no surprise to Sarah and myself when Steve, Tony and Leonora resigned at the end of the first half of the tour and left our lives; Steve to become a playwright, Tony to die not many years later and Leonora.... who knows?

Sarah and I, instead of having a much-needed holiday, spent the next four weeks re-casting and re-rehearsing. We reduced the acting company to four – Anne and myself were joined by Brian Carter and David Shackleton, both amiable people. The second half was a pleasure. We began on the River Nene, with its formidable locks and steep bends and finished at Abbey Park in Leicester on the River Soar. Brian was neat and fastidious and *Hood* became a haven of tidiness. David was slightly scatty and had a tendency of slightly altering the script whilst acting, thus completely altering its meaning. Example: "I'll fill your bellies full of bread and your pockets full of gold" was rendered as "I'll fill your bellies full of lead and your pockets full of bread."

Survival had been the name of the game. Now was the time to decide whether Sarah and I wanted to continue with this mad enterprise or should we give up now. "It was a good idea but it's too difficult. We have a son to bring up, our marriage to keep going. Get out while the going's good."

4

THE *FLOWER OF GLOSTER* AND THE LEARNING CURVE

We decided there were enough pluses to outweigh the negatives. These were early days – we needed to gain more experience ourselves in running a boat-bound theatre company. We would be able to help new members of the Company to appreciate the way of life and the enjoyment we were bringing to our growing audiences.

But we had no boat or boats with which to continue. Rod and Joss really did want to carry coal – quieter and less cantankerous than actors. A few years later they went to carry cargoes on the continental waterways. *Fazeley*, the butty, is now part of the Captain Cargo Carrying fleet. *Hood*, a wooden boat, is no more. The "tom-tom" system reported that there was a Michael Sampson of Liverpool who had a boat he was prepared to hire out to us for £40 per week It was the wooden, ex-Ovaltine boat *George*, now re-named the *Flower of Gloster* after starring in the eponymous series. We had no choice. It wasn't a palace but we were going to be able to steer it ourselves. (We had never been let loose on *Hood* or *Fazeley*).

We needed three new actors – we found Anna Bentinck and Richard Robinson with no difficulty but recruiting a third member was proving to be not so easy. We had two more people to see. They came to audition in our flat. (Sarah, Sam and I lived in a refurbished ground floor GLC flat in Bermondsey). The first fellow had come from a circus background and, although he was very willing to push or pull a narrowboat around the canals, his acting ability was, to put it politely, not his strong point. "Keep your circus job" would have been an appropriate reply but, of course, we just came out with the usual "We'll let you know."

So it was all down to this other fellow, Alan Bridger. He came into our living room – a striking figure, very tall, masses of hair, and an unforgettable face. He was gawky but very charming and, even more importantly, appeared to have some vague knowledge of the art of acting and played the guitar to boot. We offered him the job with just one proviso: that he met the other members of the Company so that he and they could decide they wanted to work together.

A few nights later we all met socially at the Albany in Deptford. It was apparent that we all were very sympathetic to each other and that we might have the makings of a talented and happy company. Alan was to spend the night with us. Sarah's mum was staying with us, so Alan, Sarah and I had to sleep on the floor in the living room. All was fine until some time in the early hours. I woke up hearing what I thought was quite heavy rain. I sat up and my mouth fell open. There was Bridger (as he became known to us all) standing at the window, peeing all over our collection of paperbacks which were stacked up on the window ledge. The job finished, he turned round, climbed back into bed and went back to sleep.

Sarah was also awake by now and pointed out that it might be a good idea to clear up the mess before the morning and before we told Bridger that he no longer had a job. We switched the light on to start the process. "Switch that damned light off, will you" was the response from Bridger's bed before he resumed the previous sleeping posture.

When Bridger awoke in great spirits the next morning, he was oblivious to the night's happenings. He was, of course, abjectly apologetic when we told him of our night's adventure. He explained that the flat where he lived was on the second floor where there was no toilet and he was in the habit, if he had had a few pints of an evening, of opening his window and peeing out on the garden! All this was told with such humility and grovelling that we forgot to tell him that he had been sacked before he started work, and thus began Bridger's two years with Mikron.

On reflection, and even at the time, 1974 was a momentous year for Mikron. We introduced a second show into the repertoire. It was not the anticipated Pinter one-act play or a small-sized Shakespeare. We had realised that there was a vast wealth of material to be mined from the story of the waterways – a subject which no other theatre company had ever covered and which so fitted our method of travel and our venues, the canalside pubs, many of which had been built for the benefit of the working boatpeople. So myself and the three other actors in the Company rehearsed and wrote a show called *Keep Yer 'ands Off* which told the story of the canals from the view of the boatpeople. We traced the origins of these proud people and showed how family boating began on the waterways. The show was excellently written with much humour, and we had great fun rehearsing it as we travelled on *Flower of Gloster* on the first stage of our tour.

Flower of Gloster proved to be the other momentous part of 1974 – she and our struggle to steer her along the canals. None of us had had any experience of handling a full-length ex-working boat. Sarah and I had been on boating holidays so we were designated "Captains". But, although we knew vaguely how to steer a boat in a straight line and get into locks, even we were not prepared for the problems to be encountered trying to negotiate an old wooden boat around the system, particularly when we reached the narrow canals. These are the earlier canals, many engineered by James Brindley, pioneer of canal building, with locks of just sufficient size to fit one seventy-two foot long, seven foot wide narrowboat and built on the contour principle – that is, if you have to go up or down a hill, build a lock or a flight of locks or a tunnel, but if possible follow the contour lines and avoid going up or down. Result: go and have a look at the summit of the Oxford Canal where the canal bends alarmingly. At one point you spend an hour going round all sides of a farmhouse. Distance by canal – a mile; distance by crow – 250 yards. The cut and fill technique – cuttings and embankments – was to come later in the history of canal building.

We were convinced in 1974 that it was impossible to steer a 72-foot boat around the bends on the Oxford summit between Napton and Fenny Compton. A trip which now takes us two-and-a-half hours took us seven.

Then there was the wind – we seemed to have much of it blowing over the canals in 1974. And blasts of it would blow the *Flower* on to the bank. We would try to push ourselves off with our long boatpole (or shaft as it is more properly called) and just as we thought we'd pushed the boat back into the channel the wind would blow us back on again. And so on... Richard Robinson was often to be seen scrambling through knee-high nettles and brambles on the off-side of the canal in order to be thrown a rope to try and pull us back into the middle.

Then there were the mistakes. This was the year of the learning curve and Bridger probably had more learning to do than anybody. So many of the events seem to have involved him....

At the wharf in Wigan (we started the tour on the Leeds & Liverpool Canal at Haskayne), we were tied up alongside a very smart boat called *Duchess* which belonged to the, then, chairman of the Inland Waterways Association, John Heap. Bridger waved his friendly farewell to all those on land and proceeded to set off steering the Flower. He had, unfortunately, forgotten to ask anyone to untie the ropes; so he was moving full ahead, except he wasn't. He was attempting to take *Duchess* and Wigan Wharf with him.

I shall pass quickly by the other events: putting diesel in the oil-tank; crushing our bicycle, which lived on the roof of the boat when not being used , under a very low bridge (my fault that one); getting stuck on the edge of a weir on the River Soar (Richard this time who went catatonic, like a hedgehog in the middle of a busy road, when he "blew" a bend); Anna setting fire to the cooker; Sarah falling in with the week's wages in her handbag (there were notes hung out to dry all over the cabin of the boat) – and move to the question, what is a cill?

A cill in waterways parlance is a stone platform at one end of the floor of a lock. It acts as a dam with the gates above it and when a lock is emptied juts out into the chamber of a lock. I knew about cills from my holiday boating days. We had been given warnings of the dire consequences of getting the back (or stern) of the boat caught on one of these while descending in a lock. Sarah and I thought we'd told the rest of the crew about cills but, when what happened happened, the cry went up from Bridger: "What's a cill? No-one told me about cills. I've not been in a downhill lock before."

There we were on a day off, proceeding down the Staffordshire & Worcestershire Canal (a "day off" only meant we didn't do a show in the evening; we generally still had to move the boat). All is peaceful as we enter Dimmingsdale Lock. Sarah and I open the bottom paddles and the boat starts to drop. There are moments on the canals when you have to move from slow, precise movements to very fast and panic-ridden action. The front of the boat was dropping but the back of the boat was staying where it was – on the cill. We drop the paddles and are running to the other end to raise the lock again, when there is an almighty splash as the back of the *Flower* drops into the water. We realise with horror that the rudder has snapped off and dropped into the bottom of the lock.

So it was that, that evening, we pulled the *Flower* out of the lock. Bridger, courageous, remorseful or whatever, volunteered (!) to go down into the dank, dark, slimy bottom of the lock to search for the missing rudder. Without a rudder, we were rudderless – we were a theatre company going nowhere.

Dimmingsdale Lock never seems to get any sunshine. It has a drop of nine feet. Bridger is six foot three but of slender build. So the only result of Bridger's search with his feet for the rudder (he was standing in five feet of water) was a shivering, shaking mass of humanity, who, with teeth chattering, was sent to have a shower on a neighbouring boat (no such luxury on the Flower) and given a large slug of brandy. We spent a glum night on board the Flower. Bridger had manfully offered to go down again early the next morning. We couldn't begin to face the prospect of what would happen if he failed. The only idea we came up with was to hire a diver.

At six o'clock the next morning, I took the condemned man – sorry, Bridger – a cup of tea. "It's a lovely morning, Bridger." "Yes, but it's still bloody cold and dark down in that lock." We wished him luck and in he went, shivering almost instantly. He walked along the bottom of the lock feeling with his feet. "I've got it," he cried. He bent down and pulled, and the top of a five-barred gate broke the surface of the water. Bridger came out for a warm. Sarah and I were all for calling in a diver but Bridger, bold to the last, said he would have one last try. "I've got it, I've got it" appeared to be what Bridger was saying through chattering teeth. It was flat, steel and heavy and impossible for Bridger to lift, whatever it was. We lowered him a rope. It had to be the rudder for there was a hole in this object and rudders have holes so they can be lifted. Out came the rudder, a piece of steel two feet square and out for the last time came the triumphant Bridger. He allowed a smile to cross his pale, chill face – he may have caused the problem but he also had solved it.

Well, not completely. We had already contacted a boatyard and asked them if they would be able to repair the rudder. They said that, once found, they would take the rudder and rudder post away and weld them. And they would be able to replace the whole thing with the *Flower* in the water. There would be no need for dry-docking. So it came about that an hour or so later we said goodbye to Tim Cashin of Water Travel Boat Company at Autherley Junction and set off to try and make our venue for that night, the Navigation at Greensforge, ten locks and several miles away... We arrived at nine o'clock, an hour late for the show but the audience was still waiting for us. We had already got into our costumes and the show went on.

1974 was a year fraught with difficulties, some of these caused by our own inexperience, others caused by the decrepitude of both the canals and the boat.

The backlog of maintenance on the waterways had by the early '70s reached crisis proportions. In the August edition of *Waterways World*, the editor, Bob Shopland, wrote: "It is perhaps ironical that in what is likely to be a boom year for inland waterway cruising much of the canal system is incapacitated due not only to water shortages but also engineering difficulties such as the prolonged closure of Harecastle Tunnel and the Anderton Boatlift. It all underlines the need for a considerable injection of capital to overcome the backlog of engineering work required to enable the system to meet the ever growing, all year round, demands now being made on it."

The estimated cost of overcoming the backlog was £30m. This state of affairs was even more remarkable when one remembers that 1974 was *the* year of openings, that is canals and rivers that had been allowed to fall into dereliction and had now been restored using both voluntary and professional labour. 1974 saw the re-opening of the Upper Avon, the Peak Forest Canal, the Ashton Canal and the Caldon Canal. So, while the Queen Mum was at Stratford unveiling a plaque and John Betjeman was reading a poem to commemorate the opening of the Upper Avon Navigation ("...*the lock you will re-open will set free/The heart of England to the open sea*"), Mikron was struggling along some of the ditches laughingly described as canals. We limped along the Erewash Canal, through huge growths of duck-weed, which were so thick we eventually abandoned our attempts at clearing the prop every few minutes and bow-hauled the boat to our venue at Langley Mill; we took two hours to unravel a large bumpy mattress from our blades, which we had caught going under a bridge in the suburban squalor of Handsacre on the Trent & Mersey Canal. We displayed the shredded mattress to our audience, expressing our view that the canals were still regarded as very convenient linear rubbish dumps.

In July, we were struggling along the South Oxford Canal. On this particular day, we needed to reach Claydon before 4pm when the flight closed in order to conserve water supplies. We sent Richard on a two mile run up the towpath to see if he could talk the lock-keeper into letting us through after time. We were going to be late and beyond the locks lay our venue at Fenny Compton. En route, he tripped over a fisherman and broke his brand new rod.

We arrived at the bottom of Claydon to find several boats tied up for the night. We steered past them and took *Tyseley* up to the lockgate, but the padlocks were on and a very exhausted Richard informed us that the lock-keeper wanted nothing to do with us. He just wanted to go home for his tea. It was beginning to look as if we might have to miss a performance for the first time ever. But, fortunately, help arrived in the form of two old ladies who happened to be walking along the towpath. They offered to give us a lift to Claydon to see if we could find the lock-keeper. Sarah and I joined them in their Beetle. As we were driving along, one of the ladies told us that she had been a very well-known actress in her day and was now living in an Actors' Benevolent Fund Home along with Robertson Hare and Fay Compton. "Book your place, dear. You'll need it someday."

Nobody had heard of the lock-keeper in Claydon. Sarah phoned the British Waterways Section Inspector in Oxford who said he had no objection to us going through if the lock-keeper agreed. He lived in a village about three miles away. We set off in search, with one of the old ladies driving in the manner of a movie car chase. In the village, we turned up a track and suddenly found ourselves in Cold Comfort Farm – a run-down cottage with toothless old men and women sitting in the kitchen eating hunks of bread and supping mugs of tea. The lock-keeper emerged, but was very reluctant to help until we told him his boss was agreeable and that we would pay his overtime. He immediately picked up his windlass and, before we could turn round, he was on his bike and away.

We drove back through the narrow lanes to the canal. A few minutes later, the lock-keeper arrived and unlocked the bottom gate. We were up the flight of five in less than thirty minutes. We gave our saviour his £2 overtime and set off along the Fenny pound. We had no trouble along this stretch and tied up outside the George & Dragon at eight o'clock. We were already in our costumes and there was a huge crowd waiting for us. The show went a storm in a wonderfully informal atmosphere and finished in near darkness with the aid of somebody's car headlights.

In these early days of touring we also performed in some unusual venues. Not that we thought the Opposite Lock was going to be unusual. It was obviously going to be a canal pub with a name like that. It was also situated in some converted canalside stables in Gas Street Basin in the centre of Birmingham. It wasn't until we entered the building that we realised that it wasn't a pub but a club, and it wasn't a venue full of nostalgia for the canals but, being Birmingham, it was a shrine dedicated to the adoration of the motor vehicle. The walls were scattered with steering wheels and there were photos of fast cars in every nook and cranny. "Opposite lock" is what you do when you are trying to get out of a skid.

We performed a show about the history of the canals in this nightclub setting with red lighting. As the club filled with people, it soon became apparent that not only were a large number of the clientele not interested in watching a live show, they were also intent on stopping it. We kept getting messages from the management saying "Stop now!" but, because I never like to admit defeat and because there were people who had come especially to see the show, we ploughed bravely (or madly) on to the end, with Sarah doing her bit at the back, telling the well-heeled customers how appallingly rude they were. We danced all our tensions away at the disco afterwards.

Our fifty-year-old wooden narrowboat *Flower of Gloster* was not in the best of nick, to put it mildly. I used to lie in my bed during the night with my hand dangling on to the floor. I would wake up if my hand became wet. This was the signal to tell me that the bilges were getting very full and that I was to arise, start the engine and run the bilge pump. When the water was emptied it was again safe to go to bed without worrying about sinking before the morning, particularly disturbing when tied up somewhere like the River Severn with many feet of water under you.

This situation could not continue for all of the tour, so eventually we had an automatic bilge fitted which kicked into action when the water rose to a serious level. We discovered after we'd finished the tour and handed *Flower* back to her owner that, although the boat wasn't fully water tight, we hadn't helped by not putting grease in the stern-gland which prevents water coming in through the stern-tube. Another learning curve!

All the trials and tribulations of taking a full-length ex-working boat on tour for the first time were considerably eased by the high morale of the Company, and the skill and effort they put into the performances. "Some segments of the production were positively brilliant" said the *Banbury Guardian*.

Bridger, Richard and Anna were a delight to tour with. Anna, daughter of Count Henry Bentinck, although she had a boyfriend who later became her short-lived husband, flirted her way round the waterways with a beguiling prettiness and charm. Lock-keepers and even some members of the Company were amongst those who fell madly in love with her. She has continued to be involved in theatre and is now happily settled with a partner and three children. Richard learnt to paint roses and castles, the traditional decoration for narrowboats, while he was on tour and the collection tin and parts of the back-cabin still show his work. He probably had more time for his hobby as he did not possess quite the same love of pubs and beer as the rest of us. When he did turn out though and when there was a piano, he would entertain the locals with skilful renditions of Scott Joplin's ragtime music. He went off after this tour and formed his own pub theatre company, the Covent Garden Community Theatre. He is married to Thirzie who toured with Mikron in 1975. More of her later.

Bridger and I did not like leaving pubs, especially if the landlord and landlady were hospitable and conversation and drinking continued into the early hours. Bridger was once seen at 1.30am reaching up from a stool he had just fallen off. Brave lad. His words were "Just one more Pils." Everything was not always sweetness and light. I remember having a row with him (over what I cannot recall) and he stormed out saying "I'm off!" Hastily, I called him back saying "No, Bridger, you can't just leave in the middle of a tour!" "No," he said, "I'm off for a walk – to cool down."

Bridger had, and still has, a wicked sense of humour. Just before we entered Netherton Tunnel on the BCN (the Birmingham Canal Navigation), I was regaling the others with the story of the young woman who had drowned in the tunnel many years before. Her ghost is still to be seen or felt in the tunnel as she tries to grab the tiller of a passing boat to pull herself out of the eternal murky waters.

So, I'm taking the *Flower* into the tunnel. Bridger joins me on the back. "I want to see how you handle these tunnels and I'll be a bit of company for you!" We enter the tunnel and we stand in companionable silence, me steering, enjoying the eeriness of the experience – the reflections of the roof in the water giving you the impression you're travelling through a tube, the occasional drips of water on the face and the reassuring chug of the engine. We're about halfway through with each end just a pinprick of light in the distance. Bridger says "I don't expect you believe these tunnel ghost stories, do you?" "Certainly not," I reply a little too quickly. Silence again for a few moments. Then suddenly without warning, the tiller starts to shake and judder and I feel the chill of pure fright envelop me. Then almost as quickly I feel a complete fool as Bridger takes his hand off the tiller – the hand he had stealthily been moving behind me in the blackness.

I'D GO BACK TOMORROW

A great tour with tremendous response from public and press – just the encouragement we needed to continue with this way of life. We had to keep going now. We were fulfilling a need for good theatre in unconventional surroundings and we were fulfilling our ambition to introduce theatre to a much wider audience. Sam was going to have to grow up as a "boat-child".

5

THE SUMMER OF THE RAGING BUM

Our immediate problem, during the long winter months, was we didn't have a boat for our 1975 tour. *Flower of Gloster* was not available and, even if she had been, we were not certain that we wanted to keep her afloat for another year.

Possibilities arose and then simply evaporated. So we were getting quite desperate when, one evening, there was a knock at the door of our Bermondsey flat. It was John May. John had been very helpful when I was running the Gulbenkian Theatre in Canterbury. He had worked for free as my front-of-house manager and Sarah and I had become great friends with him and his wife, Penny.

He was passing and wanted to say hello. We hadn't met for quite a while, so it was great to see him. Over a glass of wine, we caught up on each others' lives. John, it turned out, was in a dilemma. His uncle had sadly died but had left him quite a healthy chunk of money. He wanted to do something positive with this bequest and not just fritter it away but hadn't come up with any good ideas. "John," I said to him, "Have you ever thought of buying a boat – a narrowboat?" I explained our predicament and suggested that he might like to buy a boat and rent it out to Mikron for some of the year. "That's a very interesting thought. Give me a day or two to think about it." The following day, John rang us to say if we could find a suitable boat he would buy it and we would be able to use it for the 1975 Mikron tour. Sarah started ringing around and using the canal "tom-tom" system. We were put in touch with Malcolm Braine who ran a boatyard at Norton Canes on the BCN. "I've got just the boat for you – she's not too expensive 'cos she's a bit...greasy. She's called *Tyseley*."

So it was that John, Sarah and myself went up to look at *Tyseley*. She had quite a history. She was built in 1936 by Yarwoods of Northwich, as part of the Grand Union Canal Carrying Company's fleet of Town Class boats. She was what is known as a "small Northwich". She carried all manner of cargoes and, during the Second

World War, was on the "Guinness Run" – a vital part of the war effort taking Guinness in barrels from the Park Royal Brewery in London to Birmingham. Guinness was considered to be a premium product and was "fly-boated", which meant the boats ran day and night and had priority at the locks over other craft. When the waterways (or most of them) were nationalised in 1947, *Tyseley* became part of the British Waterways fleet and finished her carrying days on the "Cement Run" from Long Itchington to Sampson Road depot in Birmingham. In the 1960s she was converted into the first-ever canal restaurant boat and operated out of Thrupp on the South Oxford Canal for ten years.

The brochure read: "Stephen and Patricia Woolford invite you to wine and dine afloat on the motor narrowboat *Tyseley*. Enjoy a leisurely meal as the boat is navigated through locks and narrow bridges along the Oxford Canal and the river Cherwell. *Tyseley* has been converted from a cargo boat to carry 12 passengers in comfort, with a sun deck and glass observation dining saloon. The vessel is heated in cold or wet weather and there are toilet facilities on board. The vessel is fully licensed. Our cruises start from the picturesque inland harbour of Thrupp." The cost of a three hour cruise and four course meal was £2 10s (£2.50) per head.

Tyseley had been lying at Malcolm Braine's boatyard for nearly two years. Her butty, the unpowered boat that is pulled by the boat with an engine thus giving a total of fifty tons carrying capacity, *Gertrude* was being lived on but poor *Tyseley* – it looked as if the chef and the rest of the crew had finished work one night and then just abandoned her. There was a little touch of the *Marie Celeste* about her – the portable toilet was still half full, the cookers and the working surfaces had layers of grease liberally smeared on them and the dining area still had some mats and place settings on the tables.

Sarah was always able to make the imaginative leap in circumstances like these and, instead of saying "This is no use for Mikron", she had a pencil and paper out and was sketching the new lay-out of *Tyseley*. The kitchen was to become the back bedroom, the store area the bunk room and the dining area the living room and kitchen. It all made perfect sense and John and I both agreed that the large foredeck, which had wooden seats for the guests to sit outside and take their aperitifs, would be ideal for Mikron and we were all delighted that the original engine-room and back-cabin were still intact. The back cabin of a working narrowboat is only eight feet by seven feet but in there the woman (it *was* the woman) had to cook, work and look after her family. Sarah and I lived in the back cabin while touring for many years, but we were never able to comprehend fully how a whole family (husband, wife and two or three children) managed to live together in this tiny space.

Mikron had very little money, so Malcolm Braine agreed to convert the boat according to Sarah's design but at as low a cost as possible. "I don't want my name on the side of the boat, you understand. The quality of the work and materials won't be up to my usual standards," he said.

But it was going to be paradise for us – a proper workable layout and, heaven, a shower. John agreed to let us have free use of the boat whilst touring on condition we paid for all maintenance costs and that he and his family had use of the boat for the rest of the year. So he bought *Tyseley* for £4,000. That knock on the door enabled Mikron to tour again. *Tyseley*, so loved by us all, is still carrying Mikron safely and efficiently around the waterways.

After eight weeks researching, writing and rehearsing a new show called *Up the Cut* and revamping *Keep Yer 'ands Off*, we went up to the Cannock Extension Canal to pick up *Tyseley*. We couldn't believe our eyes...taps with running water, a fridge, a lovely tiled floor and curtains! We treated ourselves to a glass or two of champagne (or was it sparkling Spanish wine?) and began to settle in.

This year, in addition to the team of myself, Sarah, Bridger and a now three-year-old Sam, we had Thirzie Robinson and Dan Caulfield. I had worked with Dan before during my stint at the Manchester Library Theatre. He was a fellow ASM. He was also much older than the rest of us...an antique 48 years old. How was he going to cope with the cramped conditions of a narrowboat? Thirzie was the girlfriend of Richard from the previous year. Later to be married but already, coincidentally, with the same surname, Thirzie had decided not to audition with Richard but to try for the following year. She was highly talented with great comic skills and proved to be an ideal replacement for Anna.

So on Monday May 5th 1975, we made our first move on *Tyseley* down the short Cannock Extension Canal to our first pub venue. It was very windy and cold. We were all nerve wracked for the performance of *Keep Yer 'ands Off* but it went passably well.

The next day was devoted to steering along the BCN. I have to say that I steered beautifully round the Whirly (the Wyrley & Essington Canal) to Catshill Junction. Dan had his first lesson and quickly picked up the technique of steering. About two miles before our first lock we caught something very large round our blades. It was a great lump of wire. Wirecutters made no impression on it and it was too cold to go in the water. So, with the help of two people from a nearby boat club, we bowhauled the boat to the lock. Bowhauling involves pulling the boat along with ropes. It was very windy and progress was slow and painful. We lowered the pound between the first two locks, sat *Tyseley* on the mud and a magical man with enormous magical wirecutters cleared the blades. He also straightened the tiller which we had broken coming out of the lock. We tied up for the night at Bell Bridge totally exhausted. We had no performance that night. Praise be.

I'D GO BACK TOMORROW

Our third day was pretty eventful as well. More locks on the Rushall Flight, pulling a dead dog out of one of them; the journey beneath Spaghetti Junction (the only way to see it properly); the horrendous slog up the filthy oil-covered Garrison Locks and our final limp along the Grand Union in the pouring rain. All that hard boating became worthwhile when we performed in the Boat at Catherine de Barnes (Catley Bar to the boatpeople) to a large appreciative audience.

This first week was fraught with difficulties. Due to our inexperience, we had organised very long moving days. We fell in (well, Thirzie did, and very cold and humiliated she looked); we crashed into bridgeholes and bends (well, mainly Dan – we changed to a tin teapot after this); we had engine problems (it was drinking oil at an alarming rate); we jammed the tiller under the lockgates and had to borrow some oxyacetylene equipment in order to straighten it out; and, at the same time as all this, we were trying to fit in rehearsals of our new show, *Up the Cut.*

Up the Cut is the story of the canals since the last World War – the end of carrying by narrowboat (almost), the formation of the Inland Waterways Association and the start of canal restoration. Our main character is an ex-boatman. He is now a long-distance lorry driver and, as part of his working life, drives over canals every day and remembers fondly how good boating life was. He is very largely based on John Saxon. John and his wife Phyl had both come off the boats in their teens and they were the first boatpeople we got to know well. They saw our shows, respected our work and were very forthcoming not only by supplying us with some wonderful stories of their boating lives, but by introducing us to many ex-boatpeople who now lived on "the land" in the Coventry area.

But, despite all these problems and despite Alan falling in one night when returning from the pub and losing his script and despite a dreadful, truly dreadful, dress rehearsal, we did give the world première of *Up the Cut* at The Admiral Nelson on a bright but chilly evening to a huge appreciative crowd.

The tour now began to settle down into a rhythm. The boating improved, the shows matured. We found a launderette which was a great relief to us and probably to the front few rows of our audiences. A beautiful evening, with us performing with a dramatic sunset behind us, boats tied up for the evening and cows grazing on the hillside, would be followed by a day of torrential rain, resulting in us performing in a small public bar in front of the dartboard to those who had managed to cram themselves into a space a tenth of the size of a West End actor's dressing room.

Talking of darts... You would be amazed if you knew the reaction of some pub locals to their being deprived of their precious dartboard for an hour or two on one night of the year. "You can't do your show there.

Not there. What are we going to do? We won't be able to play darts."
It was not as if we were asking them to hang up their arrows for ever
– just for an hour. But no, there was always much weeping and wailing
and downright ill temper. Now, I like a game of darts along with the
best of them but such obsession cannot be good for a person.

Our finances were now looking healthier. We were in receipt of an
Arts Council grant. Official recognition. The main thanks for achieving
this must go to Bridger who, towards the end of the previous tour, had
personally contacted members of the Drama Panel, some of whom had
come to see our shows when we were in London. They finally realised
that we were not just a group of middle-class semi-hippies tootling
around the waterways with our fingers dangling limpidly in the languid
water, but serious minded and talented actors with something to say
and a very original way of getting that message across.

So we had to forgive Bridger many things because of this. If he
asked if truffles would be available in Loughborough for a particular
recipe he was planning to cook, we had to smile patiently and tell him
we thought it unlikely and why didn't he try Egg Curry instead. If he
fell in love with Lesley Judd from *Blue Peter* at the same time as me,
I had to indulge his whims. He obviously didn't stand a chance but it
would have been ungallant of me to tell him so.

Lesley Judd features in this story because she and Peter Purves were
the presenters who filmed a piece with us for *Blue Peter* on the South
Stratford Canal. The director of the film was going to shoot our
progress down the canal over a period of two days and had written
himself a little scenario. Lesley and Peter were to help us move the
boat, set up for our shows and with our daily routines. But Sarah's
strong personality and the uncertainties of canal travel meant he was
going to have to tear his script up or not get a film.

The director wanted me to steer the boat with Peter helping and
Sarah to cook the meal with Lesley. Sarah insisted it should be the
other way around. "You don't want *Blue Peter* viewers just to watch
stereotypes, do you?" she said. Thus were the young viewers able to
watch Sarah and Lesley steering the boat and Peter and myself
preparing a spaghetti and mushroom dish. What the littlies didn't see
was Sarah and Lesley having a fag every time they were off camera,
nor them trying to keep warm on the second day of filming because the
temperature had gone down ten degrees but they still had to wear
bikinis for continuity purposes. The action was all meant to take place
on the same day. They also didn't see Peter and me trying to cook in a
tiny space – the rest of the kitchen being taken up by lights,
microphones and technicians.

The South Stratford Canal also played a vital part in the filming.
The canal in those days was owned by the National Trust. It had been
restored by the indomitable David Hutchings with very little money

and resources, using volunteers, prisoners and the Army. It had been re-opened by the Queen Mother in 1964 but to be frank it had been a bit of a "curate's egg" of a job. And parts of it were already starting to collapse. Unlike the scripted version of *Blue Peter*, we stuck completely while coming out of Lock 44. The director was able to film the real live action of myself, Sarah, Dan, Thirzie, Lesley, Peter and many people off other boats waiting for us to get out of the lock so that they could get their boats through. But, despite hauling on ropes and pushing on the lockgates and sides, we were stuck solid. The lock walls had bellied out just in exactly the same place where *Tyseley* had suffered middle-aged spread. So it wasn't until German Pete and One-Armed Pete had arrived and several hours of valuable filming time had elapsed that *Tyseley* finally slithered free from Lock 44. Pete (who was German) and Pete (who did have two arms but one of them had a hook on the end) worked for the Trust and they used a Tirfor to slowly but surely winch our boat out inch by inch. By the time this had been achieved, to the accompaniment of cheering from the gathered crowds, the director had run out of filming time and that was the end of that. Except that Lesley (I love her, oh, and so does Alan) and Peter had taken to this boating lark so well that they decided to boat with us all the way to Stratford.

It ought to be said at this point that their enjoyment and commitment was in stark contrast to John Noakes, the other star of *Blue Peter* in the 1970s. A year or so later, we were filmed as part of *Friendship*, a series in which the intrepid Noakes walked the Pennine Way, went to the Moon and, for our programme, was boating round the Cheshire Ring. Now John may have walked the whole of the Pennine Way and completed every inch of his other tasks, but I can only report that our little piece was filmed on the Market Harborough Arm of the Grand Union (a long way from Cheshire or its Ring) and that John returned to his hotel (oh, yes, he wasn't staying on any old narrowboat) hours before the performance which is shown on the programme, with John smiling delightedly at our antics and Shep sleeping contentedly under his seat. All this was filmed separately well away from us. All one's illusions were shattered when the director warned us to keep our four-year-old Sam away from John as he didn't like children. John also treated Shep terribly (Shep had a stand-in for a lot of the shots, by the way) and, when stepping aboard our boat supposedly having met us along the Cheshire Ring, he asked us a couple of inappropriate questions like the give-away "Where are you going?" and then turned to the director and said "You'd better cut. I can't think of anything else to say." He showed no interest in us whatsoever. The fact that we were fellow actors bothered him not one jot.

Other highlights of the first half of the 1975 Tour were meeting Joe and Rose Skinner, and my raging bum. Joe and Rose were famous amongst waterways people. Their boat *Friendship* was the last boat to carry cargoes along the Coventry and Oxford Canals pulled by a horse. They had only resorted to a horse because their mule (who "had been in the Army and was very obedient") had fallen in the cut and died a few days later of pneumonia. They still lived on their boat tied up at Sutton Stop at the junction of the Coventry and Oxford Canals. They also had a little cottage which they used to sit in during the day but every night they would retire to the back-cabin of *Friendship*. They never slept on the land. We met them, as many did, with their heads poking out of their cabin waiting to chat to passers-by. Joe, his eyes twinkling, would regale us with stories of their days on the cut. One of my favourite moments was him listing all the stables there used to be down the Oxford Canal: "Napton, Fenny, Cropredy..." – it was pure poetry.

My bum was not very poetical. It was a pain in the bum, in fact, or severe itching at least. Maybe it was nerves. Maybe it was the hot, sweaty weather. But I could not stop my bum raging. At night it was so severe, I used to stick it outside the back-cabin to try a catch a passing, alleviating wind. Rather like modern day "mooning". I visited several doctors *en route* who plied me with potions and tinctures but all to no avail. Thirzie's dad was a doctor and he gave me some lethal looking suppositories which seemed to do the trick. But I shall always remember 1975 as the Summer of the Raging Bum.

The second half of the tour was notable for our circumnavigation of the Cheshire Ring (remember John Noakes). This had only re-opened right through in 1974 and taking a full-length narrowboat along the Peak Forest and Ashton Canals and through the middle of Manchester was still pioneering stuff. We crawled along the ditch they called the Lower Peak Forest Canal at not more than one mile per hour. We reached a railway bridge where our passage was blocked. All five of us jumped into the water and spent an hour or more clearing out fifty or so railway chairs and sleepers which had been dumped into the canal by kids from the disused railway above. Of course, when we came back the following year, they had all been thrown back in again. Hireboats had been able to skate over the top of them but not us with our three foot draught.

It was obvious we were not going to make our venue by water. Sarah managed to contact a member of the Peak Forest Canal. He said he'd arrange road transport for the actors and he'd get some help for Sarah who with Sam was going to try and get down the Ashton Flight into Manchester. We were taken off to Worsley and when Sarah reached the top of the flight there were dozens of male volunteers waiting for her.

There are (or were) quite a few canalside pubs down the Ashton, and at every one Sarah bought her motley crew a pint and dished out her Piccadilly fags. They sailed down the flight with Sam sleeping peacefully, Sarah elegantly steering and her lockwheelers getting slowly pissed.

These people, many of whom became our friends and remain so today, formed the solid core of Waterway Recovery Group (North-West). They were the first set of Mikron groupies. They came to many shows, helped us out many more times and Tim Noakes and Ian McCarthy were invited to become members of the Mikron Council of Management, a post that Ian still holds today.

On the Sunday morning they were there again – this time to help us down the Rochdale Flight which was notorious for its loose gates and leaking pounds. It was a bizarre experience boating through the middle of Manchester, through a lock which is underneath a skyscraper block called Rodwell Tower, past the Playboy Club and the gay quarter of Manchester. The locks had to be operated carefully, otherwise you could flood the towpath. As we approached the bottom lock we realised it was getting ominously close to two o'clock. Pubs used to shut at two o'clock on a Sunday. I ran ahead to the nearest pub in Deansgate and, slightly out of breath, muttered to the barmaid the immortal line: "Twenty two pints of mild, please, three pints of bitter and a whisky." It was one minute to two. She uttered the equally immortal line: "Are they all for you?" Reassured she bravely began to pull the many pints of beer and, as the disparate crew straggled in all slightly out of breath, she said, not unkindly, "Could you get in a little earlier next time, please."

Our trip took us along the Leeds & Liverpool Canal towards Liverpool and for the first time we ventured as far as Bootle to perform at the Old Roan Inn. A mistake. Sarah had to have police protection when she was on the boat with Sam whilst we performed to a group of very drunk Irishmen. They didn't listen to a word but the landlord seemed delighted. "Wonderful show. You will come back, won't you?" he said, as he thrust a fiver at me. We haven't. Been back, that is.

Our year can be best summed up by an encounter Sarah had with a man at the Navigation, Gathhurst. Looking at the show and the actors, he said, "It's all right for you students swanning around doing this sort of thing but I couldn't do it though, not with my responsibilities." Sarah replied, "It's very flattering of you to think I could be a student but that's my husband performing over there and this is our job." "That's all very well but wait until you have children... yes wait 'til then." "Our son, Sam, is fast asleep on the boat tied up outside." The man did not reply.

It had been a successful year, a year in which Mikron's work had expanded – our audiences were growing, our "house-style" was emerging. Dan left to seek his fortune. He is still acting today, mainly in touring theatre. But he, like many actors, had to do his "National Service", that is a year's contract in Agatha Christie's *The Mousetrap*.

He played the "one that did it", but I will not reveal the secret in case you are still planning to go and see this epic. Thirzie married Richard Robinson, worked with the Covent Garden Community Theatre and is today a co-ordinator and planner of arts festivals.

As for Bridger... He decided that he was either going to have to work for Mikron for ever or become a lawyer. After tossing a coin, his fate was sealed and he was destined to become successful and rich... as a solicitor. More of this later.

The world of theatre didn't lose Bridger to the legal profession immediately though. He performed in a panto for the Covent Garden Community Theatre, a production which toured the local pubs and clubs. Alan is tall and striking and he was playing the dame, and very fetching he looked in drag. But the night Sarah and I saw the performance he seemed to have forgotten everything he had learned with us. When you are acting in a small space, like in front of a fireplace or a darts board, it is essential to stay as still as possible whilst "offstage" which can often only be a couple of feet from "onstage". Bridger went off after a sparklingly witty scene as the dame and, to the total distraction of his fellow performers and to the amazement of at least myself and Sarah and probably all the audience, proceeded to stand by the mantelpiece and in full drag light up his pipe for a relaxing "offstage" smoke.

6

THE YEAR OF THE DROUGHT

We thought we had encountered a few problems in the first four years of Mikron on the waterways. We had seen nothing. 1976 was to become known as the Year of the Drought, as the year when the waterways system ground virtually to a halt. A year we shall not apparently see the like of again for five hundred more years.

The year didn't start well. Sarah went down with what we thought was a bad attack of flu. She was left feeling very weak and hardly able to eat or drink. One doctor said it was post-flu debility. She would improve. She didn't, and was now unable to even take down water and was weakening fast. Another doctor arrived and immediately diagnosed glandular fever. Sarah was so dehydrated that it was feared she would have to go into hospital and be put on a drip. But, with a dose of a very powerful painkiller, she was able to drink water and take down a few solids. It took several weeks for her to feel better and it was over a year before she was finally given the all-clear. It was ten years before she really felt her old self again.

It was not many weeks after the initial diagnosis that we needed to audition for the new season for three new actors to join Sarah, Sam and myself on the 1976 Waterways Tour. We wanted to get this over with as quickly as possible. So we didn't interview many actors. We made quick decisions – Ruth Tansey, Mark Steeves and David Brett – and it was by pure chance that we got it two thirds right.

The new play was to be about the building of the canals, with particular emphasis on the canal navvies. This amazing breed of men had been totally neglected by canal historians up until 1972 when Eyre Methuen published *The Canal Builders* by Anthony Burton. In this book, Anthony Burton not only chronicled in fascinating , well-researched detail the fight to build canals, the arteries of the Industrial Revolution, with battles between promoters, financiers and engineers and administrators but he also shed light on the lives of the workers – the navigators, or navvies, who worked with pick and shovel to construct this new method of transport.

THE YEAR OF THE DROUGHT

This book was to be our main source and inspiration for the writing of *Puddle It*, along with the first two novels in Tony's trilogy, *Master Idol* and *The Navigators*. We were even more encouraged when I contacted Tony who said he had already enjoyed our shows and would be delighted to let me have access to his research material. He wanted Sarah and me to go and stay with him and his wife, Pip, in Islip near Oxford and thus began a long, deep friendship. Tony became Chairman of our Council of Management.

Puddle It and *Up the Cut* were rehearsed in London and the tour opened at the White Lion, Marsworth near Tring on the Grand Union Canal on May 3rd. At this time, we had no indication of the troubles to come. The weather was usual May-style weather, sometimes hot, sometimes cold, but with significantly little or no rain. Maybe we should have taken more note that we were struggling along the Grand Union, a canal usually deep and wide. By June, we were creeping along the Northern Stratford Canal and getting stuck on the Southern Stratford (oh yes, including being winched out of Lock 44). The sun came out and stayed out (with breaks for clear, cool nights, of course) until September and of rain there was none.

The Staffs & Worcs Canal had never been the deepest of canals but it excelled itself for shallowness and bumpiness this year. We had almost reached Stourport one day when *Tyseley* landed on a large object, tipped over to an alarming degree and came to a very definite halt. It was only later we were to discover that the large object was a gravestone which had fallen or been pushed from an adjacent cemetery. It took over four hours to dislodge *Tyseley* with help from other boats pulling and pushing us, ropes on to the bank and much rocking from us stranded on board. At one point the boat was tilting so much that Mark had to pour water into the engine to keep it cool, as the intake for the water cooling system was high out of the water. There was a horrible moment when Sarah asked me where Sam was. I said I thought he was with her. Immediate panic. The dread of all parents – not knowing where your child is. Sam was only four. I started shouting his name out loud, convinced he must have fallen overboard while we had all been concentrating on the task in hand. After what seemed like hours, Ruth emerged to say Sam was happily playing on his bunk with his toys, apparently oblivious to our plight or keeping out of the way at such a difficult time.

From then on, Sarah and I always needed to know where Sam was at any particular moment. If one of the members of the Company wanted to take Sam off for a walk or to the shops, they must let us know. We had heard and read so many stories of the boatpeople's children lost overboard or drowned in a lock or crushed by the prop. If we were to continue touring with a growing child, Sam's safety had to be paramount. To this day, when Sam comes boating with us, I'm always aware of where he is even though he's a grown man and a very skilful boatman.

By the time we had refloated *Tyseley*, it was apparent we were not going to make our venue in time by boat. We still had to lock down Stourport Basin and travel down the Severn to Grimley. As so often on these occasions, help was at hand; a man appeared on the towpath and said "I'll take you and your kit in my Land Rover, if you like." We may not always reach our destination by boat but we've never cancelled a show because of our failure to arrive. We get there – be it by Land Rover, van or horse and cart (I made the last one up).

Our journey northwards via the Shropshire Union Canal was remarkably incident-free and we arrived in Ellesmere Port, where the old narrow canal joins the "modern" Manchester Ship Canal, on the 12th June. We had been invited to perform at the inaugural opening of the Boat Museum there. The remaining decaying buildings of this large interchange port had been saved and they were to house waterways archives and artefacts. In the basins themselves boats and barges were to be restored to their former glory as living exhibits.

Sonia Rolt, wife of the late Tom Rolt, author of the classic book *Narrow Boat*, opened the proceedings with a very grand speech. We were slightly nervous when we began our performance of *Puddle It* on the deck of the ex-tar boat *Gifford*. The opening scene was a very smart lady making a very grand speech at the opening of a canal. It sounded like a pastiche of Sonia's speech. Or maybe she had taken a sneaky look at our script beforehand! I've since got to know Sonia well (more of her when we come to *Imogen's War*), and she became one of Mikron's patrons.

It was when we moved on to the Cheshire Ring that we began to realise the full implications of this most un-English of summers – that there would be a price to pay for such glorious days of unbroken sunshine. Nothing comes free. Water levels were dropping fast, lock-opening hours were being severely reduced and there were mutterings that some canals would have to close completely. The six miles from Marple to Whaley Bridge on the Peak Forest Canal took us thirteen hours. We congratulated ourselves on actually making it, only to realise that we had to go all the way back. At least we knew it would be easier through one bridgehole – we had pulled out a recently stolen motor-bike.

On our return we used Mark as a depth-sounder. He walked down the middle of the canal wearing just swimming trunks; if we could see his trunks, we knew *Tyseley* hadn't sufficient depth to get through. We cleared out several bridgeholes, enlisted the help of a man and his tractor, who was quietly minding his own business in a field, to pull us through the "impossible" sections, and we never once (I'm crossing my fingers at the moment) thought that the same journey would take 10 minutes in a car. We were determined to get to our venue in time

THE YEAR OF THE DROUGHT

and after fourteen hours of sheer slog, *Tyseley* arrived at the top of Marple locks. Mark was catching the rope I'd thrown him and, with a burst of exhilaration stemming from extreme fatigue, he shouted to the world, "We've fucking made it." Man with child immediately appeared on the bridge: "We don't want that sort of language around here, particularly in front of children." "But we've just..." Mark was too exhausted to explain. He, like the rest of us, had still a one-and-a-half hour performance to do.

The remainder of the Peak Forest from Marple to Dukinfield, where we joined the relatively deep water of the Ashton Canal, was nightmarish. Our passage was hindered by all manner of objects not least those railway chairs again and our *pièce de résistance*, a Mini, all of which had to be removed from the canal before we could get *Tyseley* through. We were not too impressed either at our performance space at the very first CAMRA pub, the White Gates in Hyde. It was a scruffy piece of land behind the pub adjacent to a bonemeal factory. It was a miracle that neither us nor the audience vomited at some point during the show – the stench was horrendous.

What a relief to reach the deep water of the Bridgewater Canal and the Leeds & Liverpool. We now had enough time in the day to rehearse a longer version of *Puddle It* which we were going to perform at Lymm Cruising Club. There could be seen the bizarre sight of us with topcoat and hats above the waist and shorts with bronzed legs below, strutting our stuff on the Sahara wasteland that used to be known as the Wigan coalfields.

Our journey this year was not only to be impeded by water problems but also by road building. Stoke Council had closed the canal through their city so that they could build their state-of-the-art inner ring road. This meant *Tyseley* could not get through to the Caldon Canal where we were finishing the first half of our tour. The Council were very helpful and, when we asked for an alternative craft on the right side of the blockade, they went out of their way to oblige. We arrived at the "parking site" for *Tyseley* – a fenced area with security guards – and were provided with transport to move us and our gear to our new temporary home, or rather homes. There were two boats to greet us, *Captain Flint* and *Maid o' Warwick*, two small, very small, cabin-cruisers or "noddy boats", as they are affectionately known. Cabin-cruisers are given the nomenclature not because they sometimes look as if they are out of the pages of one of Enid Blyton's books, but because, in the early days of pleasure cruising when there was still considerable commercial traffic, the captains of these small craft were so nervous at passing a loaded pair of boats that, when the skipper of the pair shouted "good-morning" to them, all they could manage, while gripping the steering wheel tightly, was a nod.

We managed to pile ourselves, props, costumes, food and drink into

33

the boats and set off on our journey up the Caldon. *Captain Flint*, although not a boat in the mintest of conditions, pottered along steadily and was very easy to steer – unless the slightest of breezes got up, when it veered from one side of the canal to the other like an old sea-dog who had had one too many. *Maid o' Warwick*, on the other hand, would only steer straight if the engine was wound right up. The subsequent following wave was large enough to surf on and pulled every remaining piece of towpath along with it. The only solution was to travel at tick-over and then it appeared that *The Maid* had visited the same hostelry as *The Captain*.

All this was very amusing to us "narrowboaters" with our tillers and 16hp National engines but the adventure was worthwhile. The Caldon Canal is a beauty. It had only been re-opened in 1974 and was relatively little-used. The trip up it is a gradual change from the heavy industrialised Potteries through suburban Hanley to the grandeur of the Churnet Valley, a little-known area on the edge of the Peak District. I am loathe to tell you this but one of my very favourite spots on the whole canal system is Consall Forge. After a one-mile trip along a very bendy section of the River Churnet, you arrive at the Black Lion. The pub and a few houses stand in isolated splendour alongside the canal, the river and the railway with tree-filled hillsides rising up to seven hundred feet on either side. It is a tranquil oasis and, until recently, the only access for pub customers was either to arrive by boat or walk along the railway line (which used to have two or three trains a day carrying sand to Froghall) or down the hillsides from the nearest roads over a mile away. We've always had large audiences there, people considering it a challenge to find the pub. But sadly "progress" has meant there is now a car park in the valley bottom, the toilets are inside the pub and there are signs outside saying "No dogs" and "No dirty boots". It's still a wonderful place but why, oh why can nothing be left unspoilt?

We went off for a week's holiday knowing that the water situation was deteriorating rapidly. We knew we weren't going to be able to make Peterborough by boat for the National Waterways Rally. We arranged to borrow a van from the ever-helpful Waterway Recovery Group. We knew that the chance of *Tyseley* being able to reach all our second-half venues was remote.

At Peterborough, we performed in the usual festival-style marquee. At the end of the first performance, we asked if there was anybody out there who was prepared to lend us their boat so that we could continue our performances on the River Nene by water. Amazingly enough, a family of bakers from Tottenham stepped forward and offered us *Festina Lente*, their modern fifty-foot narrowboat. So, gratefully, we all squeezed on board and travelled by water, as is always our intention, from Peterborough to Northampton. They were grateful for having their boat moved up the Nene and we have never forgotten their generosity.

Water, water, not everywhere; more like trickle, trickle in some places and increasingly less so. Canals *were* closing completely; those that were open had ridiculously short lock opening hours and water levels that were sometimes a foot or more down. We struggled on until the beginning of September but finally tied up at Fazeley on the Birmingham & Fazeley Canal. We knew that if we didn't lift *Tyseley* out of the water and move her down to the Thames, which was still navigable, we were going to be locked inside the Midlands canal system.

On September 9th, *Tyseley* was lifted out of the water by two cranes, eased gently on to a flat-bed lorry and taken, with a police escort, to Oxford, where she was put into the Oxford Canal at Jericho. On the day of the lift-out it was raining for the first time since June! This delicate operation had cost Mikron £600. It was thus even more important that we attracted audiences. At most of our performances we didn't charge an entrance fee but took a collection on the way out. We made it clear, though, that we were not asking for coppers – we expected to be properly rewarded for an evening's professional entertainment. For the venues between Fazeley and Oxford, we again used the WRG van leaving Sarah and Sam behind every evening and travelling like a "normal" touring company.

By September 19th, we were again moving by boat on a River Thames where water was being pumped back upstream to keep it navigable. The rest of our tour was on the Thames and the southern Grand Union and boating again became pleasurable without the daily grind of heaving on ropes, pushing on poles and leaping into the canal to clear out yet another bridgehole.

One special event in October involved a trip by road to Yorkshire. We had been invited to perform at an event in Malton to draw attention to the restoration of the beautiful Yorkshire Derwent. Robert Aickman had lent his support to the project which was being co-ordinated by Heather and Graham Smith. The whole enterprise became a *cause célèbre*, when several landowners objected to the restoration and won the support of many organisations who were against having boats again moving on the upper reaches of the Derwent as they had a hundred years previously. These included the Yorkshire Wildlife Trust, the Royal Society for the Protection of Birds, the World Wildlife Fund and predictably, many angling clubs. (It is said that every fisherman in Yorkshire had been asked to contribute 50p to keep the boats away). The case went all the way to the House of Lords, cost many thousands of pounds and was eventually lost by the Yorkshire Derwent Trust in 1991, when the House of Lords overturned the Appeal Court ruling that a right of navigation existed on the river.

This judgement could potentially affect other rivers which do not have a clearly defined legal status. Even worse is the effect it has had on the lives of people like Heather and Graham Smith who devoted many, many years to trying to re-open a river for navigation in order that it could be enjoyed by the public at large. We all owe them a great debt for giving up so much of their time and energy. To lose the struggle after getting so close to winning must be devastating.

The tour finally ended on October 23rd, after six long months, at the Bedford Arms, Linslade. It had been a fascinating tour. Our battle to keep *Tyseley* moving had taken much of our time. The rest of our energies had been devoted to performing well. It is vital that your audience feels that the show is for them; it has to sparkle however many times you have done it before. But there was still some energy left for looking after Sam and for the interaction of personalities. Sam was now four. Half of his life had been spent on a boat and it was quite natural for him to be with five adults. He loved it, particularly when he was taken on special treats – a day at New Brighton with Mark and David, for example. Ruth didn't enjoy being with Sam and Sam spotted this and played her up. (When she met him a few years ago, her first words to him were: "Oh, you were a naughty boy, Sam")

Sam loved dressing up and acting out scenes from our shows (which he knew by heart). He also loved steering the boat – not when we were on the move but when we were safely tied up. He would get on the back counter, put the tiller on complete with tiller-pin, put on his cap, get his Nicholsons' map and off he went. He wasn't moving – he couldn't see over the top of the boat – but it was all real for him. Too real one day when, from the front of the boat, I heard a splash. I don't remember climbing off the boat and running to the other end. The first thing I remember is being in the water and lifting Sam out with his cap still on his head. Sarah had also heard a splash but what she had heard was me jumping in. Sam had pushed the tiller a little too enthusiastically and had slid into the water. When we recounted this close shave to our assistant administrator, Sue, she said she would have him swimming by the next tour. She did.

At the end of an exhausting day, Sam may have been reluctant to go to sleep but, when he did, he would sleep right through the night hardly ever being disturbed by the comings and goings of the older people on the boat. When the boat was tied up outside a pub we all used to take turns, when we were having our post-show drinks, to check if Sam was all right. We would be tied up only a few yards away, but we used to make a habit of checking him every ten minutes. We were having a small amount of "after-hours" with mine friendly host at the Boat, Berkhamsted, one night when there was a knock at the front door. John, the landlord went to the door, whispering to us to hide our glasses. Standing there was not a policeman about to give Mikron some unwanted publicity ("Actors caught in late night drinking raid") but Sam. In the short period from the last visit to the boat, Sam had got up, very sensibly put on his dressing gown and wellies, and proceeded to the pub. Of course, he was then the star of the evening, sitting on a high stool at the bar with a glass of lemonade and a straw, and regaling the illegal customers with his stories of life on the cut. In all the years of growing up on the boat, that is the only occasion I can remember Sam waking up and giving us a visit.

Mark and Ruth were married. Not to each other, I may add. We had enough with having to cope with one marriage on the boat. They had both recently married and, by the end of the six-month tour, had spent longer with Mikron than with their spouses. Ruth never told anyone she met, fellow boaters or members of the audience, that she was married. Several of them, including a lock-keeper and a boatyard owner, fell madly in love with her and pursued her round the country. She encouraged them and enjoyed her star status. One poor fellow told me excitedly towards the end of the tour that he was engaged to her.

David had a very soft spot for Ruth but the rest of us, including Sam as I said, found her increasingly mannered and irritating. She "gave the sink a birthday"; she "saw you on the ice". She talked in clichés. She made you sandwiches when you didn't want them, even though she rarely ate anything herself – she did drink lemon verbena tea – and, worst of all, she was a terrible steerer of the boat. All my frustrations came to the surface on the last day of the tour. She managed to put us heavily aground on a very deep section of the Grand Union. I ran up to the end of the boat with the intention, I think, of throwing her in the canal. Instead, I took a deep breath and threw her coffee cup in instead, with the words "You'll never steer this boat again!" Vain words on the last day of moving.

Ruth did go back to her husband and became a dancer. She now has a child of her own.

Mark would have loved to have done another year with us, but he wanted to save his marriage. He now works with much bigger boats – oil tankers – moving them around the oceans of the world from the comfort of his office. David worked next with Major Road. It was there he started the *a capella* work which eventually came to fruition with the group *The Flying Pickets* and their No1 hit *Only You*. He has now returned to being mainly an actor, touring regularly with companies like Oxford Touring Company.

7

"SOMETHING'S DIFFERENT THIS YEAR"

Ruth may have been not one of our best choices as a Mikron member. We didn't expect to make further mistakes. We hadn't reckoned on 1977.

Apart from myself, we were going to have to recruit a new acting company for the 1977 tour. Early in the New Year we advertised, as usual, in the actors' newspaper, *Stage*, and the response was excellent. We saw quite a few people and from these chose two men and one woman whom Sarah and I felt were going to make a good team. We were certainly right about the writing, acting and musical skills of the trio – what we had got horribly wrong was the living-with factor, at least as far as the two men were concerned. All of this would gradually reveal itself as the year progressed.

Mikron was now five years old. During those years we had met a number of boatpeople. Most of them were no longer working on the canals but they had been born into boating families and had worked either as children or adults on narrowboats. They still lived in towns or villages close to a canal and there are places today like Braunston, Coventry, Bedworth, Leighton Buzzard and Middlewich that have communities of ex-boatpeople.

We decided to write a show about the life of a woman on the boats. We spent two weeks visiting ex-boatwomen and men and recording their memories on tape. We ended up with hours and hours of fascinating material. Now, normally, the most difficult moment in writing a new show comes when you have to decide on a title. But this time, it became apparent quite early on in our research that our title had picked itself; over and over again, most of the people we met said they would never forget their lives on the boats and that, given the opportunity, they would go back tomorrow.

I'd Go Back Tomorrow was written by the four of us in two weeks, including eight new songs. The leading character was Alice. She was an amalgam of three remarkable women – Nell Cartwright, Annie Palin and Phyl Saxon. ("I'm not educated but I've enough to take me through the world." "I didn't like the gaffers." "I've emptied twenty-five tons of corned beef, thirty-one tons of copper and spelter, twenty-five tons of timber; to me work was nothing. I couldn't care less. I don't even today. I don't care how hard it is." "I'd do it all again, exactly the same as I have, with the horses, the boats and the loading.")

In the play, Alice is in her eighties and takes us right back to the beginning of the century when, as a young child, she was responsible for taking the horse over the top while the boat was being taken through a tunnel: "At seven years old, I was leading the horse. We didn't let her baccer, 'cos I was there of course. Along the winding towpath with no-one near to bother me, always walking with our Kit, riding bareback with the wind in your face. Wait for the boat out of the tunnel, you knew your place."

We felt confident that we had produced something rather special. The summer tour would prove whether we were right.

Since 1972 we had written and compiled over fifty songs for our shows and people had begun asking why we hadn't made a record. In early 1977, Eric Tomlinson and Peter Murray of Raymar Music Company had managed to persuade eight ex-members of Mikron and myself to gather at the Halfway House, now called the Horse and Barge, on the Grand Union at Harefield to record some of the songs in front of an invited audience. Of course, at that time, pubs had to close at two o'clock. So it was an unusual sight to see a group of actors without recourse to alcohol working their socks off to record a whole LP in five hours. Gathered there were Danny from '72, Alan, Richard and Anna from '74, Thirzie from '75 and Ruth (yes, despite my threats of water immersion), David and Mark from '76. Eric Tomlinson did wonders. He is the two-track maestro and had won an Oscar for his recording of the *Star Wars* music. With him and Peter, Sarah and I co-produced the album and it was released on the PBR label in time for our summer tour.

As we anticipated, *I'd Go Back Tomorrow* proved to be a tremendous success. The show was both amusing and moving. The music and songs captured just the right atmosphere. And what was most rewarding, the boatpeople themselves loved it and declared it to be a remarkably accurate portrayal of their lives on the boats. We were also delighted that John Saxon wrote the lyrics for the song *I am a Boating Man*. The production was seen again in 1978 and revived by popular demand in 1981.

Buffy Davis was the new female member of the Company. She was a superb Alice in the show and equally excellent in her varied parts in *Puddle It*. She had been born in Vancouver, Canada, but moved to Cheshire in 1967. She was not particularly experienced when she joined

Mikron but she had natural talent and musical ability. She had loads of red hair, was ebullient and witty – a positive asset to the Company.

Derek Harman and Matthew Marsh were the other two members of the Company. Derek had performed with companies like Theatre Mobile and Open Air Theatre Company, Cardiff, but it was Matthew's professional debut. They were both good actors and were excellent in the shows but...

When you perform in non-theatre venues, you not only perform at close proximity to your audience, but you meet them before and after the show. There is no quick escape through the backstage entrance. Nor, generally, would you want there to be. It's a small price to pay that occasionally you are invaded by the theatre or waterways bore, to be able to talk about the performance at first hand with members of your audience over a pint or two. In fact,we have made many friends as a result.

This year people would be chatting to Sarah and myself after the show and they would say: "Something's different this year. I can't put my finger on it. The shows are excellent, as usual, don't get me wrong...but it's to do with the atmosphere...the spirit of the shows."

That was it. True the shows were well-written and performed as ever. They were fast-moving and zingy, but what was lacking was true team spirit, the feeling that we were all working together for a common purpose, for something we believed in. The reason the audiences, or at least those who knew Mikron and had been following us for several years, felt this was because it was lacking. Our everyday life on the boat was being reflected in the performances. For the first time since the disastrous first half of 1973, two members of the Company were pulling in a different direction from the rest of us. Matthew hated living on a boat, was prepared to put up with it for the sake of gaining some very valuable experience but was not prepared to offer anything towards the social good of the rest of us. He also disliked pubs and rarely drank – a pretty lethal combination when touring with Mikron! He tried to set up a conspiracy of discontent with Derek. But Derek was so completely different from him in character that that never really worked. I think Derek found the world difficult and relationships particularly so. He is the only person I know that, when we were having our communal meal in the evening before the show, would sit crosslegged on the sofa with a copy of the *Guardian* in front of his face and never say a word. Mealtime was when we were supposed to get together, discuss the events of the day, or anything else that was concerning us, and listen to a briefing from me about the night's performance and the following day's journey. You try briefing a copy of the *Guardian*.

Life with Mikron progressed with Matthew throwing himself into learning how to cook (he went from a baked beans man to *haute cuisine* in a very short time) and into the pursuit of fresh coffee. He often walked miles to find a shop where he could buy high quality freshly ground coffee. Derek threw himself into falling in love with Buffy. She didn't reciprocate, but she was such a good-natured person she was never unkind to him.

Both of them enjoyed taunting 5-year-old Sam. Derek had no time for him at all but Matthew was more subtle in his cruelty. One moment he would be lifting Sam into the air in a playful way; the next he would be taking Sam's football to play with Derek and refusing to let Sam join in. Still, we gritted our teeth and got on with it. So much of the time you're working so hard, you almost don't notice that it is not as enjoyable as it had been in previous years.

We journeyed down the tidal Trent for the first time in order to visit the Chesterfield Canal and the Fossdyke and Witham Navigations. Although, scenically, the tideway has very little of excitement, the thrills come from navigating the river without accident and from the sight of ships and barges – commercial traffic. There are various hazards on the tidal Trent which can catch out the unwary once they have left the safety of Cromwell Lock. These include a sunken island, Dunham Rack (a long spit of gravel in the middle of the channel) and also the daunting sight of a laden gravel barge charging round the bend, seemingly straight at you.

Our first trip went off without incident (beginner's luck?). We went through Gainsborough where there were several coasters tied up loading and unloading, and in five miles we approached the entrance to the Chesterfield Canal at West Stockwith. Getting into West Stockwith Basin proved to be as hair-raising as the pundits predicted. Going downstream on a tide you have to steer past the lock entrance which is on a diagonal to the river. Then you start to turn and the really exciting moment is when you travel downstream sideways for what seems like an eternity before finally coming round to face upstream. You struggle, particularly with a 16 hp engine like ours, against the tide and, with a little bit of luck, you reach the jetty wall where a helpful lock-keeper and other volunteers take your ropes and drag you into the welcome still water of the lock.

The Chesterfield Canal is a delight; a winding, narrow waterway with delightful rural scenery for most of its length – and some of the most taxing bends for the steerer of a 72 foot narrowboat in the country. But it is a very under-used canal and severe weed growth makes for slow progress. We made it to all our venues, though, including the Chesterfield Canal Bicentenary Rally at Worksop, at that time the limit of navigation. Sections of the canal between Worksop and Chesterfield are now being restored.

We met more commercial traffic on the Caldon Canal, or rather we bumped into a cargo-carrying boat. *Tyseley* was being steered beautifully round a steep bend when from the other direction came a boat loaded with plates – of the earthenware variety. Neither boat could reverse in time so there was a minor collision. The crockery rattled and shook and then settled down again without a single breakage. The boatman seemed completely unruffled by the incident. He knew that, despite the odd encounter like this, carrying by canal had reduced breakages by two thirds and was also much cheaper than by road. Two boats were operating for Johnson Bros called *Milton Maid* and *Milton Queen* between their Hanley and Milton factories. The traffic continued until July 1995.

In July we were on the Macclesfield Canal performing, amongst other venues, at the Royal Oak in Bollington. Bollington is an industrial village. The canal passes above it on an aqueduct and looks down on dozens of little streets with alleyways and courtyards, with mill chimneys dominating the landscape. Sarah and I went for a walk along the canal. As we gazed down on to the village, we began to talk about our lives. We both agreed that, the longer we continued touring on the canals every summer, the more difficult it was becoming to readjust to life back in central London every winter. When you have been used to the quiet and tranquillity of the canals and to visiting many towns and villages all with their distinct characters, London presented a brash, hectic face on our return. All our friends who lived there seemed to be running around chasing their tails. They were constantly dashing about and constantly worried. For the last seventeen years, London had been an exciting place for us with so much to see and do. Samuel Johnson said that, when you are tired of London, you are tired of life. But we felt quite the opposite. We now realised that there was a whole world out there which wasn't London. And we liked a lot of what we had seen on our travels. Should we be thinking of moving out of the capital, away from the hubbub? Wouldn't it be better for Sam, not to have to go to school on the Tower Bridge Road? "If we did move out," said Sarah, "it has to be to somewhere like this, a large village or small town surrounded by hills and beautiful countryside." "With a canal nearby," I replied jokingly. We walked on and said nothing more about it.

For the first time, Mikron was to travel on the section of the Leeds & Liverpool Canal between Wigan and Leeds. The locks are only 62 feet long. So it was necessary for us to trans-ship on to another vessel for this epic journey. Our new craft was *Weaver*, a Leeds & Liverpool short boat especially designed and built for the waterway. These boats were 62 feet in length and 14 feet 2 inches wide and were decorated with delicate scroll work and subdued colours. *Weaver* was owned by Derek Bent, a passionate lover of boats and waterways. He was to be our captain. We were to be "housed" in the hold.

Under the sheets or canvas of the boat, life was pretty basic. The six of us, including Sam, bedded down on pieces of foam laid on the

An early publicity shot of Mike Lucas at Little Venice in 1972.

Danny Schiller and Karena Mond in Still Waters at the King's Head in Islington, 1972.

Mike Lucas and a early tankard for Sam, at the Bridge Inn, Branston in 1974.

Leaving the Northampton Water Festival in 1973 aboard
Hood and Fazeley.

Performing Still Waters for the Hillingdon Environmental
Action Party in 1973. Cast from left: Steve Whittaker,
Leonora Keogh, Anne Wells and Mike Lucas.

Rudder trouble above Dimmingsdale Lock, Staffs & Worcs
Canal, 1974: Tim Cashin, Alan Bridger, Mike Lucas, Sarah
Lucas and Sam.

Getting ready for a performance, Wolvercote Green, 1974
(P.J. Alexander)

Taking part in BBC's Blue Peter, 1975.
Above: Stuck in a lock on the Stratford Canal – Lesley
Judd, left foreground.
Below: Peter Purves and Mike Lucas get to grips with life in
the galley.

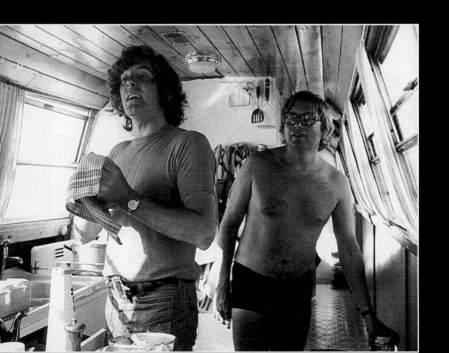

Tyseley travelling along the Caldon Canal in 1975. Alan Bridger, Sam, Mike Lucas, Sarah Lucas, Dan Caulfield and Thirzie Robinson.   (Harry Arnold)

A performance of Keep Yer 'ands Off outside the Canal Museum at Stoke Bruerne in 1975.

Puddle It at the Wise Alderman, Kidlington in 1976. Mike Lucas, Matthew Marsh, Derek Harman and Buffy Davis.

(P.J. Alexander)

Matthew Marsh, Buffy Davis, Derek Harman, Mike Lucas, Sam and Sarah Lucas at Apsley on the Grand Union Canal in 1977.

wooden floor of *Weaver*. There was a small cooker, a sink with cold water and a small "tent" containing the Elsan, which is a toilet consisting of a large bucket with a toilet seat on top. We were used to this system on *Tyseley* and I still consider this to be the simplest and the best despite the innovation of porta-loos and pump-outs. It would cost Mikron about £150 a year to have a pump-out toilet emptied regularly at boatyards. A visit with the bucket to a British Waterways Elsan Disposal is quick and free.

Life on board *Weaver* was great when the weather was fine. It was just like camping really. If the sun shone you could open up the sheets and sunbathe on your bed. If it was raining your "home" was damp and gloomy. In 1977, the weather was kind. The Leeds & Liverpool has to be my favourite of all English canals. It has everything – stunning Pennine scenery, backdoor views of towns and cities like Leeds, Liverpool, Blackburn and Burnley, big heavy locks and a staggering array of swing bridges, some of which are for a farmer to get his cows from the field to the milking shed, some are on very busy roads and most of them are hard and difficult to shift. There is one notorious stretch between Skipton and Bingley where there are eighteen swing bridges. But this is all part of the excitement, and I always felt I'd deserved my pint or two after a day moving *Weaver* followed by a performance in the evening.

Buffy had to use all her diplomatic skills and her powerful personality to keep the two Dereks from indulging in fisticuffs on the towpath. You see, both were now in love with her and, as a result, couldn't stand the sight of each other. Charismatic gal, our Buffy.

Our journey on *Weaver* also took us on to the Aire & Calder Navigation – the major commercial canal in the country. We were fortunate to see many barges either on the move or loading and unloading – there was coal for Ferrybridge and sewage on its way from Bradford and Leeds to disposal at sea. And when we arrived in Goole, where the canal joins the Ouse, there were not only ships from Russia and other countries in the port but a train of Tom Puddings being loaded. Sadly no more, Tom Puddings were a superbly efficient way of moving coal – floating iron boxes about 20 foot by 16 each carrying 35 tons. As many as fifteen at a time could be towed by a tug. It was wonderful to see a train snaking along the canal. You had to get out of their way – otherwise they would just push you up the bank.

The fall in the demand for coal by industry brought the life of the remaining Tom Puddings to an end in 1986. Only one of the hoists and a few pans remain as a reminder of the importance of getting coal in a steady flow to the ever-demanding factories and mills of the Industrial Age.

This year we were not able to get to the National Rally by boat. We had to rely on the generosity of Waterway Recovery Group. They were to transport us there in one of their red vans. John Palmer, their transport manager, was to drive us. What a journey we had. The van was quite poorly and after a few miles came to a halt. It was a fanbelt problem; so John utilised a pair of Buffy's tights as stand-in belt. This would work for a few miles – then the tights would snap and another pair had to be fitted. So we progressed, taking nine hours to complete the journey from Bradford to Reading. Needless to say we were late for our performance.

The weekend didn't really improve. It rained constantly, the site was turned into a mud bath and the general public stayed away in their droves. The one consolation for us was that we were packed for every performance, as events like the best-behaved dog and the march of the majorettes had to be cancelled. Our audience was almost solely people off boats who were trying to find any distraction from the sheer misery of the occasion.

Matthew was a complete pain in the bum – he did nothing but moan, even complaining that he hadn't got a separate dressing room. Buffy laughed at him. Sarah and I tried to be diplomatic whilst being severely tempted to slap him one.

In September, we were filmed by Harlech Television for a half-hour documentary about the life and work of the Company. It wasn't a bad effort although not really representative of a typical day on the canals (struggling along an undredged ditch), as it was filmed on the deep and wide River Severn and Gloucester & Sharpness Canal. Derek talked about the lack of space on the boat, employing his favourite expression "so be it" several times in the interview, and Matthew was filmed cooking, talking about his newly-discovered skill and his addiction to coffee. There were some delightful scenes of Sam reading a story and buying his mum a birthday present and, all in all, I'm sure it upped our profile with the general public.

At the end of September, we travelled by road to Huddersfield to give a performance as part of the Canal Festival. We enjoyed visiting the "North" again, the show went well and we even managed a visit to a beer festival in the splendid town hall. At the time, little did Sarah, Sam and I realise the significance of this trip to Huddersfield.

I can remember little of the latter part of the tour, only that it was beginning to seem very long. One highlight was our performance inside Dudley Tunnel. We travelled into the tunnel with the audience in an electric boat. It was very eerie travelling along, with just the gentle whirr of the engine and the slopping of the water. After a brick-lined section, the canal opens out into a rock-hewn cavern and we performed there to our very first captive audience.

It wasn't until we were back in London that Sarah and I realised what a strain the last six months had been – gritting our teeth and just getting on with the job. We had managed to keep our marriage together

– just. But for Sam it had also been a difficult season and I know he felt ignored and disregarded by Derek and Matthew. It's not that we don't warn people. We tell a potential company member that we have a young child and ask them how they would cope with that. "Oh, I love kids...I've got a younger brother," they would say. Well, I suppose you do if you're desperate for a job. But you have to be prepared to rue the consequences if you're lying. Or, perhaps, they really believed it at the time. Thank goodness we had had Buffy with us, a delightful person in every way. I'm only sorry that she didn't get a better deal with fellow cast members. She has continued to mature as an actress and is often to be seen on television or in the theatre. I've seen Matthew several times since 1977 – on the television that is. He's a good actor. I've no idea what has happened to Derek.

8

THE MOVE NORTH

The question Sarah and I had to ask ourselves and answer was: did we wish to continue with Mikron? It had been a great idea and we had been pretty successful in carrying out our aim of taking professional theatre to places where you wouldn't normally expect to see it. But were we prepared to carry on touring year in, year out in pursuit of an ideal? Were we prepared to put up with egocentric actors whose only reason for touring with us was not that they identified with the ideal but that they wanted an Equity card or another credible entry on their CV? And what about Sam? Was it fair on him? True, he generally seemed to enjoy the life and he seemed to be developing into an interesting and sensitive child. But what about his schooling? True, the infants school in the Tower Bridge Road had accepted that Sam would be missing from school for six months every year and were satisfied that we would keep up with his schooling. But for how long? What would happen when he was seven and moved to junior school? Were we being selfish, dragging him along with us and were we being fair to our own marriage? We had had five years at it and proved a point. There would be no shame in ducking out now.

We thought long and hard and finally decided that we loved the life. It was great to have a job where the three of us could be together. Sarah and I were equally responsible both for the bringing up of Sam and the nurturing of a company. We were just beginning to get good at it. There was heaps of potential for Mikron yet. Why let two male actors put us off our stride?

We decided to carry on but that we would have an acting company of two men and two women, and the prime consideration when choosing the new team should be that we like them and that we think that they are going to be easy to live with on the boat. Hopefully, they will possess considerable acting and musical skills, but that would come secondary to their acceptability as members of the human race.

Back in our council flat in London we were again feeling discontented. Despite the rigours of the last tour, we still missed the boat and the peace and quiet of the countryside. Our minds went back to our walk along the towpath in Bollington. Sarah said to me one morning, " I wonder how much houses are costing in the North. They're probably outside of our price bracket but it won't harm to check it out."

As it happened, I was travelling into Soho that day to do some work in a sound studio. I had become quite an expert at the art of dubbing and over the years I had earned most of my income from putting English voices over foreign films and from voice-overs for television ads. Some of these films were of the soft porn variety. My voice for the randy hero of the Swedish film, *Exposed*, ran for two years in a Leicester Square cinema. Sarah's mum used to love telling her friends in Leeds that her son-in-law was appearing in the West End. I have spent mornings in a darkened studio dubbing the sensual grunts of a lusty youth. Apparently, foreign grunts are different from the English variety.

This particular morning I think I was dubbing for a Belgian children's series which was scheduled to be shown on the BBC. Sarah said "On your way back, pick up a *Yorkshire Post* at the station." I said "You won't be able to get a Yorkshire Post at Charing Cross Station. King's Cross possibly but..." "Just have a try," she said.

After a morning earning as much as I could in a week with Mikron, I went into the newsagents at Charing Cross Station. There staring up at me, begging to be bought was a crisp, fresh edition of the *Yorkshire Post*. As soon as I was on the train, I opened the paper. Amazingly, it was the Houses For Sale page. I looked at it, and the first thing I saw was a little box: "Canalside Cottage For Sale. Marsden. £3,500". We had never in our wildest dreams thought of living in a canalside cottage. It's not the sort of residence that poorly paid actors can afford. But £3,500, that might be feasible. We got out a map and looked up Marsden. It wasn't listed. It was somewhere in Yorkshire but on what canal? Certainly not one we had ever been on.

Fate now took another twist. It so happened that the following weekend we were due to go to a Waterway Recovery Group party in the centre of Manchester. We were going with others, including Graham Palmer, the redoubtable leader of WRG, in a hired mini-bus. If we found out where this Marsden was, we might be able to persuade the others to stop off *en route*.

We phoned. Yes, the house was still for sale. Yes, we could visit at the weekend. Marsden turned out to be eight miles from Huddersfield, on the road to Oldham, and the house was alongside the Huddersfield Narrow Canal. A little research revealed that this was the third of the trans-Pennine canals after the Leeds & Liverpool and the Rochdale. Both the Huddersfield Narrow and the Rochdale were now mainly derelict.

So it was, the following Sunday we managed to cajole some well-hungover fellow passengers to delay their return to the capital with a visit to Marsden. What swung it was the lure of looking at a canal nobody really knew anything about, except Graham, who said, "There are some enthusiasts who want to restore it. But it has 74 locks in twenty miles and a three-and-a-quarter mile derelict tunnel under the Pennines. It's a non-starter."

It was a miserable, grey November day as we came "over the top" from Lancashire into Yorkshire and descended into Marsden at the head of the Colne Valley. Nevertheless, the sweep of the wild moorland with a few sheep dotting the landscape and the sight of the village itself nestling in a curve of the land was impressive. We soon found the house, a few hundred yards from the centre, at the top of a steep hill.

Sarah and I had no clear idea of what we were expecting. We were sure that the house was going to be semi-derelict with thousands of pounds needed to be spent on it. It had to be for that price. In 1978, you'd expect to pay at least £6,000 for anything decent. But there it was, an attractive cottage from the outside, attached to a larger building on the old canal wharf. At the back was the canal, a trickle of water finding its way between the trees and undergrowth which flourished in the bed of the once-navigable waterway. Nearby was some old paddle gear and a hump of grass underneath which would presumably be the remains of a lock.

The people in the house next door were selling the house. They explained that it had been the lock-keeper's cottage and where they lived had been the warehouse for the loading, unloading and storage of cargo. They said that the house had been empty for nearly two years, that several people had looked at it but the only people to have put in offers were those who wanted it as a second home for weekends and holidays. They wanted a family to live in the house full-time.

Inside, the house was small – basically a two-up, two-down – but it was perfectly liveable in and not in any way derelict. We looked around for a few minutes and, without even consulting each other, we said to the sellers, "We love it. It's the only house we have ever looked at but we would like to buy it." We asked about schools and transport and shops, we explained that, although it would be our only house, because of our job, we would be away for six months of the year, and we told them that we weren't even sure if we could get a mortgage or a loan for such an amount. Everything about the house, the place, the hills seemed right. The view had to be worth the asking price. Our neighbours-to-be said, "If you like it on a day like today, wait until the sun shines and, if the house feels right for you, you'll feel right for us."

A few days later, back in London, we went to see our bank manager, rather grandly situated in Berkeley Square, to see if he would give us a loan. It turned out he was from the North-East and was himself applying to return to a bank there. He had had enough of London and agreed with us that the quality of our lives would be improved if we moved. The loan repayment terms were equivalent to what we were paying in rent for our council flat.

THE MOVE NORTH

A month or so later we were owners of a canalside cottage in Yorkshire and our lives were to change irrevocably. There was no going back. We would never again be able to afford a place to live in London. Were we really going to enjoy the life of "country bumpkins"? It gradually dawned on us what an important decision we had made. Leaving all our friends behind to go and live in the cultural wastelands of the North.

All this was to come. In the meantime, we had a new season to plan and a new company to assemble. We auditioned, and chose two women and a man who we thought would be easy-going and pleasant to live with and would enjoy the life on the canals and the presence of a very lively 6- year old. They were: Jo Fitzgerald from London, Carmen Lynn from Hull and Hilary Rikof, who had Swedish/Welsh parents but had been brought up in Bromsgrove in Worcestershire. It was Jo and Hilary's professional debut. Carmen had worked in fringe theatre and had been a singer/guitarist in theatre restaurants.

We were reviving the highly successful *I'd Go Back Tomorrow* and researching and writing a new show. This was to be a musical journey through inland transport, past, present and future, starting with Roman roads and ending in 2050 with the royal opening of a long-derelict but now re-opened M62. The modern day research was particularly fascinating as we met people like William Rogers, the Minister of Transport, Bob Harrison, National Secretary of the Transport and General Workers Union, and went on a trip up the Thames as the guests of the crew of one of the latest Thames tugs.

The show was called *What a Way to Go*, and was rehearsed in London in late March and early April along with *I'd Go Back Tomorrow*. But, before we had our final dress rehearsals, there was an important matter to sort out – moving all our worldly possessions to Marsden. There they were going to stay until we joined them in November.

Neither Sarah nor I could drive. It had never seemed necessary to be able to do so. London is much easier to get around by tube, bus or taxi, and a car became completely irrelevant as soon as we went on the boat. So, early one April morning, a friend called Lesley arrived in a hired van and we loaded our "home" aboard. It all fitted easily into a box van. A couple of neighbours and some friends stood outside our flat in Bermondsey and toasted us and our new life with a glass of champagne (or was it just sparkling wine?). Sarah was suffering with her neck, which she had pulled moving furniture and was in some pain. But our spirits were not to be dampened and we set off up the M1, leaving London and the last eighteen years of our lives behind.

Marsden was welcoming or rather the local pub, the Railway (one of many), was. We unloaded all our gear into our new cottage. It was cold and not a little damp, so we (including Alan Bridger of 1974-5 fame who now lived in Bradford and had come over to help) found sanctuary in the hostelry. The landlady, Muriel, immediately recognised Sarah and myself. "You're the people who are moving in, aren't you? Well, welcome. You're going to love Marsden. Four pints of bitter, is it?"

We spent a cosy, if not exactly warm night on the living room floor, had a quick look round at the canals and the surrounding hills the next morning and then set off for Aylesbury where we were to join the others on *Tyseley*.

This was to be an unusual introduction to canal life for the new cast. We weren't going to be moving anywhere for a week. We were going to be tied up in Aylesbury, down the end of the very pretty and rural arm off the Grand Union. They were going to get used to life on board whilst making the final preparations for our first performances.

The first performance of *I'd Go Back Tomorrow* was in a community hall on Monday, May 1st. It went moderately well but the show had lengthened considerably from the previous year and that was with exactly the same script. The reason was all too apparent – Hilary's performance as Alice, the boatwoman. Hilary looked like a boatwoman both when being eighty and eight; she sounded just like a boatwoman (her Bromsgrove background meant she was able to capture those Midlands vowel sounds perfectly). She really was Alice to a tee – which is where the problem arose. She used no artistic licence. It was a full method performance. When she was being eighty, she spoke in very slow, considered measured tones as an eighty-year-old would. It took for ever. The narrative sections were interminable and at times I felt the show was just going to grind to a halt. Something had to be done. It took a few performances to sort it out; for Hilary to realise that, however good she was at getting right under the skin of Alice, this was useless unless she communicated it to the audience. If she didn't project her character and use stagecraft to put it across, we were going to have audiences walking out. "I can't hear her. She's so slow. I'm off for a pint."

But when she did crack it, it became a superb moving performance and it was a joy to act with her.

Sarah was in a great deal of pain with her neck. We weren't far from Stoke Mandeville Hospital, where they specialise in spinal injuries. There she was told that it would slowly get better, but she would need to wear a neck brace for a few weeks. We must have looked a strange bunch as we set off on *Tyseley* up the Aylesbury Arm. For Jo, Hilary and Carmen, it was their introduction to the art of boat-moving and they were immediately presented with 16 narrow locks as their first challenge. Sarah, resplendent in a white neck collar, was instructing the novices aided by Sam, who, at the age of six, was already a veteran. The others ran about like headless chickens, obeying orders, opening paddles and pushing on lockgates, and we progressed up to the Main

Line at a reasonable pace. When we reached the venue, the White Lion at Marsworth, Jo confessed that, although he had enjoyed all the dashing about, he had no real idea of what he had been doing and still did not understand how a lock worked.

They were all to get even more confused a few days later when we arrived at Hunton Bridge. There was no way through. There had been a breach; that is, a hole had appeared in the side of the canal and the water had just poured out into the river below. British Waterways had already put stop planks in and had begun repairs but this didn't help our immediate predicament. What was going to happen to our schedule? How were we going to get to our venues the other side of the breach and, if and when it was repaired, how would we ever catch up on ourselves?

The new members were beginning to wonder what sort of venture they had got themselves into. You work like mad up and down locks which you are just beginning to understand; after a hard day's slog, you arrive at your venue; then you do a show; then you set off again only to have your way blocked by a closed canal. Wouldn't short trips along motorways in a van be much easier on the body and the mind?

They were soon to find out. Sarah and I spoke to the waterways manager in charge of the repairs; well, we didn't speak to him – we almost broke down in front of him, telling him that our livelihoods were at stake. He listened carefully, was obviously moved by our very real concern and then promised to provide a British Waterways van complete with driver to take us to our venues until the repairs were finished. After about five days trundling around in a van, I think Jo, Carmen and Hilary were mightily relieved to be told that the breach had been repaired and that the next day we would again be moving by boat. They then had the experience of flyboating – that is, moving a boat day and night without stopping until you reach your destination. *Tyseley* was a flyboat during the Second World War, when she was carrying the most important cargo from London to Birmingham – Guinness. We had two days before our next show; so we boated like mad down into London and finally the boat was where it was intended to be according to the schedule.

The new members now were beginning to get the feel of how exciting boating could be – and how unpredictable. They were proving to be just the sort of people we needed after the traumas of the last tour. They were kind to us, each other and Sam and easy to rub along with. The overall standard of performance may not have been the best we'd ever had, but everyone was competent and the shows were going well. Carmen had a lovely, pure voice, despite being completely deaf in one ear, Jo played a mean guitar and harmonica, and Hilary's Alice continued to grow in stature.

Jo was a very laid back person. When he thought I was starting to panic or over-react about a situation, he would say to me, "Calm down, dear boy. Calm down." He had become solely responsible for the emptying of the Elsan, the toilet bucket. He said he positively enjoyed doing it. Everyone was quite happy for him to take on this role, and we ceased to see the sight of members of the Company emerging from the disposal point with handkerchiefs round their mouths looking a ghostly shade of pale. He would not be daunted by a blockage – quite frequent in the old-fashioned porcelain Elsan disposals. For the normal person there was usually a stick provided so that the sewage could, by prodding, be persuaded to drain away. Not for Jo. He would use his bare hands to aid it on its way. Now this bit may or may not be apocryphal, but it seemed a peculiar coincidence that the day Jo was bucket emptying was the day that he was preparing his marinade for his tandoori chicken. Jo's tandoori chicken was the tastiest and most flavourful I've ever had.

Jo was so laid back that, even when he was in extremity, he remained calm almost to the point of indifference. The first of these extreme moments occurred on the Thames. We were travelling downstream from Newbridge on the Upper Thames above Oxford to Duke's Cut which gives access to the South Oxford Canal. Parts of this stretch are notoriously bendy and it was while negotiating a particularly vicious twist that the very strong wind blew us on to a sandbank. Now, on a canal, when you find yourself aground, you can either push yourself off by means of poles and rocking the boat or walk back to the nearest lock and give yourself some more water. But the only solution we had on the river was for someone to jump in and to try and shove the boat back into the deeper water. Jo was an eager volunteer as was Ray, our graphic designer, who was travelling with us that day. In they went. It was a warm day and, with a great effort, they managed to push the boat across into the channel.

In order to avoid being blown aground again, I had to put the boat into forward gear. But, somehow, we had to get Ray and Jo back on board. Ray held on to the gunwhales and managed to haul himself through the sidehatch into the safety of the boat. Jo, for some incredible reason, thought he would climb on to the back counter or stern. As he started to put his legs under the counter so he could get a grip with his arms, I screamed at the top of my voice, "Nooooooo", and at the same time twisted the control wheel into neutral. I was a gibbering wreck as we hauled the rather whale-like body of Jo aboard. He was just as calm as ever, maybe not even realising that, if his legs had connected with the moving propeller, they would have been chopped off.

Whilst we were on the South Oxford, we had a booking at a most extraordinary venue – the RAF base at Upper Heyford, better known as one of the USA's airbases for their B52 bombers. Ostensibly, the base still belonged to the RAF; so, every so often, they would have Anglo/American evenings and Sarah had managed to get us booked in to provide the entertainment, a performance of *What a Way to Go*.

We were collected from *Tyseley* in a very large jeep, driven by a very tall black airman from Texas. We immediately began to feel we were in some Hollywood movie, probably *Mash*. These feelings increased as we drove on to the base. It was completely self-contained – a little America in the heart of the Oxfordshire countryside. Everything the guys needed from Coca-Cola to T-bone steaks was flown in from the States; dollars were the only valid currency and in the bar cocktails were definitely shaken and not stirred. We were told that we would be performing after they had eaten and, like the travelling players of old, mere underlings, left in a side room without even a sandwich while they (USAF and RAF officers and their wives) proceeded to do so.

As we stood around the bar area not even able to try a Manhattan or a Screwdriver, due to our imminent performance, we noticed that there were some airmen who were also not drinking. They all had cards pinned to their chests saying "On Alert". We discovered that these were the men on duty, the men who, if the four-minute warning came, were to climb into their B52s, roar into the sky and drop nuclear weapons on Russia. It should have made us feel cosy, safe and protected but it didn't. It was simply chilling, realising that we were a plane ride away from a full-scale nuclear conflict.

We converted the price of our programmes and records into dollars, erring on the side of capitalistic opportunism and performed to a replete, if not wildly extrovert, audience. There were a few comments of "Gee, that was not bad" and then we were whisked back to the canal – and England. After a couple more years of this, we took a moral stand and decided that, if we were in favour of the removal of American airbases (which we were), we should discontinue our relationship with Upper Heyford.

Jo's second encounter with extremity came on the Macclesfield Canal on the 28th of June. We had just begun our climb up the Bosley flight of locks. It had been raining and everywhere was slippery. Jo, wearing a large overcoat and big boots, jumped off to open the bottom gates for us. I steered *Tyseley* in and waited while Jo closed the bottom gates, and walked up to the top end to wind up the paddles to fill the lock. No-one else had got off to help.

My attention must have wandered for a second or two. The water is starting to come into the lock and Sam is shouting to me from the front end of the boat, "Dad, Jo's fallen in!" There's no sign of Jo. I manage to haul myself on to the lockside and run to the top end. At first I cannot see Jo. Then, I look down and there he is. He is clinging by his fingertips to the paddle post. All but his head is in the water. The rest of his body is being sucked down the paddle hole. I am just about to lower the paddle to release the pressure of water when Sarah, who is now on the bank, screams, "Don't do that! You'll break his legs." True. His legs would have been caught by the descending paddle. So I grab hold of his arms and with great difficulty hold on to him until the lock is nearly full and the force of the water has died down. We are then able to pull him on to the lockside.

Jo seemed completely calm although he was shivering after his immersion. We put him in the shower and poured ourselves a restorative tot of whisky. Jo said that, when I reached him, he felt his fingers getting numb and he was about to let go. If he had have done, he would have been pulled down the paddle hole, jammed halfway and drowned. He was in fine fettle when he came out of the shower, only remarking that he ought to get a pair of boots that didn't have a flapping sole. The rest of us worked up the remaining nine locks slowly and carefully, never once crossing the top gates, which have no guards on them, looking distinctly pale and contemplating our own mortality.

Our trip across the Leeds & Liverpool this year was on another Leeds & Liverpool shortboat, not *Weaver* but *Lune*, skippered by Geoff Wheat. We were to get to know Geoff very well over the next few years. Our maiden trip with him was relatively uneventful. No-one fell in love with anybody else but we did encounter the Yorkshire llamas. The Anchor at Gargrave had a small zoo in the fields surrounding the pub and, sure enough, there were llamas grazing alongside the canal. As we progressed down the canal, we told a man on the front of a passing boat, "Watch out for the Yorkshire llamas further up the canal." And, as we disappeared round the bend, we could hear him telling his fellow crew members very knowledgeably about this new breed.

The 1978 National Waterways Rally was held in the Black Country. It was our first venture up the Titford Canal and, via the six locks, into Titford Pools, where there was plenty of space for the hundreds of boats that attended. All the traditional boats were tied up underneath a viaduct over the M5. We thought it was going to be dreadful but it turned out to be the quietest place on the site – just a bit of a rattle from the juggernauts pounding overhead oblivious to their transport ancestors bobbing underneath. It was the first time that Waterway Recovery Group had been involved in the organisation of a National Rally. Graham Palmer's logistical skills resulted in one of the best "Nationals" ever.

It had been an enjoyable tour. The new Company members had been easy to live with and Jo had ceased dicing with death. Carmen had even acquired a boyfriend *en route*, Paul who also lived on a boat. It was a natural phenomenon which was to provide us with our final hazard – the River Trent.

THE MOVE NORTH

We managed to avoid the sunken island again on our trip down the tidal Trent, but we headed too soon for the willow trees on the opposite bank shortly after Dunham Bridge and landed on the dreaded Dunham Rack – the wide, shallow section of gravel in the middle of the river. It really is shallow. I walked around *Tyseley* with the boatshaft and prodded. She appeared to be sitting in a few inches of water. We tried pushing with poles but *Tyseley* remained steadfastly still. We waved at the fishermen who were on the far bank but they were much too involved in the contemplation of their unmoving rods to be concerned by a theatre company with nowhere to go on a tidal river. Finally, with a great deal of effort, we managed to push the bow into deeper water and, suddenly, the tide took it and we swung around ninety degrees into the deep water. We were facing the wrong way but, at least, we were on the move again. We turned again and continued on to Torksey. On our way back upstream, we were let out on to the tideway very early in the morning at Torksey Lock, only to discover that the Trent was covered in a thick mist and that visibility was virtually nil. A small cabin cruiser who came out with us, very sensibly, immediately turned round and returned to the safety of the Fossdyke Navigation. We had no such choice. We had to go. We were performing at Newark that night.

We moved very slowly upstream trying to stay near enough to the bank to see where we were but not so near that we would go aground. Our biggest fear was that one of the many gravel barges would be coming downstream and would not be able to see *Tyseley* in time. Rather forlornly, we placed Hilary's boyfriend (visiting, poor boy) in the bows and instead of playing his clarinet, we got him to blow the boat horn continuously. We needn't have worried. The gravel barge captains were far too sensible and when we passed them they were all tied up waiting for the fog to clear.

We had two terrifying moments. The first one was when we heard what sounded like the horn from a barge blasting out as it bore down on us. As we drew closer we realised it was the lowing of a cow. Much more life-threatening was when a dredger, moored in the middle of the river, loomed up at us. Now dredgers have a white disc or flag to indicate the safe side to pass. The red disc is the side where the chains holding the dredger pass under the water on to the shore. Our problem was we couldn't see the discs. The dredger was getting closer and closer. I would have to make a decision as to which side to pass. "Which side?" I screamed. "Right" someone shouted. Perversely, I steered to the left. Call it captain's instinct, but it was the right decision and a mighty pile-up with steel hawsers was avoided.

9

SNOWING AND TOWING

The tour ended at the end of October and, for the first time, Sarah, Sam and I went back to our cottage in Marsden. After living with four other people on a boat for six months, meeting people every day whom we had got to know over the years, it felt very strange moving into a Pennine village where we knew no-one. It was going to take time to feel our way into the place but being regulars at the Railway helped. A pub is a place where people don't stand on ceremony, where inhibitions are soon lost and confidences are exchanged.

Sam just did what most 6-year-olds would have done in order to be liked. He conformed. He arrived with a broad London accent but within a week he was talking "Yorkshire". Not only "Yorkshire" but "Marsden" which was even a different accent from Slaithwaite, two-and-a-half miles down the valley.

Sarah and I were spending much of our time alone in each other's company at first. This, coupled with the inevitable trauma of moving house and moving to a completely different part of the country, as removed from London as living abroad really, put a great strain on our relationship. We had to take a long hard look at ourselves and each other and decide whether or not we had made a big, big mistake. Not that we could have done much about it if we had. We were living together in Marsden with Sam. This was our new life.

We tried to talk honestly to each other. We were very frank and, as a result of this self-counselling, we grew very attracted to each other again. I would say we fell in love all over again. This closeness was to stand us in good stead when, later, together we had to fight the bigotry which always seems to exist in small communities. We may have been welcomed by most people but there was a tight-knit group of indigenous Marsdeners who, over the years, did everything they could to try and destroy us.

One of the first things to strike us when we arrived in Marsden were the large signs just outside the village which said "SNOW. When red light is flashing, be prepared to stop." It sounded really dramatic. Could the snow really get that bad? Yes. The winter of 1978/9 was very cold. The canal outside our back door was frozen over for more than two months and there were heavy falls of snow. We thought it was great. Sam, especially, had never seen snow like it. It lay on the ground for weeks. There was tobogganing, snowballing and skiing. There were huge drifts. Small lanes were blocked and the red signs often flashed. We thought this was quite normal for Marsden but, sadly, we've not had a winter like it since.

One of the casualties of the heavy snow was the Electric Cinema in Marsden. One of the first cinemas in the country, it had remained open until the early 1970s. Sarah and I had already started to dream of re-opening it as a community arts centre. If we were going to live in this community, we felt it was important to give something back to it. The Electric Cinema was one of the very first to have been built in England. It had not closed until 1974. The day it collapsed, because of the weight of snow on the roof, I was the last person to take photos of it. The screen was still intact, the seats were covered in a thick layer of snow, there was a poster advertising *Alfie* in the foyer and, in the glass-fronted ticket booth, were a pair of round National Health spectacles and a ticket roll. Within twenty-four hours, the building had been demolished and the screen and seats had vanished. It was as if it had never been.

During the winter we went into a studio and made our second record, *I'd Go Back Tomorrow*, which had songs from that show on one side and from *What a Way to Go* on the other. We also auditioned in London for a new company. Jo, Carmen and Hilary had all decided not to do another year. For the first time, the Company had to live and rehearse in Yorkshire. They all stayed with our very kind neighbours, Keith and Margaret – Sandra Moore, Chris Whittingham and Carol Prior. At the final auditions, we discovered that Sandra (or Snad as she became known) and Chris were partners. They had got together relatively recently when they worked with a children's theatre group. Snad had trained as a biologist and Chris was a qualified doctor. How another couple on the boat was going to work out, Sarah and I were not at all sure. Certainly, the cry "Is there a doctor in the house?" would be responded to quickly. Carol had studied drama at Bristol University and had helped found a community theatre in Bristol. Despite this experience, she turned out to be incredibly naive. It was left to Sam to explain the world to her, like that the sun was a star and that water ran downhill.

We were going to research and write together a show very relevant to Marsden. The Huddersfield Canal Society had been formed a few years before with the aim of completely restoring to navigation the now mainly derelict and filled-in canal. Sarah and I had become members as soon as we moved to Marsden. Many locals could not imagine that the canal could be restored. They just saw it as a linear eyesore that needed filling in. So I decided to write a show telling the story of the rise and fall of the Huddersfield Narrow Canal and to highlight its restoration potential.

It was fascinating research. Apart from studying books and documents, we spoke to many people who had worked on or been connected with the canal. There was Wilf Donkersley who had helped to move the *Ailsa Craig* along the length of the canal and through the three-and-a-quarter mile long Standedge Tunnel with Robert Aickman, Tom Rolt and Elizabeth Jane Howard on board amongst others. There was Charlie Holroyd, a lovely old boatman who had been through the tunnel many times. There was Dr Morphy of Huddersfield Polytechnic, who claimed the return of boats would wipe out a breed of snail which had come over in cotton bales from America and was unique in England to the Huddersfield Narrow. There were many others who contributed their memories and views.

The show was eventually called *Where's Our Cut?* We told the story of the canal from the viewpoint of the Diggles. These were mythical creatures invented by members of the Canal Society. The story goes: thousands of years ago the Diggles, a shy, homely race, were driven from Scandinavia by the marauding Wegis. Eventually they settled deep in natural caverns at Standedge. This place is known today as Diggle. For generations the Diggles kept to themselves, living off mushrooms which they grew in their caves and brewing fungal ale, until one day men began digging a hole through the hill to accommodate boats.

Our Diggle suits were made from nylon fur fabric bought off a market stall in Bradford and Snad and Chris had the job of creating them. They looked great but we were often mistaken for Wombles and they were hell to wear, especially in the hot weather. They were very itchy and they didn't breathe. Hence at the end of the show you were sweat-sodden. I spent two years wringing my underpants out at the end of performances.

We rehearsed at the Conservative Club (the Con). As my neighbour said, "Mike, you have to leave your principles at the door when you go into the clubs in Marsden." Needless to say, there was also the Soc (Socialist) and the Lib (Liberal) Clubs. Not to mention the Legion, the Bandroom and the Cot plus twelve pubs. Marsden has a population of around four thousand.

We were also busy purchasing *Tyseley* from John May. He had decided to sell as he was giving up teaching and was putting all his resources into setting up a wholefood shop in Abingdon. He had given Mikron first offer. We were able to raise £8,000 which John very kindly accepted even though he knew he could get over nine.

Unfortunately, John had allowed some friends to live on the boat over the winter. They had not looked after her, and now rats were living with the friends and the friends had forgotten to drain the water from the engine during a very cold, frosty spell and the block had cracked.

Orchard Cruisers in Oxford said they would have a go at mending it; so we left *Tyseley* with them while we rehearsed in Marsden. When we returned in early May to start our tour, Sarah and I were not very reassured to see that the block had had dried mustard powder poured into it to seal the cracks. A traditional remedy, they said.

We said nothing to the newcomers as we stuttered up to Wolvercote Green for our first performance. The engine sounded terrible and finally gave up altogether. There was nothing for it. We needed a new block. So it came to pass that Snad, Carol and Chris's first experience of boating was steering *Tyseley* butty-style behind *Hadley Rail*, a motor borrowed from Mikron fans. At Braunston, the wonderful-sounding Balliol Fowden was to remove the engine-room roof, lift out the engine on pulleys and put in a new block. All this was to cost a considerable amount of money which John May very kindly paid for as he accepted responsibility for the errant behaviour of his friends.

We finally said goodbye to *Hadley Rail* at Long Eaton on May 26th and *Tyseley* was again under her own steam. We'd had a few exciting moments with the pair, not least my escape from death. Coming down the Napton Flight, I was taking *Hadley Rail* ahead while the others bowhauled *Tyseley*. On the longer pounds I would wait at the bottom of the lock, ready to pull *Tyseley* down to the next. To keep the boat steady while waiting, I would leave her in reverse gear hard against the bottom gates.

At one of the locks, I jumped back on to the boat just as the turbulence of the water coming out of the lock swung the boat's tiller hard round. It swept me into the cut without a by-your-leave. As I broke the surface on the way back up, two things happened: I thought, "Ooh, my glasses are still on" just as they disappeared into the murky depths, and my legs were dragged ever nearer the still-revolving propellor. Instinctively, I grabbed for a foothold in the adjacent brickwork and held on desperately until Sarah was able to climb on the boat and put her out of gear. A narrow escape and a great shame about a fine pair of gold-rimmed glasses.

Another traumatic day was when we moved from Stoke Goldington on the Ashby to Alrewas on the Trent & Mersey on a so-called day off. This was going to have been a very long move anyway but with a pair of boats, a reduced crew and very high winds it was cruel. Bowhauling *Tyseley* down Atherstone was interminable. We also spent many an hour stuck to the bank. No sooner would we push the two boats into the channel than the wind would blow under *Hadley Rail*'s cloths and we would inexorably be back where we had started. Carol who had not had the nous to take the day off the boat, was heard to say at one point in the day, "This is not what I came into theatre for."

Boats other than *Tyseley* were to feature prominently on this tour. *Hadley Rail* was our rescue boat in May. In July, we trans-shipped on to a Sheffield boat in order to go from Chorley on the Leeds & Liverpool to Sheffield Basin where we finished the first half of the tour. *Charlie Williams* was unconverted and we lived in the hold, at the bottom of a very steep ladder and amidst unswept droppings of sand and grain from previous commercial trips. Sam loved it, of course. I'm not sure about the rest of the Company.

We had to complete our tour in October in *Lindisfarne*, another converted narrowboat. One of the Thames locks was closed for emergency repairs. Again acquaintances came to our rescue and lent us a boat. I think Chris, Snad and Carol were a mite confused by the end. Certainly none of them returned for a second year.

It was a good tour, however. There were some problems with having another couple on the boat. Carol felt isolated from the other two a lot of the time. Quite naturally, they were kept very busy getting to know each other. But it meant Carol kept seeking Sarah's and my company, although she did have a good relationship with Sam. All in all, it worked out. We had our first mini-tour in Scotland as part of the Scottish Inland Waterways Rally of Boats in Edinburgh and we performed *Where's Our Cut?* in a cavern inside Dudley Tunnel , a natural home for the Diggles. Snad and Chris were married a year or so later and they now have three children. Carol is I know not where.

10

THE DIGGLE FAREWELL

After another winter spent in Marsden, it was again time to look for yet another new company. We auditioned in London and after a final recall we ended up with a Mark, a Sarah (this was to become confusing) and a Julie. Sarah Wilson was from Burley-in-Wharfedale and had a drama degree from Exeter University. Julie Brennon was from Blackpool and had trained at the Guildhall School of Music and Drama. Mark Strickson was Stratford-born and had been a member of the National Youth Theatre before graduating from RADA in 1979. For all of them it was their professional debut.

Where's Our Cut? was to continue into its second year. Our new show was to tell the story of the restoration of the waterways particularly through the eyes of members of WRG (Waterway Recovery Group), the voluntary organisation mainly responsible for the rebuilding of long derelict canals. We spoke to many of them in the course of our research and visited restoration projects like the Droitwich, Basingstoke and Huddersfield Canals.

We spent one weekend on the Montgomery Canal at Frankton working with members of WRG on repointing the walls of Lock No 1. This gave us first hand experience of both the commitment and sheer sense of fun of these volunteers, many of whom didn't have boats or even go on waterway holidays. They just felt that the canal system was too important to lose and wanted to do their bit to restore and maintain them. Many of them were "shiny bums" – they worked in sedentary jobs during the week and looked forward to weekends of physical effort and to getting away from vegetating in front of the telly. Mick Golds was different. Not for nothing was he called "Mick the Brick". He spent his working week bricklaying and his weekend leisure time... bricklaying.

Mud in Your Eye opened in Marsden in early May and we began our Waterways Tour in Wigan on the Leeds & Liverpool Canal. The first two weeks went as smoothly as any first two weeks of a tour could, bearing in mind that we had three new company members. It was the Macclesfield Canal that provided our first major obstacle. It is a shallow canal at the best of times although scenically one of the most interesting in the country. This year we had little time to appreciate the views of the Cloud and White Nancy and Lyme Park. The water level was two feet down and so our progress was painfully slow – one mile an hour at the best and we would get stuck under every bridge. There are 98 bridges on "The Macc", the details of which I now know intimately. The delay at a bridge was anything from a few minutes to an hour depending on how much grot was in the bridgehole. Sometimes, we were able to get through with a combination of pulling on ropes and pushing on the bridge itself. At other times, we needed the help of all the people whose holidays we were delaying. Boats would push, pull and nudge us, children and grannies would haul on ropes and no-one seemed to get too upset. They accepted it as part of the adventure of a canal holiday. We gave them one of our Mikron badges as a thank you. They came to a performance and many of them became Mikron fans. Our greatest thank you had to go the driver of the tractor who came from a nearby farm to pull *Tyseley* through a particularly recalcitrant bridge. It was a mighty relief when we arrived at the "deep" waters of the Trent & Mersey Canal at Hardingswood Junction.

The tour progressed well. Sarah Wilson soon became very popular with the Mikron regulars. Although neither a highly skilled actress or musician, she had total commitment to the job and had a charming and beguiling personality both on and off stage. Mark also was highly charming and many a female member of the audiences fell for his smile and red hair. But Julie had already won his heart and it looked as if we were heading for another Mikron couple.

Mark developed a very good relationship with Sam who was now eight. On the first day he arrived in Marsden, he took Sam off for a bike ride and returned with Sam minus part of his front teeth. They had gone down a very steep slope and Sam had crashed. Sam never seemed to hold it against Mark and on the boat they would fish together and on some days go off on adventures. It was after one such day off that disaster struck. Mark and Sam had gone ahead to camp in the fields near to our next venue – the Camp House Inn at Grimley. This is an idyllic pub set on the banks of the River Severn near to Bevere Lock, a few miles from Worcester. It was the Royalist Camp during the Battle of Worcester and the furthest point up the Severn reached by the Vikings. More to the point, it is a family run pub with a great atmosphere serving a vicious pint of scrumpy.

Sarah and I arrived at the pub the following day by boat. We had a couple of pints of cider and then decided to visit Mark and Sam's campsite. It was a field or two away from the pub and when we arrived, we were offered a cup of tea. The kettle was boiling away on the camp fire and Mark decided to demonstrate to Sam how, in the countryside, you used a stick to hold your kettle when pouring boiling water into a teapot. Now, at this point, I should point out that Mark had injured his hand a few days previously whilst demonstrating to Sam the skill required to make the bell ring on a punchball machine at Stourport Fair. He had hit the ball so hard that he had pulled the ligaments in his hand. It was this hand that was now demonstrating the kettle pouring technique.

Unfortunately, the injured hand did not hold the stick steady enough and the boiling water went all over my foot and not in the kettle. I screamed very loudly. There was a great deal of water and it was all over my foot, which had a sock on neatly retaining the heat of the liquid for the maximum length of time. I tore at my sock. "You need cold water," shouted Sarah. I ran as fast as I could down to the river and sat with my foot in the water for over an hour, trying to keep down the temperature of the raging piece of flesh that used to be known as one of my feet.

I was able to perform that night because a Mikron fan called Jean arrived. She was a nurse and she dressed the wound and put on some soothing cream. I somehow managed to squeeze into my show boots and it was business as usual. But it was a not quite up to par team appearing in the lounge bar of the pub – myself with severely scalded foot, Mark with torn ligaments (it was jarring agony every time he played the guitar – only just you might say), Julie with a swollen eye and Sarah Wilson with acute cystitis. Add to that Sarah's bites and Sam's cuts across his top lip from running into a barbed wire fence and we were a sorry sight.

I hobbled around for the next day or so and then took myself to Gloucester Hospital where a nurse proceeded, without a by-your-leave, to tear off the damaged skin leaving me with a totally raw foot, which became more painful by the day as the nerves started to re-grow. It was six weeks before it was properly healed.

Our journey on the Gloucester & Sharpness Canal was not without incident. Sadly, today very little commercial traffic uses the canal (more of this state of affairs nation-wide later) but in 1980, there were still quite a few ships travelling up to Gloucester, particularly the oil tankers to Quedgley. It was an awesome sight – a ship apparently travelling across the fields or passing within a few feet of the people having a pint outside the Berkeley Hunt at Purton. The coasters would squeeze through the swing bridges with inches to spare and it was at one of these that we had an almighty fright.

We arrived at Parkend with the bridge open but a red light against us. We noticed a coaster approaching through the trees; so we pulled in to let it through. Julie was on the back of *Tyseley*, the rest of us on the bank, some of us holding ropes, others cameras. We watched admiringly as the skipper steered his vessel through the narrow gap. We raised our cameras to record the event – but at that moment *Tyseley* started being sucked forward by the surge of water around the bridge. The skipper leaned out of his bridge many feet above us and shouted "What the hell are you doing there?", and the stern of the coaster moved ever closer to *Tyseley* as he tried to bring his ship around the bend immediately beyond the bridge. Julie put on full reverse but *Tyseley* continued her forward progress. Julie was next to be seen hurling herself on to the bank. She was obviously not going to go down with her ship.

Miraculously, *Tyseley* survived the ordeal of being clumped by a coaster. If she had been wooden, it might have been a different story but the only memento we have of this incident (there were no photos – it all happened too quickly) are a few scratches on the brass rings of the back cabin chimney.

The tour generally went well. Mark and Sarah decided to return for a second year. Julie didn't but was later to marry Mark and live with him in Australia.

It was the end of the two-year run of *Where's Our Cut?* but not quite the end of the stars of the show – the Diggles. I had grown fond of playing Napoleon Diggle over two seasons, despite the discomfort of wearing an animal costume made out of very cheap fur fabric. The show had been very popular with children. In the autumn, I had a request from a teacher. She was bringing a class of seven- and eight-year olds to Tunnel End in Marsden. Would it be possible for me to turn out in my costume at the tunnel, greet them as a Diggle and tell them the story of how these furry creatures came to be living inside Standedge Tunnel?

So it was that one sunny November morning, I could be seen walking up the towpath from my house to the tunnel wearing my Diggle costume. As I came round the bend just before Tunnel End, I noticed that the children were already there. I slipped round the back and slithered down the hillside towards the children, scratching my ears and behaving generally Diggle-like. But what was strange was not only did the children not seem to know who I was but the teachers didn't either. A quick word with one of them revealed that they were not the right school party. I mumbled an apology and retreated back up the hillside.

Eventually, the right group arrived and I again ran down scratching and preening myself. This time the reaction was staggering. One of the children spotted me: "Look, there's a Diggle." I was immediately surrounded by little children who asked me searching, pertinent questions about my life in the tunnel and completely accepted that I was a Diggle and that I lived on mushrooms and brewed fungal ale. I took them up to the mouth of the tunnel, and told them that if they listened very carefully they would be able to hear other Diggles singing as they went about their work in the tunnel. We all leaned out and, sure enough, I could hear them singing as well as the children.

A week or so later I received letters and drawings from the children. They had remembered so much of their visit and sent very fond greetings to Napoleon Diggle.

11

YEAR TEN

During the winter of 1981 we recorded our third album. We were privileged to be able to use Abbey Road Studios in London and the very same studio where the Beatles recorded their Abbey Road album. Our oeuvre may not have received as much publicity or sold quite as many copies as the Fab Four, but *Waterways World* did describe it as "...a fine recording of a memorable and frequently moving show, one of Mikron's best... Musical accompaniment throughout is by the ever versatile members of the Company performing on guitars, banjos, harmonica, mandolin and even a penny whistle and spoons."

We were also organising for our tenth tour of the waterways. To celebrate our success in managing to keep a small theatre company going for so many years, building the body of our work and developing our audiences every year, Sarah and I decided to revive an old show for 1981. We very much wanted to revive *I'd Go Back Tomorrow*, the story of life on the working narrowboats since 1900, seen through the eyes of a boatwoman called Alice, which had been so warmly received on our 1977 and '78 tours but, first, we thought some of the members of our audience should have a say. We asked readers of *Waterways World* to write in and say what show they would like to see again. *I'd Go Back Tomorrow* easily came top.

We needed a new Alice and thus the two Sarahs, Sam, Mark and myself were joined by Thea Bennet. She had recently been seen on BBC1 playing Poll in *A Little Silver Trumpet* and had written the book of the series. She had studied classics at London University and drama at Webber Douglas. She was an intelligent actress but I felt that she never really got to grips with the boating life. One instance of this was when we were on the shortboat *Lune* for our crossing of the Leeds & Liverpool Canal. We were sleeping on the deck, under the sheets, as usual for this trip. When we arrived in the very attractive market town of Skipton, Thea announced she was going to stay in a hotel for the night where she might get a comfy bed and a bath. Admittedly, it was pouring with rain at the time and the cargo space of an old boat might not have seemed the most enticing of bedroom prospects; but that it is all part of canal touring – the weather, the ever-changing venues, different canals and rivers, different boats.

That did happen in August, some four months into the tour. Perhaps she had been gritting her teeth up until then. She did seem happier with the relative comforts of *Tyseley*.

Our trip across the Pennines began in Leeds at the IWA National Rally held in the old docks, which have since become part of the waterside redevelopment of Leeds with smart housing, hotels, restaurants, the Tetley Wharf Museum and the Armouries. I think Leeds should still be a major inland port for barge traffic from the Continent, with the exciting sight of boats being loaded and unloaded and the knowledge that, as a result, there were less lorries trundling across the M62 and polluting our environment. But, if there isn't sufficient imagination to make that happen or rather if the road lobby continue to hold such political sway, then the present redevelopment does give the river a presence in the city and a pleasant area for people to walk, eat and relax, rather than it being a rat-infested wasteland.

The weekend in Leeds was much improved by the presence of the Campaign for Real Ale National Beer Festival. There one could sample some of the 150 beers and stouts on offer. We were slightly hampered by the fact that we had to remain sober enough to give a nightly performance, but we did manage to slip down a few halves of the likes of Timothy Taylor's Landlord and Theakston's Old Peculiar. CAMRA is a great organisation. I have been a member for many years and, just as there would probably be no navigable canals today if it had not been for the campaigning of the IWA, without CAMRA we would all be drinking fizzy keg.

In September, we made our first trip up the Wey Navigation. We had been invited to the Godalming Water Festival which is at the top end of the river. We were also performing in Weybridge and Pulborough. All was fine until the day of our show in Godalming – the day the river decided to flood after an almighty storm which blew up while we were performing *Mud in Your Eye* in a marquee. The wind threatened to lift the tent off the ground, the large audience responding rather hysterically to all references to the weather in the show. Many of the display stands were blown over and destroyed, and Mark was in the gents mobile toilet when it collapsed. He slid gently sideways while peeing, but the man in the cubicle was heard to say, very appropriately, "Oh, shit" as he fell off the Elsan.

We were delayed for two days before the water receded sufficiently for us to get under the bridge.

Our trip up the Grand Union in early October was interrupted by the closure of Blisworth Tunnel in Northamptonshire. The tunnel, at 3056 yards in length, proved exceptionally difficult to build and delayed the opening of the then Grand Junction Canal by several years until 1805.

It had stood the test of time well, but now had been closed for urgent and expensive repairs. We were left with no alternative but to arrange for *Tyseley* to be lifted around the tunnel and, on the bright but chilly morning of October 21st, the 24-ton boat was plucked out of the canal by crane on the Stoke Bruerne flight and carried by low loader to Gayton Junction where it was refloated. The country roads were very narrow and it must have been bemusing for the owners of some of the cottages to see a very long boat travelling along their hedge or wall. The only mishap was on one very steep bend when two glasses fell off a table in the boat and broke. Thanks to the help of a local firm, the total cost of the liftout and in was only £160. We were able to complete the last two weeks of our tour as we had always intended to – by boat.

Our experience with the closure of the Blisworth Tunnel highlighted many of the problems with the British waterways at that time. The neglect of many years was coming home to roost and now tunnels, embankments and locks were all collapsing at the same time. The British Waterways Board was unable to keep up with the backlog of maintenance – Blisworth Tunnel was to cost £4.25m, Preston Brook Tunnel £750,000 – and many people felt that the waterways were fighting for survival. A couple of bright features at the start of 1982 were that the Government was giving the British Waterways Board an extra £7m for maintenance, and that £10m was to be spent improving the Sheffield & South Yorkshire Navigation so that much larger commercial vessels would be able to reach Rotherham and Mexborough.

Nearer home, we felt it was time to commit ourselves fully to the area we lived in. Sarah and I had already joined the Huddersfield Canal Society and the Marsden Community Association, and were taking a keen interest and part in the campaign to have our local base, the Marsden Mechanics, refurbished so it could be used as a community centre and as a focus and venue for arts activity of all kinds – theatre, music, dance and the visual arts. For the first time, we decided to tour locally by van for the first four and last two weeks of our season. This was to be called the South Pennine Tour.

12

THE BROKEN
SHOULDER

Sarah Wilson happily entered her third year with Mikron. Mark went off to play the Doctor's assistant, Turlowe, in *Dr Who*; Thea I know not where. New auditions produced Robert Edmunds and Eluned Owen. Robert had trained with the National Youth Theatre and the National Youth Theatre of Wales (he was from Swansea). He'd played his guitar in a few wine bars in London but Mikron was his first professional engagement as an actor. Eluned (pronounced Alinid) was from London and had been to the same drama school as myself (Webber Douglas) after graduating in drama and French at Bristol University. She had already had some experience in fringe and community theatre.

I'm afraid Robert's inexperience showed and he never managed to achieve the standards expected of a Mikron actor. He proved to be highly irritating while we were touring – never being there when you wanted him, steering the boat badly and professing to be a vegetarian. There's nothing wrong with being a vegetarian but he was a non-vegetable-eating vegetarian. Cooking for him and by him was a nightmare. He seemed only to like chips and sweets. His greatest delight was to dip a Mars Bar into a pint of bitter. He was a very childish person and, perhaps because of this, he got on very very well with 10-year-old Sam. The bad side of this was his obsession with sex. We discovered he was showing Sam a notebook where he listed all the girls he had "had". Fantasy or not, it wasn't quite the sex education Sarah and I had envisaged for Sam.

The good part of his relationship with Sam was how he introduced him to ornithology and the love of birds. (Sarah and I were quite happy with the feathered variety). They went bird-watching together, and to this day Sam retains his knowledge and love for wild birds.

At our auditions we sometimes ask people if they have any funny (ie peculiar) habits that might make them difficult to live with. Eluned had answered negatively to this question but, on the day she was offered the job, she took me to one side and said, "I'm a practising Christian. Would that be a funny habit in your book?" I replied, "Well, Sarah and I are both atheists or at the very least deep agnostics. But we would have nothing against you having such beliefs yourself...unless you start preaching to us every day and trying to convert us to the Good Life." Eluned certainly never did that. She was a vivacious, witty person and a good actress. We did let her teach Sam RE though, which he enjoyed immensely, including readings from the Bible.

I had decided that we should research and write a show tracing the development of transport over and through the Pennines and the impact that it has had on the landscape and the local communities. This would reflect our growing interest and commitment to our local area. So, we started with the Romans and their incredible straight roads and progressed through packhorse roads, canals, coach roads and railways to the M62 motorway. Robert, Sarah, Eluned and myself researched and wrote the show together, including the music and lyrics. Robert's writing varied from the naive to the downright bathetic and much of it went at the editing stage. This sounds very cruel and Robert never knew, but we kept his edited sections and occasionally, after a few drinks, entertained ourselves with dramatised readings from them. I wish I still had them now to quote from but, alas, they are nowhere to be found.

Over the Top and a revival of our show about the evolution of family life on the narrowboats, *Keep Yer 'ands Off* formed the repertoire of our 1982 tours. Although I had reservations about the quality of some of the performances, the shows were both well-received and well-reviewed by the press: "The cast switched roles, taking turns to act, sing and play musical instruments with a panache and professionalism which made it invidious to single out individual performances" (Rochdale Observer).

One "epic" journey of this tour was on the Chesterfield Canal in July. We had been informed by British Waterways that they were closing the canal for a day in order to spray the water with a special chemical, hoping to rid of the thick weed growth which was making it increasingly difficult for a boat to travel up the canal without the crew having to stop every few minutes to clear the prop.

In order to be at our next venue, the Boat Inn, Hayton, the following night, we would have to travel the ten miles from Misterton during the night. For those of you who know the Chesterfield, it's not the easiest of canals to navigate even in daylight – it's windy and shallow. Everyone became very excited about night boating and even Sam was going to stay up for the trip. We stocked up with beer from the Packet Inn, our venue and we set off just before midnight. Sarah was steering and we had bacon butties and real ale for sustenance. Two British Waterways men saw us through the two locks, then went home to bed.

Sarah said, "I thought there was a very bendy section near here." I replied, "There is and you've already done it." She had negotiated several hairy bends with consummate skill and with just the aid of a tunnel light, without noticing. The night wore slowly on and gradually "the crew" (who were going to stay up all night) slipped off to bed. First Sam, understandably enough; then Robert and Eluned. Even Sarah Wilson deserted us, leaving Sarah and myself, the veterans.

After Drakeholes Tunnel, I took over steering from Sarah. She stood at the front of the boat for a few minutes and then she too joined the slumbering ones and I was left alone to guide *Tyseley* to her destination. I soon became used to the dark and to picking out the towpath and the bridges with the headlight. I enjoyed the eerie stillness of the night and marvelled as night turned to day and the sun began to burn through the early morning mist. I never felt tired and only once did I blow a bend. I went to the front of the boat and shafted myself off with a pole and back into the channel. No-one stirred. We arrived at our venue well in time! Six o'clock in the morning. I rested for a couple of hours, then joined Sarah for a day of office work on an improvised desk on the pub lawn.

For myself, the major event of 1982 was the breaking of my shoulder. I had broken a shoulder before – back in 1970 when I had hit a patch of oil on my motorbike and myself and bike had parted company. You would have thought that to break one shoulder was unfortunate, but to break two has to amount to downright carelessness.

On Monday September 27th (oh, I remember it well), we were travelling down the one section of the River Cherwell that forms part of the South Oxford Canal between Bakers Lock and Shipton Weir Lock. It's very different from the rest of the canal – it's deep and wide although in parts very bendy. It's an opportunity to " wind 'er up a bit". *Tyseley* always moves faster in deep water.

We were approaching the diamond shaped lock at the end of the section but Eluned, who was steering, hadn't seemed to realise that, while the river continued onwards (unnavigable after a few yards), our route lay through the lock. It turned out later that she wasn't wearing her glasses and hadn't seen the sign saying that the lock was to the right. I tried to warn her both to slow down and to go to the right. She did slow down but the momentum of the boat was now carrying us neither further down the river nor into the lock, but towards the island in the middle; an island protected from wayward boats by concrete.

My next decision was a very stupid one. I thought that I could save the boat being damaged if I leapt off the bow and pushed her away with my body. The decision was stupid but the execution was even worse. I slipped as I jumped. The bow hit me, and I was thrown to the ground. I knew when I tried to get up that all was not completely well. Although the excruciating pain came a few minutes later, I quickly realised that I couldn't move my right arm. I had to be helped back on to the boat. It was obvious I needed to get to a hospital but we were in the middle of nowhere, and Sarah decided the quickest action was to get the boat to the venue in Thrupp and find help there. She took over steering, quickly was through the lock and managed Thrupp wide and through the liftbridge in one on sheer adrenaline. I was whisked away in a car by the landlady of the Boat, Gill. I told the others to get ready for the show and that, all being well, I would be back in time for the start.

Twenty minutes to eight and I was still waiting for the result of the X-ray. Sarah phoned the pub and told the Company to do what they could...sing a few songs from the show...whatever. The doctor who examined me said that I could be lucky and that my shoulder might only be dislocated. I wasn't and it wasn't. It was broken. There was nothing to be done. Just wear a sling, take painkillers and, in about four weeks or so, I might be able to start moving it again. We arrived back at the pub to hear Sarah Wilson, Eluned and Robert singing the last song from the show. Sam had also joined them. I was now in agony, which I alleviated to some extent with several pints of cider and a few whiskies. Better than any painkillers. It was obvious that I was not going to be able to get back on the boat that night; so Sarah and I went back to Islip with Tony and Pip Burton.

The next day the pain in my shoulder was excruciating – not helped by watching a video of *Abigail's Party*. I yelled out every time I laughed, which was often. Nor by the trip to the local, necessary for medicinal purposes, but with every step I took *en route* I was assailed by what appeared to be knives being inserted into my shoulder. But I was determined to perform that night. I wasn't going to be the cause of the cancellation of another Mikron show.

Radio Oxford arrived at Tony and Pip's and proceeded to interview me about the incident and the consequences for the Company. I said the show would go on and I would be appearing at Thrupp that night. But I would not be able to get my costume shirt on – an old-fashioned union shirt – and was there anybody out there on the airwaves who could lend me an outsized version? Within an hour, two shirts ideal for the job arrived and I was able to go on that night with my sling inside my shirt. I warned the others that it would be too painful for me to move around during the show, so they would have to come to me. But, as soon as I was "on stage" with the adrenaline rushing through me, I felt no pain and was able to move around normally, much to the amazement of the others and Sarah and Sam who were watching. Immediately after the show, I felt faint and sick and my shoulder began to throb alarmingly. Getting back on to the boat was difficult, sleep was unattainable, but Mikron had given a performance to a room full of satisfied punters.

For the next four weeks I was able to perform with my shoulder in a sling. The pain decreased, the bruises on my body became very colourful and I even cooked one meal. But, frustratingly, I was unable to steer or lockwheel and even my admin capabilities were sparse, although I did teach myself to write, albeit scrawlingly, with my left hand. I visited various hospitals for check-ups *en route*, and I was amazed on going to Wigan Hospital on October 26th when the doctor told me to throw away the sling and start trying to move my arm again. Getting mobility back was a long, slow process and I never have completely regained full use. A word of wise advice to my readers. Don't ever try to stop a 24-ton narrowboat. Let it crash. It's tougher than you.

The season ended with the completion of our first South Pennine Tour by van and the recording of our fourth LP. This took place at our last performance of *Over the Top* at the Railway in Marsden. For the first time the whole of the record was devoted to the one show with an edited version of both scenes and songs.

Robert went off to seek his fortune and the only thing I know about him is that he married a Japanese woman. I hope they are very happy. Eluned married a fellow actor, Neil Swettenham, and became a mum and now has an Alexander, an Eleanor and a Nathaniel and teaches. We often see her and her family at Mikron shows.

Sarah Wilson (known as Swiz to differentiate her from Sarah Lucas) decided she ought to pursue another course after three years with Mikron. She trained to be a teacher, bought a house in Marsden and worked locally, before being whisked away to teach in Portugal for three years and South Korea for two. She was just settling back in England when she discovered she had pre-cancerous cells on one of her breasts and was advised to have a mastectomy. She faced this bravely and with humour and was getting her life back together again when she collapsed and died while on a Fun Run in Leeds to raise funds for women with cancer. The post-mortem showed she had a faulty valve in her heart which could have stopped functioning at any time. The year was 1995. She was 39 years old and we all miss her dearly.

13

STILL CARRYING ON

Our twelfth year was upon us. What would it bring? Three new members of the Company for one thing. For the first time we auditioned in Marsden, giving potential Company members the opportunity to see the place where they would be spending thirteen weeks of their thirty-one week contract.

After a week of angst and soul-searching, Sarah and I chose an Oxbridge trio to join us. Kate Duchene was from Brighton and had just left Cambridge where she had studied French and Spanish and worked with the Cambridge Mummers. She had also toured with the Footlights in their revue *Promises, Promises*. This was to be her professional debut. Sarah Parks knew Kate from Cambridge where she studied English before studying acting at the same college as myself (although much later, of course) – the Webber Douglas Academy. In 1982, she had become a founder member of Fourcast Theatre based in London. She had also, when "resting", worked in an ante-natal clinic and as a freelance drama critic on the *Harrow Observer*. She knew the area in which Mikron was based, having been brought up in Halifax. Her father was the Manager of the Halifax Building Society – the boss. Unusually for new recruits, she knew a little about canals. Her father owned a boat.

Mark Williams was the new male member of the troupe. We had had difficulty finding any suitable men to interview, so had resorted to what we called the "B Pile" and, for some reason, had decided to interview Mark. He had had very little experience, although he had studied English at Oxford University and had been a member of the Fools Theatre Company of Oxford. He seemed to have spent most of his time doing odd-jobs – wine-bar manager, mental nursing assistant, dahlia grower and painter and decorator. In fact, the photo he enclosed with his CV was taken against a brick wall, with him in his painter's overalls. Either a humorous eccentric or a nutter!

But as soon as he walked into the interview room in Marsden, I felt instinctively he was right for Mikron. He was very unusual looking; he had a "funny" face and no chin; he was amusing, read and sang well, and Sarah and I both immediately warmed to him. At the recall he did nothing to put us off, so he got the job.

Over the Top was to continue for a further season. Our new show was to be on a canal theme. For many years I had been toying with the idea of writing the story of a narrowboat and about all the people who had worked her. It was not until I heard about Alan Brooks that I realised that there was an obvious choice of boat – our very own *Tyseley*. Alan and his wife spent many years on *Tyseley* and Alan's parents before him. He lived on the canalside at Buckby on the Grand Union Canal and followed the fortunes of Mikron and their (or, as he still felt I'm sure, his) boat. With such a contact, we would be able to trace the history of *Tyseley* right up to the present day and her role in carrying a theatre company around the cut. Hence, the title of the show – *Still Carrying*.

During two cold weeks in winter, Kate, Sarah Parks, Mark and myself researched the material for the new show while Sarah and her associate administrator, Kathryn Brierley, booked the tour and applied for grants. We visited Alan and Margaret in their canalside cottage. It was a wonderful experience. Alan was an eloquent talker and he began to regale us with stories of his life on *Tyseley*. He and his father went to watch out for their new boat when it was on its way from Northwich, where it had been built at Yarwood's. A number of Town Class boats were being constructed for the Grand Union Canal Carrying Company. The boats were late arriving, and Alan and his dad went on to the Main Line of the Birmingham Canal for several days, before, in the distance, they saw two boats coming down the straight. Alan's dad cast his expert eye over them as they approached. He shouted out to the steerer, "We're having that one, Tom." Alan piped up, "What's her name, dad? What's her name?" Dad shouted back, "What's her name?" Through the air came the word "Tyseley".

So, *Tyseley* became the Brooks' boat and, as a lad, Alan helped his parents work *Tyseley* and her butty, Uttoxeter. She was supposed to be paired with Tydd but, when they arrived to collect the wooden butty from Walkers of Rickmansworth, she had already gone off with another boat. When his parents left the cut, Alan and his wife Margaret took over *Tyseley* and they worked her until they also decided, regretfully, to go on to the land. They felt, quite rightly, that narrowboat carrying was dying and that, if they didn't leave, they would be forced off anyway.

Alan was able to put us touch with other boatpeople who had worked *Tyseley*. She had a reputation of being one of the fastest boats on the cut. "She'll get there. She always does." As it turned out, Alan had followed the fortunes of *Tyseley* through the rest of her commercial carrying days, her restaurant boat days and had regularly watched Mikron passing by on her over the years. He even had the cutting from the *Northampton Chronicle and Echo* with the photo of *Tyseley* being lifted out and taken round Blisworth Tunnel.

I'D GO BACK TOMORROW

We spoke to many people who had stories to tell of *Tyseley* and ended up with hours and hours of recollections which we used as the basis for *Still Carrying*. Everyone was given their proper name, and Alan and Margaret became very well-known as characters of a show along the waterways. It was to prove to be one of our most popular productions.

The tour began at Marple on the Peak Forest Canal. Although *Still Carrying* settled down very quickly as a show, it took a while for *Over the Top* to get into full gear. It was at the Swan, Fradley Junction on the Trent & Mersey Canal, that Sarah Parks (Parksy), Kate and Mark realised it was a funny (ha, ha) show. It was probably because they had not been involved in the writing of it.

During the preceding months, Sarah and I had been having meetings over several pleasant restaurant meals with John Thornicroft. He was a television director and he wanted to film a half-hour documentary about Mikron for Central Television's *England, their England* series. He came with good credentials; he had an unconverted narrowboat of his own and had installed a small cinema in the hold. At festivals and rallies he would show old canal films including, of course, *The Bargee* with Harry Corbett as well as classics like *Robin Hood* starring Errol Flynn. His cameraman was to be Ian Hollands, who also owned a narrowboat; so we stood a good chance of the film being made with integrity and accuracy.

We spent about five days filming with them altogether. There was footage of us travelling and working locks, of our everyday life on board and in the pubs (naturally) and of us performing. John used an interesting technique of recreating some of the scenes from the show on location – there were shots of Alan and his dad watching out for *Tyseley*, and of the family starting the engine and leaving in an early morning mist. It worked well and intercut with us performing in front of a pub audience.

Although they filmed two performances, the one shown in the film was shot at the New Inn, Buckby Wharf. It was a memorable evening and a very moving one. Alan and Margaret were there watching their own lives being portrayed in front of them. But also there were many boatpeople whose lives had intertwined with *Tyseley* and they loved it. Rene James, who with her husband Noel, had had *Tyseley* as a change boat (ie a boat you use when yours is being repainted or repaired) said it all rang very true and that "that fellow playing Alan's dad has got him just right." That was Mark, who was from Bromsgrove and whose boatman's accent was spot on. We had a standing ovation that night and many of us crowded on to John's boat *Duke* and, over several pints in the chilly hold of the boat, watched some of the classic old black and white films made about boats and boatpeople. It was an awe-inspiring sight at the end of a reel, as everyone piled off the boat, women included, to have a pee against the adjacent towpath hedge.

STILL CARRYING ON

The film was edited and eventually shown nation-wide. It's the best film ever made about us and captures the essence of Mikron and its commitment to the canals along which we travel. I only hope Douglas Yarwood was able to see it. He was one of the Yarwoods who built *Tyseley* and, when he saw the show on the River Weaver, he leapt to his feet and started shouting "*encore*". He insisted on going to the bar himself although he was ninety-two and a very frail little man.

In the film there are several shots of Sam – cleaning the brasses, helping on the locks and appearing in the location sequences as the young Alan. He was now eleven. There is a sequence where Sam plays *Still Carrying* on the penny whistle and another where he talks about the Company members over the years – "I get on with most of them very well but sometimes they don't like me." Sam's relationship with his adult fellow crew members was very important. Sarah and I had to be sure that Sam was happy with our way of life and was not missing out on his education in any way. When we moved to Marsden, we were not sure that the Infants School there would allow us to take Sam away for six months of the year as they had in the Tower Bridge Road. We explained that, during that time, we would teach him ourselves and that they could set him work if they wished. They readily agreed. A year later, it was time for him to move to the Junior School and this time we thought they would refuse. But no, they said they would give it a try. The members of the Company took it in turns to teach Sam. A timetable was pinned up and everyday Sam was supposed to have three lessons. It didn't always happen, particularly if it was a hectic boating day, but it did mean that Sam had one-to-one tuition; this year, for instance, Parksy teaching him music, Mark maths, Sarah nature study and myself English.

The school were delighted with Sam's progress. He was asked to do a scale drawing of *Tyseley* in chalk on the playground and the Head said that, if every child were able to be away from school on some project for half the year and at school for the rest, what educated, socially-aware children we would have. By travelling around the country, Sam's interest in geography and maps was easily stimulated, and he quickly became aware of the historical significance of canals as a major part of the Industrial Revolution. The decision yet to be made was what would we do with Sam when he went to the local comprehensive school. This was to be decided back in Marsden in the autumn.

The tour progressed. It was a good tour, a happy tour. There were a few boating incidents but not many. Mark hit a hire boat while turning to moor on the Trent at Newark. The hirer turned out to be the captain of a cross-channel ferry and, although he and his family were initially shocked by their cooker and various other domestic appliances moving towards them, he became quite sanguine when he realised that they were still afloat. Parksy blew a bend and was so annoyed with herself, she disappeared into the back cabin for an hour or so until she could face the boating world again.

But our real problems began on the July 14th. Mark didn't have to storm the Bastille but simply cross the Severn. At least it was a beautifully hot sunny day that Thursday. We set out from Gloucester to travel up to Twyning on the Avon just outside Tewkesbury. We had just come out of the Parting, which is the narrows which runs from Gloucester Lock and rejoins the main river three miles upstream. Suddenly, we were making very slow progress. The engine was on full power but the propshaft was barely turning. Half-a-mile an hour was our best speed. As usual in these circumstances, there was not a boat to be seen. We could see a long way upriver and it was deserted. No help, no tow.

It was Mark who bravely volunteered to go for help. He would swim across the river and try and find a phone somewhere to get assistance. It didn't much look like phone country across on the bank – more like cow and sheep country. Anyway, armed only with a pair of swimming trunks and some change in a plastic bag, Mark dived in and the last we saw of him for many hours was him scrambling, with great difficulty, up the bank and disappearing into the trees.

The river is very wide at this point and we felt rather helpless as we drifted slowly upstream in the midday sun. After about an hour or so, we looked behind us and saw a largish boat approaching in the distance. As it got nearer we recognised it as a British Waterways tug from Gloucester Docks. What good fortune!

But it wasn't fortune. Mark had phoned the docks and the tug had been sent out immediately to take us back to Gloucester. We soon discovered the reason for their haste. There was a four-foot high spring tide due that afternoon and, if it had arrived while we were still drifting, *Tyseley* would have been deposited on one of the banks and then left high and dry as the tide receded. So, our rescuers tied *Tyseley* to the side of the tug and back we went from whence we had come – the tranquil safety of Gloucester Docks.

A British Waterways engineer had a look at our engine and declared that we had a broken crankshaft – the shaft had crystallised and separated. There was just sufficient friction left to turn the shaft very, very slowly. Hence, our majestic speed of half-a-mile an hour. British Waterways offered to freight us by road to Twyning for our show that evening. In the meantime, we phoned Paul Lorenz, our boat superintendent, back at our base in Leigh on the Bridgwater Canal and apprised him of our problem. He immediately started phoning round and located a canal enthusiast in London who collected spare parts for boat engines. He just happened to have a National crank shaft sitting on the floor of his front room. We could have it for a very reasonable price.

The plan was as follows: if we could somehow keep moving, Paul would collect the spare part and assemble it as we went along. Our job was to find a boat to borrow which we could use to tow *Tyseley*. We contacted John Thornicroft and asked him if he would lend us *Duke*. He was only too willing, and even offered to get it to us on the River Severn. The only problem was that *Duke* was in the middle of Birmingham, thirty miles and 58 locks away.

John promised to get *Duke* to us somehow on the River Severn if we managed to get *Tyseley* moved in the meantime. So, the next morning, we went back up the river again lashed to the side of the British Waterways tug. When we reached Upton, where we were appearing that night, the tug set us loose in the middle of the river and we glided, not that gently, warning the moored boats as we approached that we had no power. Fenders appeared from everywhere to protect the paintwork but, with a nifty bit of ropework, we tied up against the steps without causing a major incident.

The following day we hitched a tow from one of the boats belonging to the hire company in Upton and we progressed slowly upstream to the Camp House Inn at Grimley. In the meantime, John had set off the previous evening with a friend called Sean to start the trip down the Worcester & Birmingham Canal. Sean is a very large, strong man with enormous hands, which make a pint glass of beer look like a half. He was to prove invaluable on this trip with just a crew of two and so many locks to get through on the journey down to the Severn.

We had tied up outside the pub. It was a hot day and we were swimming in the river at about four o'clock in the afternoon when up the river came *Duke*. They had been travelling non-stop through the night. John and Sean were both totally exhausted but delighted that they had been able to come to the aid of Mikron so promptly. A few pints of scrumpy were going to be in order later that evening.

Because of, or despite, the Camp House's reputation for brilliant head-banging scrumpy and for providing an hospitable late night atmosphere after the shows, various of our friends always used to arrive there, purportedly to see us and the new production but, I suspect, just to have a guaranteed damn good time. They would bring tents and camp (very appropriately) on the Camp House lawn and that's exactly what happened this year.

It was a very late night. One of the traditions of Mikron visits was that, as the night wore on and the singing and playing got louder and more out of tune, the pints of scrumpy were laced with gin. For anybody who has never tried this concoction, let me recommend you do. Gin and cider go excellently together. This recommendation, however, comes with a warning. It does make you very drunk and it does produce a strange feeling the next morning. In the context of this venue, we have named it "The Grimley Gorilla". It appears, when you wake on the morrow, that you have a large gorilla sitting on your back, holding on to your head and breathing foully down your neck .

I'D GO BACK TOMORROW

Despite foreknowledge, every year, tradition has to be maintained and so it was that, the following morning, I was brought abruptly to my senses by the sound of whistling. It took me a few moments to realise that it was the kettle boiling in the kitchen. Dragging myself and the gorilla out of the back cabin I ran (staggered) to the front of the boat. There, sure enough, was the kettle steaming away but everyone around or near it slept on. I turned it off just before it burnt dry. As I did, I noticed the time. We should have left an hour before. Now, we are, as a rule, very good timekeepers. We have a rota system for steering duty on the boat and whoever's turn it is to do the first of the day (usually a period of an hour-and-a-half) wakes up everyone else with a cup of tea, half-an-hour before departure time. Generally, as we leave, all of us are up ready to set locks, make breakfast, whatever. I can't honestly remember whose turn it was that day. It might even have been mine. We discovered later that one of our friends who had been camping nearby had decided to make us all some tea, but had been so gripped by the Grimley Gorilla that they had had to depart to throw up somewhere quietly. I ran (staggered) to the engine room of *Duke*, handcranked the engine and quickly informed everyone we were leaving forthwith. Thus, I steered *Duke* upstream towards Stourport with *Tyseley* in tow and with the Grimley Gorilla grinning maniacally. Death, at the time, seemed preferable.

The reason for the unseemly departure with ropes badly coiled and bodies badly co-ordinated was that we were due to give a lunchtime performance at the Black Star in Stourport. The idea of arranging a daytime show immediately after the Camp House must have been Sarah's way of having a bit of fun during the long winter of planning. She, nevertheless, had to suffer along with the rest of us.

The news of our late arrival had been conveyed to Tony and Pip Burton who were waiting for us at Stourport. They organised for us to pass through the broad barge locks into the basin rather than the long haul up the staircase narrow locks. We went on ahead with our costumes and props piled hastily into a car, leaving Sarah and Tony to bring the boats up through the basin to the pub. We were only a few minutes late starting the show to an audience of about fifty. About an hour later, Sarah pulled in on *Duke* and, a few minutes after, Tony, sweating profusely, bowhauled *Tyseley* alongside.

It was a hard show. It was very hot and sunny and the heat (or was it the Grimley Gorilla?) glared off a white wall behind us. And, of course, we had another show to do in the evening. The afternoon ended, after we'd finished the show, thank goodness, with a tremendous storm with large hailstones bouncing off the roof of the boat. We mustn't forget that, during all this, Paul was working away like mad fitting the new crankshaft.

It was a few days later, having travelled up the Staffs & Worcs performing in Stourport, Kinver and Wombourne and at Autherley and Brewood on the Shroppie, Paul said we were okay to travel under our own power, and we pulled in to our venue at Gnosall as if nothing had ever been wrong.

We made one trip on this tour which was to prove to be historic. As before, we went down the boatlift at Anderton which drops boats 50 feet from the Trent & Mersey to the River Weaver below. Little did we know that we were to be one of the last boats to do so. Shortly afterwards, an inspection found the structure to be so corroded that it was declared unsafe and closed. It remains so to this day but later I shall deal with the efforts to restore and re-open this unique monument to Victorian engineering.

Our Waterways Tour ended at the National Waterways Rally at Wigan Pier. We were due to commence our South Pennine road tour three weeks later but not before we had researched, written and rehearsed a new show. For the first time, we were to have three shows in repertoire. *From Where I Stand*, as it was called eventually, was about hilltop farmers in the Colne Valley. We renamed the village Standen, to avoid any possible litigation, but it was really about Marsden and the hills that surround it. The words of the final chorus went:

> From where I stand
> All the valley's spread out below,
> The mills lie still, just a shadow of years ago,
> And now life's not the same
> As it used to be on farming land,
> I must look ahead to see the future –
> From where I stand.

We spoke to many of the local sheep- and cattle-farmers still trying to earn a living from the hills and, in the show, we compared their lives in the 1930s to the present day when their livelihoods are being threatened by pollution, tourists, and those people who buy hilltop properties near to the city they work in so they can keep horses and pretend to be farmers – known as the "comers-in". It was the first time I had not appeared in a Mikron show. I co-wrote and directed it, but it was performed by Mark, Parksy and Kate. The *Halifax Courier* described it as "touching, comic and magical" and said "history presented this way should really be in schools too; it's worth a thousand textbooks."

Shortly before Christmas, Sarah and I went over to Diggle to join other members of the Huddersfield Canal Society. We were to walk back to Marsden over the top of Standedge Tunnel via Boat Lane, the route considered to be the one used by the boatmen to take their horses across the moors, while the boat was being legged through the tunnel. As some of the walkers approached from Uppermill, I jumped down from a wall (not a very high wall) to greet them. As I landed, I shouted out loud. It was a strange sensation but I felt as if I had jumped into a hole. The truth was much more ominous. My leg had given way under me and I was unable to move. Sarah told me later that my knee was wobbling around in a frightening fashion. I was given a cup of coffee, and someone ran to phone an ambulance. They took quite a while to arrive and, when they did, quite a while to get me on to a stretcher and hauled up the steep banking to the road above. I was taken to Oldham Hospital. I spent quite a time on a stretcher in a corridor but, when I was finally examined and X-rayed, they told me that a ligament had snapped in my knee and that I would need an operation as soon as possible to join it together. Sarah pointed out that we had no car, and how was she going to be able to visit me when there was virtually no public transport between Oldham and Marsden? Was it not possible to transfer me to Huddersfield?

Phonecalls were made and, before long, I found myself being whisked across the Pennines in an ambulance. I was in surprisingly jaunty mood (must have been the shock), chatting away to the ambulance man and imitating the nurse's Scouse accent, when waiting outside the operating theatre. I don't know whether she hit me or not. The next thing I remember was waking up in a ward.

I spent five days in hospital. They let me out when I was able to demonstrate that I could manage stairs on crutches. (I now had a plaster on my right leg from thigh to ankle). When I told Sarah the good news of my homecoming, she said "Oh, no, I'm not ready for you. There's Christmas to organise and I'm pulling down the partition wall upstairs. Can't they keep you in for a bit longer."

14

THE DEEPEST
CUT OF ALL

I did go home and I did help to cook the Christmas dinner whilst on crutches and I did develop the most awful infection in my knee wound and I had to have a little window cut in my plaster so my suppurations could be seen to. Over the months, I had to learn to walk again with visits to the physio and many exercises. In the meantime, Parksy and Kate had left us; so new auditions had to be held. Mark had stayed on for a second year. Parksy had left in order to attend to her marriage and Kate to further her career. More of Parksy later. Kate still keeps in touch. She works regularly and spent several years with the Royal Shakespeare Company.

The auditions produced Caron Pascoe and Sue Dyde. Caron had studied drama at East Anglia University and, after graduating in 1982, she spent some time teaching drama at a school in South West France. She had just finished touring with a theatre-in-education company. Sue graduated in drama at Loughborough University in 1980 and then became involved in the setting up of Rompers, a touring theatre company in Nottingham. Both she and Sue were enthusiastic and easy to work with.

We began research on the material for our new show, which was to be the story of the Manchester Ship Canal. Fortunately for us, the Manchester Ship Canal Company had a wealth of archive material in their company office and we were allowed to dip into this at our heart's content, whilst also interviewing present day and ex-employees and taking a trip down the canal and across the River Mersey to Liverpool on one of the grain barges. Out of all this emerged our new musical play, *Manchester-Super-Mare*.

We began rehearsals on this and our second production of *Still Carrying*, little knowing what storms were brewing and what troubles lay ahead. We knew that the Arts Council was reviewing the development of the arts in England. We knew changes were in store, but we had been given not even the merest hint that we would be affected. We had spoken to our Drama Officer – everything seemed fine.

I'D GO BACK TOMORROW

One morning in March 1984, I went downstairs to make a cup of tea as usual, picked up the *Guardian* from the door-mat and saw the headline on the front page: "Arts Council axes grants of theatre companies". Even then I was not particularly worried, only in the sense of not wanting any theatre companies to have their grant cut. I gazed down quite a long list and, to my horror, there was the name of the Mikron Theatre Company. After this year, we were to lose our Arts Council grant.

It was a terrible shock and it took me several minutes to take the news in. Without this major grant (well, major to us – it was the smallest by far of all the Arts Council Drama revenue grants), we would almost certainly be unable to continue. And there had been no warning. The news in the *Guardian* was a leak. We were to be officially informed by special delivery letter the following morning.

I rang Peter Mair, our Drama Officer, in London. He was awfully sorry we had heard the news by leak. He hadn't been allowed to let us know before. Of course, he said, he had fought our corner for us but, when I asked him why he hadn't resigned as a matter of principle, he said he wasn't able to do that as he had too large a mortgage to pay off!

Sarah and I, Mark Williams and our assistant administrator, Kathryn, sat in our office at the Marsden Mechanics the next day and read the official letter. It came with a copy of *The Glory of the Garden – a Strategy for a Decade*. We read sentences like: "Foremost among these developments are the upgrading of companies due, in the course of time, to be brought into the programme of regional development, the strengthening of touring companies, increased funding for project awards and increased funding for new writing" and "Many of the companies on the list have done good work. But the Council does not place their achievements in the highest class" and "The strongest argument of need is the existence of a demand for art which springs up in response to supply" – and we wondered why we had been chosen for the chop. Were we just too small, too insignificant? It couldn't be the saving of money. Our grant of £28,500 was a mere third of what it had cost the Arts Council to print *The Glory of the Garden*. Perhaps their thinking was that no-one would notice our disappearance or that somehow we would manage to survive.

Well, we immediately decided that we would fight back. We were not going to disappear at the end of 1984. We had a right of appeal and we would put all our energies into winning that appeal. We drafted a letter and sent it to the national newspapers. It was printed in both the *Guardian* and the *Sunday Times*, in the latter alongside two photos of us. Part of the letter read: "Even after twelve years of creating a demand for theatre in venues and regions of the country which could aptly be described as ' empty' and 'neglected', we are painfully aware of our vulnerability in terms of our work being largely unknown to the 'cognoscenti'. We feel that, as well as reaching very high artistic standards, our touring network actually reaches those audiences which grant-giving bodies claim they are so keen to expose to live drama. Of the total grants-in-aid awarded to the Arts Council, our company will receive this year 0.034 per cent, ie £28,000 – a comparatively small sum but, without which, the Mikron Theatre Company cannot survive. And, of course, at the end of the day we will be missed by a mere 20 odd thousand people a year who will recognise that we are in the same boat as they feel themselves to be in when it comes to having any real voice or clout in choosing the kind of entertainment they wish the Arts Council to fund on their behalf. The idea that large building-based companies could ever fulfil our function in our absence is tragically misguided. The Arts Council, in either its ignorance or downright disdain, has taken the decision to put us out of business without consultation of any kind with ourselves or our public."

We launched a petition, which in the next three months was to be signed by 10,000 people, and we encouraged both sympathetic organisations and audience members to write their own individual letters of protest to the Arts Council. A lot of the organisation of our appeal had to be left to Sarah as we had two shows to take on tour. We gave our first performance of *Manchester-Super-Mare* at our Marsden local, the Railway on April 14th to an even more enthusiastic audience than usual. They could not believe our grant had been axed and were desperate to sign the petition.

The first night of our Waterways Tour was at another Railway, this time at Appley Bridge, near Wigan on the Leeds & Liverpool Canal. The *Artful Reporter*, the newspaper of North West Arts, described the loss of our grant and the potential closure of Mikron: "It is a Tuesday night in Appley Bridge. Seventy five people and one black Labrador are crammed into the backroom of the local pub to see *Still Carrying*. The age of the audience ranges from six years to sixty and that includes the dog. People are standing, sitting, squatting. Children are on parents' knees, apparently allowed in for the duration of the performance only, courtesy of the local PC who turns a 'blind eye'. In one corner of the room, in a space no larger than six feet by eight feet, the members of the company are preparing to start the show. One stage light on a collapsible stand is the only gesture to technical sophistication. Scenery is two boards propped against the wall. The dressing room is right there on stage...The episodic nature of the piece requires quick changes – slick and executed with the deftness of an impressionist's switch of persona. The show is punctuated with music and songs...As I left the pub at the end, what stayed in my mind was the picture of a rather plump nine-year-old who had been sitting on one side of me and one of the pub's older regulars who'd been sitting on the other. Both had chuckled away throughout the evening, both had watched the serious parts with concern, both had clearly had a good time. When the closing song came, the little girl followed the lyrics in her programme with the straw from her coke bottle, the man with a pint of bitter in his hand, and both sang heartily the refrain, '*Still carrying, still carrying, still carrying on*'. In the circumstances, could there have been a more ironic conclusion to the evening."

Virtually every member of the audience signed our petition at every show, and hundreds wrote personal letters to the Arts Council. Newspapers wrote editorials about us with headlines like – "Last Voyage for Mikron?", "Theatre Boat Holed Below the Water Line", "Swan Song?" and "End of an Era?". Our local authority, Kirklees, pledged to continue to support us and the West Yorkshire County Council gave us a small grant of £1,500. But none of this would be of any real use if we didn't win our appeal to the Arts Council. *Manchester-Super-Mare* was going down well with audiences and critics. *The Northampton Chronicle and Echo* said: "The fast-moving, lively show was a delight even to the jaded palate of a regular theatre-goer like me. The Arts Council are showing a lack of vision that the Victorians would never have understood." The *Oxford Mail* said: "The show, in the form of an end-of-pier show, unfolds with a shoestring simplicity that grand master of seaside entertainment, Clarkson Rose, would have envied."

Sarah, meanwhile was back in Marsden, co-ordinating the campaign and seeing Sam through his pre- GCSE year. For both of them, it was the first time they had not been on the boat full-time. I missed not having the family on board and we tried to get to see each other most weekends.

At the end of June, Mark, Sarah and I went to appeal on behalf of Mikron at the Arts Council in London. We presented them with thousands of signatures from our ongoing petition and we knew they had received many letters. They ranged from brilliantly-argued pleas for our survival, with clear illustrations of our uniqueness and quality, to a letter from an eight-year-old who said, if the Arts Council did not restore our grant, he would personally go to London and stab Sir William Rees- Mogg, the Arts Council Chairman!

Luke Rittner, the Secretary General of the Council listened to us for over an hour, and a month later ignored all our pleas and turned down our appeal. That was the end of the matter. There was no other route to go down. Why did they make this decision? The official letter said that we were having our subsidy cut on "strategic" grounds: "The Council would wish me to make it clear that there is much to commend artistically in the company's work and very much hopes that other sources of income will be found to enable the company to have a viable and creative future." We were also told that our company was excellently administrated. So what did "strategic" mean? We have never been able to get to the nitty-gritty of that little word.

THE DEEPEST CUT OF ALL

I cannot remember the details of this particular tour – no harrowing incidents on the canal, although I'm sure there were. All I remember is angry members of the audience reacting in disbelief to the Arts Council and its remoteness from many people. Not the season ticket holders at Covent Garden, nor the invitees to the latest exhibition at a London gallery, but the people who valued the work of companies like ourselves who worked outside of London, often in rural areas and at non-theatre venues, providing exciting, provocative but accessible theatre at affordable prices. It is interesting to note that the other companies whose appeals also failed were 7:84 Theatre Company (England) and C.A.S.T. Presentations, both small-scale companies with similar aspirations to ourselves.

The Waterways Tour finished and we embarked, feeling exhausted and under siege, on our South Pennine Tour by van. We were immediately uplifted by an article by Val Javin in the *Huddersfield Examiner*: "If the Arts Council had seen the company at work, their opinion would undoubtedly have been different. Mikron's performances are irresistible...This is an intelligent, imaginative company which genuinely takes theatre to audiences rarely able to see live entertainment. Many make the claim – few live up to it quite so convincingly as Mikron...For sheer entertainment value, Mikron are a hard act to follow. This is a company which cares about the subjects it chooses and it shows...They are professional to the core. Catch them somewhere on the road – you won't regret it."

We finished our South Pennine Tour at our local pub, the Railway on November 10th and, shortly afterwards, we heard that we were to receive a grant of £10,000 from West Yorkshire County Council, who had recently discovered "The Arts" and had a very positive funding policy towards them. The real instigator of our funding was the Chairman of the Recreation and Arts Committee, John Sully. He was quoted as saying: "I believe our grant will save this company. They have toured the country with a show which gave the history of the Huddersfield Narrow Canal and it would be ironic if the company should be forced to cease at the same time as the restoration of the Narrow Canal became a reality. There is a total lack of understanding from the Arts Council about the quality and importance of the work of Mikron." We now had a lifeline and we had to build on that. We launched an appeal to the general public for funds with the co-operation of the magazines, *Canal and Riverboat*, *Waterways World* and *Narrowboat*. This got off to a slow start but in the end brought in £5,000, a valuable contribution to our task of staying afloat. We decided to use the £10,000 to appoint a fundraiser for a year. We then received a further £11,000 from the County Council as revenue funding for 1985.

15

THE FIGHT BACK

After interviewing a few candidates we appointed Colin Anderson as our fundraiser. He seemed to have the right qualifications for the job. He had wide experience of promoting live theatre and of dealing with business and industry in Kirklees. Mark, Sarah and I were excited by the possibilities presented by having a full-time fundraiser and awaited the results with high hopes.

In the meantime, other changes were afoot. Mark Williams was staying on for a third year and was made an associate of the company. Partly to save money, but also to create tighter-written and more unified scripts, the new show was to be researched and written by just Mark and myself. In the past, I used to devise the new show and set up the research. The acting company were then thrown in at the deep end and sent out to research. Then followed hours of discussion and listening to tapes, out of which the new script gradually emerged, written by four people, some of whom may have been writing for the first time in their lives. The system had served us well, but now times were changing.

Mark, Sarah and I auditioned, and we recruited two women to join the company – Louise Waddington, from just across "the border", Delph near Oldham, who had trained at Rose Bruford College and was making her professional debut, and Jane Griffith. Jane was joining the Company as a musician. She had specialised in music at Leicester Polytechnic and worked with several dance companies. She was to be musical director and on tour would play keyboards and cello. Again, a different approach for Mikron.

Mark and I wrote *Just the Job*. It was a serious look at the so-called leisure revolution and its social effects, but it was set in the context of canals and waterway holidays. A family from Birmingham win the "holiday of a lifetime" on a narrowboat. The claustrophobic lifestyle highlights the problems the characters are having dealing with unemployment, redundancy and a changing world. The tranquillity of the canals helps them to come to terms with themselves and each other. Mark directed the show. It was strange to be just a "mere actor" for once, but I really enjoyed tackling such a meaty part as the dad,

Norman. Just before we opened, we all began to doubt whether audiences would find the show amusing. Perhaps they would just find it very peculiar. We needn't have worried. The show went a storm. As the *Tamworth Herald* said: "It took just a few minutes for three extraordinarily talented performers to ignite the atmosphere and reduce the audience to a quivering jelly of giggles."

Sam and Sarah were not on tour full-time this year. Sam was now thirteen and needed to work hard for his GCSEs the following year. I missed them a lot and was always relieved when they turned up for a weekend on the boat.

I remember some moments from this tour particularly. For instance, when Jean-Pierre Gailliez arrived from Belgium with thirty of his students. Jean-Pierre had first seen Mikron in 1975 when he came across us by chance whilst on a boating holiday. He was delighted by one of our performances and vowed that one day he would arrange a tour of the Belgium Waterways for us. He was very concerned to conserve in working order three hydraulic boatlifts on the Canal du Centre. They were to be superseded by a gigantic new lift at Strepy-Thieu. These three lifts were built shortly after the very first hydraulic boatlift in the world opened at Anderton. Jean-Pierre was a teacher by profession and he had brought his students to England on a visit but also to perform extracts in English from Mikron's very first production *Still Waters*. It was very moving to watch these young people playing James Brindley, Josiah Wedgewood, boatmen and boatwomen and singing our songs.

More bizarre was the singing dog we found at the Railway Hotel in Congleton a few days later. His favourite song was *Home on the Range*!

Later in the tour, in August, while we were performing at a pub close to Hampton Court, the police had come to the boat and told Sarah and Sam that Sarah's dad, George, had died that afternoon. He had been taken ill while sitting with his pals on a bench outside the Arndale Centre in Headingley, Leeds, and died before they could get him to hospital. He had had two previous heart attacks, but they had been several years before, and he had been a very fit and well seventy-six year old. It was obviously a considerable shock, and Sarah left the boat the next morning to go and look after her mother and make arrangements. Sam and I were to join her for the funeral. We had fortunately had a cancellation of a show, so I was able to get away.

We continued down the tideway to London and after holding off at Greenwich (I shall never forget the sight of *Tyseley* sitting on the mud at Greenwich Pier), we safely entered Limehouse Dock at 6.30pm on Saturday August 10th.

The saga began at 2.30am. I woke up to the sound of bubbling and the trickling of water. I checked our bilges. Nothing. So I went back to bed. A few minutes later, the boat started to bang, and I could distinctly hear our ropes creaking and straining. I climbed out of the back cabin and saw that our ropes were so taut they were about to snap. Somehow I managed to release them. It was then that I noticed that the water was draining out of the basin. We had already dropped eight feet. With a short shaft I could now touch the bottom. Two other boats across the other side of the basin were now hanging precariously. I dashed across and helped the owners cut their ropes to free themselves. The boats lurched and dropped back into the water. Next I ran to find the lock-keeper. He was fast asleep in his hut. His mate had gone off duty and, by mistake, had left the paddles up at both ends. If any more time had elapsed, the basin would have drained completely. Sam and our designer, Ray, were the only other people on board *Tyseley*. Sam didn't wake. Ray woke briefly and thought he heard pigeons walking on the roof!

After an attempt at a few hours sleep, it was time to set off. The basin was still three feet down but we decided to try and go up Limehouse Cut. It was fine at first, but soon we could see mudbanks stretching before us and *Tyseley* was grinding to a halt. We managed to back to the basin and make the entrance of the Regent's Canal. After half-an-hour of letting water down, we progressed from the first to the second lock. Ray was standing at the lockside holding his head. The windlass had spun off and hit him. He was very bloody and definitely needed stitches. A man appeared from nowhere and offered to take him to nearby Mile End Hospital. This left Sam as my only crew member. He was brilliant. He operated the locks for me all the way up the River Lee to Waltham Abbey. We had no time for food or breaks, but he stuck at it.

This was the year when Jean-Pierre finally managed to arrange our first Belgian tour. Over five days in early September, we gave performances of *Manchester-Super-Mare* on the Canal Bruxelles-Charleroi and the Canal du Centre. Over the next few years these tours were to become more extensive. More of these later.

For the Autumn Tour, Mark and I wrote and I directed *The British Amazon*. We wanted to write a show about a woman who had been involved with the sea in some way. We read about famous female pirates, and the adventures of Grace Darling, the lighthouse keeper's daughter, but then we were told that in the Bodleian Library was Mary Anne Talbot's own story. She was born in 1778 and, at the age of thirteen, her wicked guardian sent her off to the West Indies dressed as a cabin-boy. She spent most of her thirty-year life in the Army and Navy as a drummer-boy and powder monkey, until her sex was revealed, and she finished her days as an actress. As Val Javin said in the *Huddersfield Examiner*: "It is a fascinating story brought vividly alive by Mikron's unique blend of music and broad comedy. The material is meticulously researched, cleverly packaged and warmly presented...The performance served to confirm Mikron's place in the

Imogen's War, 1993: Richard Povall, Lucy McAra, Beccy Hall
and Rodney Matthew.   (Derek Pratt)

A Woman's Place, 1995: Edmund Harcourt and Richard
Povall.   (Derek Pratt)

Outside the George & Dragon at Fenny Compton on the Oxford Canal in 1996: Richard Povall, Vashti McLachlan, Mike and Sarah, Jo McGowan and Edmund Harcourt.

(Derek Pratt)

On the Grand Union in 1993: Richard Povall, Becky Hall, Sarah Parks, Rodney Matthew, Sarah and Mike.

(Derek Pratt)

Keep Yer 'ands Off at Wolvercote Green on the Oxford
Canal in 1975: Mike, Thirzie Robinson, Alan Bridger and Dan
Caulfield.   (P.J. Alexander)

The same venue in 1981 with Mud in Your Eye: Sarah
Wilson, Mike, Mark Strickson and Thea Bennett.
                                               (P.J. Alexander)

Beer Street, 1994: Sandra Osborn, Jo McGowan, Rodney Matthew and Richard Povall. (Derek Pratt)

Over The Top, 1983: Mike and Mark Williams.

The famous bats in Free For All at the Stanley Arms,
Anderton in 1990: Jacky Hynes and John Spooner.

Imogen's War, 1993: Rodney Matthew and Becky Hall.

Leaving the Oxford Canal for the Thames at Isis Lock, Oxford, 1998. Mike steering, Vashti McLachlan on the balance beam.

Liz Eves steers along the Trent & Mersey Canal near Willington, 2000.

Auditions! Musical Director, Janet Russell, Mike and
Andrea Walker, Mikron's Administrator.

A double birthday for Sandra Osborn and Mike at the
Anchor Inn, High Offley, May 29th 1994: Richard Povall,
Sarah, Sandra, Mike and Jo McGowan.

Tyseley goes locking down the Northampton Arm in 1993
with Lucy McAra at the tiller.   (Derek Pratt)

Narrow boat, wide river. Tyseley moored by Greenwich Pier
on the River Thames 1983.

front ranks of the country's touring companies. And it made the threat to the company's future all the more senseless."

Research for the new show had involved visits to the Maritime Museum in Greenwich and to Nelson's flagship, *Victory*, at Portsmouth. On my way to meet Mark and Jane to take a boat down the Thames to Greenwich, I began to feel ill on the tube. I was sweating profusely and I had a pain in my chest. I staggered off at Bank Station and leant against a wall. I was now convinced I was having a heart attack. Although I must have looked dreadful, no-one came to my aid and somehow I managed to change platforms and get to Embankment. Mark dashed off to find help as soon as he saw me and I sat with Jane looking at the river. I remember thinking, "If this is one of the last things I see, how right it is that there should be commercial traffic on the river at this moment." A train of rubbish barges was passing. An ambulance arrived and one of the men looked at me and said, "You're not having a heart attack if that's what you think. You'd really know it if you were. You're hyperventilating – 'ere, breathe into this paper bag." Apparently, a hyperventilation attack can sometimes resemble a heart attack. It occurs when you start to panic. You start to breathe wrongly which makes you panic even more. Breathing into a paper bag helps to correct this.

The ambulance man was not convinced that I was recovering quickly enough; so I was taken to Westminster Hospital for a check up. I had an ECG, which was fine, and the doctor confirmed that I had had a hyperventilation attack. I asked him what caused these attacks and he said they could be brought on by many factors – stress, worry, severe dehydration, for example. Knowing what is happening to you helps you not to panic more.

Over the next few years, I had several panic attacks. My doctor prescribed beta-blockers, which I used very rarely but once to great effect. It helped me relax sufficiently to pass my driving test at the first go; I was forty-five years old. We'd never owned a car but it now seemed fair to take my share of driving the Company van. Sarah passed her test in the same year.

Later, my doctor sent me to a clinical psychologist to try and discover the reasons for the attacks. It emerged that I had not come to terms very well with the death of Sarah's father. That and the usual "mid-life crisis" had started me palpitating and panicking. I've never had problems since. I've learnt to anticipate a possible attack, to breathe properly and thus not to panic.

16

FOREIGN WATERS

My performances in *The British Amazon* were to be my last (up to the
present at least). After long discussions with Sarah, we decided that it
was time to put away my box of make-up, so to speak, (although I had
never used the stuff in a Mikron show) and to concentrate on my
writing and directing. The death of George, Sarah's dad, had made us
realise how tying my having to perform six nights a week was, and
how difficult it was to get away if any of our parents became ill.

Another factor was Sarah's wish to have less to do with the day-to-
day administration of the Company and to take more of a backseat,
trouble-shooting role. She had been doing it for fourteen years and
needed a break. I was to take over as chief administrator – another good
reason to cease my thespian activities. I was going to miss it, I knew. I
relished facing a new audience every night and I had never tired of the
closeness of the contact we had with them. But I was sure that I would
soon get used to not being applauded and settle down at my desk job.

Our search for sponsorship had produced some results – a total of
£5,000 in all for 1986 from four companies, Calor Gas, Honda (UK)
Ltd, National Girobank and a local firm, Holset Engineering. Both
Holset and Calor Gas were first time sponsors of the arts; so we were
able to bring in a further £4,000 from the Government's Business
Sponsorship Scheme. Our total budget for the year was £50,000. We
could earn at least £20,000 of that ourselves from collections after the
shows, fees and product sales. The rest would have to come from
funding and, if possible, more sponsorship.

What I was looking forward to was getting back on to the boat and
doing what we were set up to do – taking theatre to the public at large
and performing in non-theatre venues. With both myself and Mark not
performing, we recruited two new members to join Jane and Louise.
Cliff Barry was from Wolverhampton. He had been in many jobs,
including a stint as a betting office manager, but had also performed in
many amateur productions. Encouraged by his friends, he trained at
the Birmingham School of Speech and Drama. Mikron was his first
professional engagement. Stephen Holmes was from Liverpool but
now lived with his wife and two children in South Wales. He too had

had a career switch. He had been a quantity surveyor for ten years, including a four-year stint in Saudi Arabia, when he decided the time was ripe for a change and enrolled at the Welsh College of Music and Drama in Cardiff.

Mark directed *Just the Job* and I directed *The British Amazon*, and Mikron was again up and running and still afloat. As it happened, I didn't particularly enjoy the Waterways Tour – it was a combination of Sarah and Sam not being on the boat all the time, still not feeling a hundred per cent fit and growing frustration at the behaviour of Cliff and Steve. Steve was an excellent actor. Cliff loved being in front of an audience and constantly upstaged the others and overacted. Socially, they both behaved like overgrown schoolboys. The women, bless them, gritted their teeth and got on with the job.

April was the wettest and coldest this century and the weather for the rest of the tour was not brilliant but, as always, there were memorable moments. We travelled on the southern Kennet & Avon Canal for the first time. We were lent *Nutfield*, a Town Class narrowboat like *Tyseley*, and went from the bottom of the unrestored Devizes Flight to Hanham on the River Avon giving performances in Bradford-on-Avon, Bathampton, Saltford and Hanham. It's a stunningly beautiful canal with two imposing aqueducts at Avoncliffe and Dundas and great views all the way. The approach to Bath takes you above the city and then, via a very deep lock, plunges you down on to the Avon. Standing on the back counter of *Nutfield* in the bottom of this lock, I wondered how long it could continue raining with such intensity. The Avon was a swirling, muddy torrent. With a bit of clever ropework, we turned *Nutfield* round using the current and battled against the stream up to Pulteney Weir (which was nearly level). What a superb tie-up – right in the middle of Bath.

On the Regent's Canal at Camden Lock, I was setting the top lock. A woman, wheeling a baby in a buggy, bent down to pick up the baby's dummy. I watched as buggy with baby slowly rolled into the canal. The woman jumped in after them. In an instant, she was followed by Albert, the lock-keeper, who had also seen it happen. Everyone was rescued and was fine, although the woman was very upset as she had been asked by a friend to look after her baby for an hour. Not to be outdone, shortly afterwards, Louise fell in off the gunwhales of *Tyseley* – her first time!

In June, we were heartened to receive a grant of £11,500 from Kirklees Council towards the touring in our local area, which boosted our chances of surviving for another year.

On August 10th, we held our first Friends of Mikron gathering at the Black Star in Stourport. We had started this up so that we could keep our supporters *au fait* with our progress, via a thrice-yearly newsletter, and to raise money from the subscriptions. Already over

150 people had joined up. What made this first get-together even more poignant was that it was also *Tyseley*'s 50th birthday party. There was a great atmosphere on the day and even torrential rain didn't dampen the spirits, even though we had to hold the event inside, including the barbecue. There were speeches, showings of our television documentaries and, best of all, a birthday cake in the shape of *Tyseley* with every detail exact (including the Nicholson's map in its plastic cover on the back slide). Louise and Jane had been working on it for weeks and we hadn't been allowed even a peek.

Before the South Pennine Tour started in November, we had another treat in store – a two-week tour of the Belgian Waterways with our production of *The British Amazon*. We travelled on North Sea Ferries from Hull to Zeebrugge, and then the following morning drove to La Louvière on the Canal du Centre, where there are three magnificent hydraulic lifts built shortly after the one at Anderton in Cheshire. Sadly, the Anderton boatlift had closed in 1983. It had become unsafe. *Tyseley* was one of the last boats to use the lift; we had no idea that the cables were in danger of snapping. It is only recently that money has been obtained to restore the lift to its full former working glory.

Back in Belgium, we boarded the *péniche*, *Peterborough* (named after the fourth boatlift in the world on the Trent-Severn Waterway in Canada). Jean-Pierre Gailliez greeted us with his usual energy and enthusiasm, full of schemes for the 1988 centenaries of the lifts and for trips to Canada and... the world. While he talked excitedly, around him people were dashing around, completing the conversion of the boat – building cabins, fitting lights, carrying in furniture. Later that day, we gave a performance of *The British Amazon* in the Italian Canteen (an ex-prisoner-of-war camp now used as a canteen and museum). It is always strange, initially, performing to a foreign audience, however good their English is. We speak much more slowly than normally and we eliminate all dialects and accents. We all speak "standard" English or as near to it as some of us can get! We were also very tired but I hope that didn't show. We went back to the boat for a few beers, a look at maps and a very early bed.

At 7.15 the next morning, with the canal shrouded in mist, we descended the three lifts. What magnificent structures they are – hymns to the grandeur of Victorian engineering. We gave our first two performances on board the boat (yes, unlike *Tyseley*, the boat was large enough to accommodate a small stage and seating space for a hundred people). The students seemed to understand most of the show and appreciated the bawdy humour.

In what became the pattern for the week, in the afternoon we travelled for six hours. We covered 35 kilometres and went through 4 locks. It poured with rain throughout the trip and night fell as we arrived in Charleroi. It had a similar feel to arriving in Sheffield –

closed steel works and coalmines. A once-thriving industrial town was now severely depressed and the number of commercial carrying boats was decreasing day by day.

During the course of our journey, we grew to like both Belgium and its people – albeit still split into two nations, the Flemish and the Walloons. We saw the attractive town of Namur, where Sarah celebrated her forty-third birthday and ate Escargots Beignet and Lotte Basilic (snails and monkfish), and it finally stopped raining.

The River Meuse is very beautiful in Namur with a citadel high on a hill and stunning churches and houses lining the waterfront. As we progressed downstream, steep cliffs and woods rose up behind the heavily industrialised banks. It's a great river, rising in France at 1496 feet above sea level. It flows 280 miles through France, 119 miles through Belgium and 160 miles through Holland to the North Sea. There are many barges going up and down some capable of carrying 1800 tonnes. Compare that to the maximum of 750 tons on a modernised English waterway like the Aire & Calder. We passed through Huy and then on to Liège which boasts the third largest inland port in Europe. It was being expanded to take vessels carrying 12,000 tonnes (then 2000) but there were ecological, economic and political problems, the main one being that the Flemish didn't want the Wallonian port of Liège to expand as this would almost certainly take trade away from Antwerp.

In between performances in Liège, Sarah and I visited the biggest outdoor market we had ever seen. Every Sunday morning, it stretches along the riverside for two kilometres. You can buy absolutely everything – bric-à-brac, household goods, carpets, crockery, meat, vegetables, cheese, spices and animals. There were live chickens for sale, ducks, rabbits, cats, dogs, pigeons and even peacocks, Canada geese and swans.

The next day saw us off down the Albert Canal. Built in 1939, it's of motorway size and very busy with cargoes up to 2000 tonnes including cement, gravel, sand, coal, grain, maize, steel, iron, timber, armaments, minerals, aggregates and mineral water. Although the locks are enormous, they do not take many minutes to empty. It was while we were dropping in the locks tied to moving bollards that I was able to have a closer look at the various péniches which were our travelling companions. The wife generally steers into the locks, while her husband deals with the ropes. Behind her is a canary in a cage, and on the cabin top is the obligatory telly aerial. The cabin windows are adorned with lace curtains, ornaments and flowers. Most of the barge people have a car on board and a rowing boat and, for their children, there's an inflatable boat and a fenced-off area for them to play in.

We turned down a large arm leading into the middle of Hasselt. We were now in Flanders and all our carefully acquired French was of no avail, as everyone was speaking Dutch. We happened to be in Hasselt for Fair Week. I have never seen a travelling fair of such size and variety – from the latest terrifying technological ride to the small side shows with "Bertha the fattest lady in the world". There were even food stalls exclusively selling snails. There were no gangs of youths roaming the streets, no drunkenness, no trouble – just fun for everyone.

In between completing the script of our new show for the autumn, I tried my hand at steering – the size of the wheel is very daunting and it's hard on the shoulders at first – and, somehow, I managed to avoid any bridges or large *péniches*.

In Antwerp, we toured the docks – very impressive, vast and still expanding. We saw all types of vessels from 280 tonne *péniches* to large sea-going tankers. The following morning, we moved through the river lock on to the River Schelde and past the old town of Antwerp looking beautiful in the early morning mist. A few minutes later we hit a blanket of fog. The barges with radar ploughed straight on but our pilot insisted that we tied up and waited for the fog to lift. When we finally got away, we found ourselves in a convoy of about ten vessels, including a coaster and a cabin-cruiser, all heading upstream.

We gave several performances in Brussels Docks, managing to fit in a visit to the centre of Brussels to see one of the finest squares in the world – the Grand Place – and to sample the excellent seafood on sale in the many restaurants which abound in the alleyways running off the square.

Then, suddenly, it was the last performance. A tearful, fond farewell to our marvellous Belgian hosts and then a mad dash to Zeebrugge to catch the ferry back to Hull. Everyone was agreed that it had been a great success; over the two-and-a-half weeks we had given twenty-one performances to over two thousand people. We would be back in Belgium next year.

In November and December, we toured by road in the South Pennines. We added a new production to *Just the Job* and *The British Amazon – Speed Your Shuttle (and change your tune)*, which was the first in what was to become a trilogy of productions about Yorkshire weavers and the woollen industry, obviously very pertinent to the area in which we lived. We told the story of a fictional family who, like many families in Marsden, had been weaver/farmers for many generations working on handlooms in their cottages and carrying their pieces of cloth to market every week. These people, as the *Colne Valley Chronicle* said in its review at the time, "were trapped in the grip of a massive historic change. The shivering apprentices, terrified of the factory bell, are still funny; the modern young man, berating his out-of-date parents, grows into a disillusioned father whose own son has been made obsolete by machines. The show is thought-provoking, moving, funny and simply grippingly human – like Shakespeare without the kings and poetry."

17

OUR FIRST BROADS

1987 began without Mark Williams and Colin Anderson. We had had to lose Colin. A fundraiser should raise at least double his salary but sadly all the grant money from West Yorkshire County Council had been spent on expenses, publicity and Colin's salary, and Colin had only personally raised about £500! It had not been a very satisfactory experience.

Mark, on the other hand, had been a tremendous success. Over his three years as an actor with us, he had grown in stature and was now a very accomplished comic actor. He had directed *Just the Job* with flair and had been an integral part of the team that had pulled Mikron out of the mire of the Arts Council axe. He now felt it was time for him to move on. And move on he has – you will recognise him as the man in the Prudential ads ("we want to be together"), as a member of the *Fast Show* team and from the films, *One Hundred and One Dalmatians* and *The Borrowers*, amongst others.

1987 also saw the return of Sarah Parks (Parksy). She had co-written the autumn show with me. It had been a success; so she was now to research and write the new show with me, with Jane Mansel again writing the music. She was also to tour again as a member of the acting company.

The new production was set in 1936 on the Tardebigge flight of locks, with 30 locks the longest narrow lock flight in the country. Called *Flight of Fancy*, it was inspired by a book written by a lock-keeper's daughter and concerns one day in the life of a pre-war canalside community. We described it as a musical evocation of rural life in the thirties. Sarah was joined by three newcomers: Amanda Edwards from Bridgnorth in Shropshire, John Elkington from Sheffield and Clive Lucas (I must hastily point out no relation to myself or Sarah) from Halifax. As well as their acting and singing skills, they were all dab hands at various instruments, including guitar, keyboards and clarinet.

We set off on tour in early May with *Flight of Fancy* and a revised version of *The British Amazon* and loaded up with copies of our new LP and cassette, *Mikron V*. Our first recording since *Over the Top* in

I'D GO BACK TOMORROW

1982, it features songs from *Still Carrying, Manchester-Super-Mare, Just the Job, The British Amazon, From Where I Stand* and *Speed Your Shuttle (and change your tune)*, sung and played by actors from all the companies since then.

All went well until we arrived at the Caldon Canal. It's never an easy canal to navigate in a full- length boat but this year the bottom seemed nearer the top than ever. We stuck in Bridge 12 but, with all of us rocking the boat from side to side, we managed to get moving again. We stuck briefly in Bridge 13, very heavily in Bridge 14 and, insolubly it appeared, in the railway bridge. This was at 11.30 in the morning. We had no such things as mobile phones in 1987, so off I trudged to find a phone-box and to inform British Waterways of our plight. Not long after, the lengthman arrived, informing us that the cut was three inches down. He was followed by the length foreman who came complete with trilby hat and many excuses – "I'm at my wits end. We can't dredge...there's nowhere to put the dredgings." The lengthman went off to send down more water and we had to sit tight and wait. Meanwhile the time available for getting to our venue was ebbing away. Finally, just before 4.30 (and after five hour's residency under the bridge), three more boats arrived and, with the extra manpower, we were able to get off. Shortly afterwards, a team of British Waterways men arrived carrying a plank!

We travelled onwards but it was obvious that we were not going to make it by boat. The landlord of the pub venue sent a van to collect the cast and props and, for the first time, I boated single-handed. In beautiful early evening sunshine, I took *Tyseley* down Hazlehurst and Cheddleton Locks. As the sun set in a red burst behind me, I pulled up outside the Boat, thirteen hours after setting off through Harecastle Tunnel. The Company were packing up after the show. Another ordinary day in the life of Mikron was over.

Two days later it was our day off, but we still had to move back down the Caldon and on to the Trent & Mersey. The pound was now nearly a foot down. We stuck in several bridges but, when we arrived at the dreaded railway bridge, British Waterways were waiting for us. They had already pulled out a motorbike. They snatched us through the bridge with their tug. When, at one point, their towing rope snapped, the foreman, instead of keeping it to splice, threw it into the canal. The lads who were pulling us through were remarkably cheerful. While they towed us to the next lock, we kept their chips warm in our oven. The tug driver remarked, "I came out this morning without my top set of teeth. Still, I'm not going to bite anyone, am I?"

We tied up at Planet Lock for the night and retired early, absolutely exhausted. I was just nodding off when a group of lads started jumping into the canal outside my back cabin. "Sorry, mate, I'm going into the Army tomorrow. I'm off abroad." They all jumped in one by one, one of them swallowing a gallon of mucky canal water. He was pulled out with much coughing and spluttering, and they all disappeared into the night much wetter, colder and probably more sober. But not, I fear, wiser.

By early June we were on the Staffs & Worcs Canal. Between Compton and Wightwick Locks, John spotted a strong black box in the water. He pulled it on to the boat and, with trepidation, we began to open it – is it a saxophone, a trumpet, a severed limb or something much worse? No, it's a selection of expensive men's leather shoes – just single samples. We spotted another box floating in the canal. John tried to reach it with a boat-hook but failed. At the next lock, he went back to fetch it but was thwarted by a vicious bed of nettles which tried to attack him after he'd stripped off to wade into the water. He was very determined, thinking that the other box might provide shoes to make a matching pair.

When we arrived at Wombourne, we phoned the police and half-an-hour later they arrived – two young policewomen in a Panda car. Naturally we invited them on board for a cup of tea to furnish them with the full details of the possible crime. Within minutes, we had them in hysterics – "Oh, my god, you don't need to do a show. You're funny enough." John and Clive were photographed wearing the women's police hats and, to cap it all, Amanda, Clive and I were given a lift in the Panda to the shops. A police car could be seen travelling along with us, a shopping trolley and the box of shoes crammed into the back seat.

Later on in the tour, I realised how useful it was that I was no longer acting in the shows. I received news that my father had had a stroke and was in hospital in Bournemouth. I was able to go and visit him. Luckily, the stroke was minor. He wasn't paralysed but his speech and sight were affected. He also couldn't remember names and reversed people's genders – about the female nurse: "He's been looking after me well." I stayed for a couple of days and left when he was back at home. He was still very weak and tired and needed plenty of rest. After a few months, however, he made a complete recovery.

That year marked our first tour of the Norfolk Broads, which was made possible by a fan of Mikron. Stephen Tillyard, a retired university librarian, had been following Mikron for a few years and it was his ambition to get us to Norfolk where he lived. He was so keen that he offered to hire a suitable boat on our behalf and to publicise the tour. We could not refuse such a generous offer and, always seeking pastures (or rather waterways) new, we set out by road to Norwich at the beginning of September. Our four-day tour was aboard the Norfolk wherry *Albion* run by the Albion Trust. It was one of the few ex-working boats of the Broads still in existence and was kept alive by the Trust as a sailing boat, by letting it out to enthusiastic holidaymakers. I say enthusiastic because, although a beautiful vessel to look at, the below decks accommodation was basic. In a small space, there were twelve creaky hammock-style beds, a large table with benches and a sink. There was no hot water and nowhere below decks where you could stand up straight.

But once we were out on to Barton Broad and the large red sail was raised, it felt great. We sailed across the Broad and continued down the River Ant with all the motorised hire craft avoiding us. (Dad hunched over the steering wheel looking as if he was driving a plastic bathroom down the M1). That night we performed at the Dog Inn at Ludham Bridge.

The following day was horrible – drizzly with very little wind. We had to quant for most of the journey. Quant poles are made of pitch pine and are 24 feet long and very heavy. You have to move the boat along with one of these poles by walking up and down the gunwhales pushing it down into the mud at the bottom of the river. It's not so difficult when you get the knack of it. We performed that night at the Ferry Boat at Stokesby, a pleasant village on the River Bure boasting the largest candle shop in the world. The weather for our journey to Thurne the next day was excellent with a fair wind. We travelled on the run at six miles per hour. We were all beginning to adjust to life without an engine when, the next day, it was time to pack and leave for Norwich where we performed to a packed and appreciative audience.

In September, we toured for the second year on the Belgian waterways. *Flight of Fancy* went extremely well. The script was even published over there, with the more difficult words translated into French and Dutch. We left with an invitation to return in April and October the following year.

18

RISE & FALL

Although staying on as my co-writer, Parksy left the acting company, as did Amanda. Clive and John were joined for the 1988 season by Katherine Dow-Blyton and Billie Reynolds. Katherine was small, spiky, very funny and from Leeds and was soon to fall for John. Billie was from Trinidad and Surrey and was very tall with a great stage presence and singing voice, and didn't fall for anyone she was going to tell us about. Two more characters on the Mikron scene were joined by a person who was to have a great influence on the musical style and standards of the Company right up to the present day – Jim Woodland.

Jim was a singer-songwriter living in London. We listened to him on record and then met him. We liked what we heard and saw, and he became musical director for our new production. This was to be on the most unlikely subject ever to be considered suitable for the entertainment of a theatre audience – the history of the first canal boatlifts! The reason? – our friend from Belgium, Jean-Pierre Gailliez. He had been campaigning for years to ensure that the four hydraulic boatlifts on the Canal du Centre in Wallonia remained open when they were replaced by the new giant lift at Strepy-Thieu. He had always hoped that Mikron would write a show about the building of the first canal boatlifts in the world. This year seemed very appropriate as it was the centenary of two of the four lifts at La Louvière and of the lift at Les Fontinettes on the Canal Neufosse in France. Particularly relevant also was the continued closure of the very first boatlift at Anderton in Cheshire. Its centenary had passed unnoticed thirteen years before and it was now in disrepair, its future undecided.

So Parksy and I went on research in England, Belgium and France to discover some of the human stories behind these majestic examples of Victorian engineering. We studied many documents and talked to people who had worked the lifts. We began to realise that the show was going to be about the problems of linking technology and conservation and the risk of spoiling life while trying to improve it. As one press review later put it: "Should the old boatlifts and the communities that thrived around them be allowed to decay or be pickled in labelled glass jars as static museum pieces? Or can they be preserved and integrated as working memorials of the times that led up to and created today?"

Parksy and I wrote the show with music and lyrics from Jim and John. There were tensions and fall-outs during the rehearsals between the cast and their musical director, Jim, particularly as we approached opening night, but all this was resolved when we opened the show *Rise and Fall* on the *péniche Peterborough*, moored in the centre of Bruges as part of the Bruges Welcomes Britain Fortnight.

The show toured for two years on the waterways of England, France and Belgium, and in the Pennines and was always well received. Simon Warner of the *Halifax Courier* said: "Mikron doesn't offer a dry academic approach to the topic. Its four furiously energetic performers turn the subject into a rollercoaster of fast-moving fun." Francesca Turner in the *Guardian* said: "If anyone had tried to convince me beforehand that an account of counterbalanced caissons, hydraulic rams and accumulators could be achingly funny, I'd have told them to cast off to the nearest basin...The skill, ingenuity and vitality of the troupe is out of all proportion to the modesty of the settings in which they appear. But don't let scale trick you into doubting their professionalism. It's scrupulous."

By luck or judgement, we had discovered a great songwriter in Jim Woodland. His ability to grasp the essence of a subject and distil this into lyrics and music is mind-boggling. He can write lyrical songs, satirical songs, sure, but no-one can better Jim when it comes to writing a song about how something works. If you want to know the principle of hydraulic lifts, look no further than:

> The ram goes through a stuffing box
> That's in the lifting pit
> And through a tunnel to the press
> Exactly made to fit. (Four foot four, not a hair's breadth
> more, is the width of the tunnel -
> Made of iron that is wrought).
> And it leads to the valve box, water-cocks and glands
> And you use it for oiling the presses and the rams.
> It's a joy. It's a miracle.
> The bells should ring
> And it gives me great pleasure
> To declare the whole thing...
> Oh, by the way, did you know...

And so on. In later years, Jim was to do the same for brewing, weaving, sites of scientific interest, canal carrying and many others.

The Waterways Tour got off to a great start for everyone but Sarah. Whilst taking *Tyseley* to Anderton, where we were to start the tour, poor Sarah slipped when jumping off the boat and badly fractured her leg. She was taken to Warrington Hospital where she was operated on. After our usual rousing performance at our local, the Railway, we moved on to the boat at Anderton on May 15th. I went from there straight to Warrington to see Sarah but she had already gone down to theatre for her second operation. (The consultant believed he could improve on the job done by his registrar – "It's like putting together crazy paving"). When I did see her, she was very whoosy from the anaesthetic and in great pain. She appeared to be more comfortable the next day and wished us luck for our first waterways performance.

It was a perfect evening and the setting completely appropriate for *Rise and Fall* – on the putting green of the Stanley Arms (or "The Tip" as it is known locally) with the Trent & Mersey Canal immediately below us and, fifty feet below that, the River Weaver and the Anderton Boatlift. Across the river, with lights blazing like a futuristic space station, spread the mighty ICI chemical works, belching out great gobbets of thick smoke, steam and pollution. Ninety-four-year old Jack Cox, who used to work the lift in its heyday, watched the show and cried. Jean-Pierre had come from Belgium. It was a memorable evening.

During the next few days, as the boat moved further south, my journeys up the motorway to Warrington became longer and, as Sarah became stronger, I became more tired. One day, I fell asleep on Sarah's bed while she watched the telly. She was not happy to discover that it would be another week before she was allowed home, but lots of friends rallied round to visit her.

The first couple of weeks were not easy. We opened our second production, *Flight of Fancy*; I started training the newcomers to steer *Tyseley*; I carried on visiting Warrington; and, back in Marsden, Sam had his first GCSE (Maths). For Sarah, it was even harder – recovery from two operations and weeks on crutches.

Boat training had its moments. Katherine was steering into Swarkestone Lock. While I was organising the shutting of the gates with John, unbeknownst to me, she was in neutral gear and not reverse. By the time I realised, it was too late and we hit the bottom gates with an almighty thud, followed by the noise of splintering wood. They parted and, for one awful moment, I thought we were going to go straight through them. Water poured through the gap at an incredible rate. We managed to lower the boat in the lock and get *Tyseley* out. Katherine was ghostly pale. A large lump of wood was missing from the gate. Otherwise, we were all sound. Well-made those gates, as I said to British Waterways when I reported the incident.

Sarah went back to Marsden on May 28th, helped by friends and Sam. I was in Nottingham performing at the Canal Museum. We were always looked after at the Museum by the attendant, Michael. Michael was a peculiar fellow. He had a change of overalls for every job and was assiduous in his demonstrations of such things as the location of the water tap. Pointing at it, he would say "Water. Tap." or the electrics, "Mr Lucas, we need to plug you in...now." He washed his hands as if he were washing all the sins of the world away, and was reputed to take all his food with him for his walking holidays in Wales – packages of cheese and pickle sandwiches.

I went back to fetch Sarah on May 30th and she finally made it on to the boat for the first time that tour. She was still feeling very tired, particularly after being carried to the pub and back by John. A few nights later and we'd improved the Sarah transportation system – a wheelbarrow.

In June, for the first time for three years, we travelled along the Leeds & Liverpool Canal, this time in a Leeds & Liverpool short boat called *Weaver*. The facilities were much better than *Lune* – a kitchen area with a fridge, a good cooker, a sink with running water (cold), a long table and neon lighting. Luxury. The boat was owned and run by Marilyn Frear and her husband, John, and son, Simon.

Once back on *Tyseley* with all her relative comforts, the tour settled down into a routine, although there's nothing really routine about life with a waterways touring company. Every day is different – like the days when we pass through a town. Like little children, with eyes glistening, we would make for the shops. A Waitrose – brilliant – we went mad and spent £72. Towns were also useful for visiting doctors. Although you have to be fit and well for tours like ours, there are sometimes niggling problems which have to be sorted. Katherine needed more birth control pills. She was given a lecture by the doctor about smoking: "You'll be dead before you're thirty-five" (thankfully, she is still with us). Clive needed more Ventylyn for his asthma. John required penicillin for his throat and Billie more diuretic pills. The doctor would not give her any. He took her blood pressure and two blood samples, and said nothing except "Ring me on Tuesday. It could be very serious." It wasn't. We didn't like this Berkhamsted medic. By the way, I was fine!

Arriving in London can be exciting. After a gentle run through the outskirts, one approaches the centre from the north through Acton and past Wormwood Scrubs and Kensal Green Cemetery. But this year, what a culture shock awaited us when we arrived at Camden Lock. Camden Town has a huge market right alongside the lock and the day we arrived it was hot and sunny. The place was heaving with humanity. There was not a spare piece of ground, not even on the locks themselves. Many of these examples of the human race were either drugged or drunk or both. Some were even jumping off the bridge into the canal. One nearly drowned and had to be life-saved. As the evening approached, they all staggered off leaving behind vast quantities of litter. We were left to perform to a select few gathered on board a trip boat called *Water Buffalo*.

Leaving London can also be exciting, particularly going out on to the tidal Thames. This year, for the first time, we went out via the Lee Navigation and its tidal mouth, Bow Creek. At Bow Locks, we waited while the highly uninviting mud banks outside were covered with a minimum of three feet of water – exactly *Tyseley*'s draught. Bow Creek is very desolate with high banks. We saw no boats except for one coaster as we approached the Thames. We did see the remarkable sight of twenty- five herons sitting in a row on a deserted wharf.

Suddenly we turned on to the Thames, a very wide expanse of water at this point busy with coasters and tankers. We had a trouble-free run upstream to the calm non-tidal waters above Teddington Lock. A night out in Teddington High Street produced a great find – an Egyptian restaurant called, amazingly enough, *Pharoah's*. Here we feasted on tabbouleh, ful mesdames, falafel and spicy lamb all washed down with Egyptian wine. Afterwards I asked for some Egyptian brandy: "Oh, my wife is French. We have Armagnac." "Any Egyptian cigars?" "Castella or Hamlet? But you must try the hubble-bubble pipe." It's a very heady experience, sucking wet Egyptian tobacco through water.

Although the Thames is a beautiful river with many delights, for us it's a bit of a problem. It doesn't have many suitable venues. Many of the pubs are very smart and very posh-food-orientated. Not Mikron-friendly at all. Unlike this year's discovery – the Bounty at Bourne End near Cookham. It's a strange place. It was used by the rich in the 1930s and even had a landing strip for their planes. But it burnt down and was replaced by what only can be called a temporary building – except that's it's still there today and run in a brilliantly eccentric way by Sue and Dave. There is no road access and, until relatively recently, no bridge. In 1988, punters either had to walk along the towpath from Cookham or ring a bell on the opposite bank and be collected by the pub ferry. We were amazed when we got quite a large audience. After the show, we sampled some of the pub games including bar billiards and lifting a very large anchor. The record is seventeen times in one go. None of us could lift it once. Long may the Bounty stay the unique place it is.

In June, we went back to the Norfolk Broads and the wherry, *Albion*. It was sad to see the Company's reaction to the boat. Admittedly, the weather was drizzly and miserable, but it is an amazing vessel and the Broads are always interesting. Not for them. They stayed down below and didn't even look out when we had to take the sail down to go under Ackle Bridge. Later John asked me if they could go off the boat the following day. It was boring.

Sure enough, the next day the Company, apart from Clive, went to Great Yarmouth for the day. I felt sorry for Stephen Tillyard who had sponsored the tour. However, we had a great day's sailing with plenty of wind and very little quanting. The highlight of the day was when we hit a hireboat fully broadside. The boat had been tucked safely into the reeds but they decided to pull out across our path. A wherry on the run at six miles an hour is unstoppable. There was an almighty crash and *Albion* completely stoved in the side of the hireboat. We heard from the boatyard later (they completely absolved our skipper of any blame) that one member of the family had been knocked out of bed, that they had packed up and gone home, and that there was a £1000 worth of damage.

After a sixteen-day break, we were back on the canals again with *Tyseley*. Shortly afterwards, on July 20th, we heard the sad news that Graham Palmer, the founder of the Waterway Recovery Group and a great mate, had died of a heart attack. He was only forty-eight but had had heart problems for several years. It was under his direction that WRG became a national organisation, closely linked with restoration groups and societies throughout the waterways. I had portrayed him in one of our shows, *Mud in your Eye* and, after that, one of his nicknames became "Garden Gnome" alongside "GKP" and "Piggy". He was a charismatic person, a deflater of fools and prigs and a hater of bureaucracy. We were going to miss him as was the whole world of waterways.

A few days later, Sarah and I went to his funeral in Shrewsbury. I had to borrow a white shirt and black trousers, tie and shoes. The vicar was not at all happy about me reading extracts from Graham's magazine, *Navvies* ("Do you think it's appropriate? I've never had such a strange request in thirty years.") He himself was dreadful in the service. He only managed to mention Graham by name once. He introduced me as "The Poet". Still the place was packed to the rafters and everyone appreciated my reading. We all had a great time afterwards at the Queen's Head, reminiscing about Graham.

In August, we ventured on to the BCN or Birmingham Canals Navigation. This can often be a daunting task with a full-length, deeply draughted boat and this year's trip was to be no exception. We stuck and rocked our way through the bridges on the Birmingham & Fazeley Canal. But this was easy compared with the Tame Valley Canal, where we stuck solidly in the middle of the channel. More water and rocking got us off. For a while we were fooled, as we travelled with no difficulty on the Rushall Canal and Daw End Branch. Even the Whirly (the Wyrley & Essington Canal) was fine until we reached Little Bloxwich where we stuck very solidly indeed in Gascote Works Bridge. It was 9am. The others slowly got out of their beds to help me. With the boathook, John cleared loads of rubbish out of the bridgehole including a washing machine, a microwave and a shopping trolley. Even with this late twentieth century impedimenta out of the way, we moved nary an inch. Two British Waterways men arrived with a rake! A look at the situation convinced them that a more radical solution was required; so off they went to Wolverhampton to get a Tirfor.

Two-and-a-half hours later we were winched out. We continued to make slow progress even though, by now, we had received reinforcements in the shape of five WRGies who were working at a nearby camp. The housing estates through Bloxwich were in a dreadful state. Everyone looked poor and badly nourished. The kids were not at school but were staring at us instead. Eight-year-olds were drinking lager and carried knives.

At last we turned into the Walsall Canal and raced down the locks. The water was quite deep but very reedy. The reeds grew right across the canal making it look derelict. We hadn't seen another boat on the move for two-and-a-half days! The Company were whisked off in the WRG van to the venue. There was no way we were going to make it on time by boat. With the help of WRG, I continued. We managed quite well until the footbridge at Moxley. Mike Palmer, of WRG, climbed into the water and, for an hour, he cleared grot out of the bridgehole – six supermarket trolleys this time, another microwave, a washing machine, a motorbike, kids' toys, breeze blocks, a whole fence, a wall and so on and so on. A row of innocent but dirty children's faces watched us from the towpath. Within an hour, all the stuff would probably have been thrown back in. I took a run for the bridge and, with everyone heaving on ropes, we managed to squeeze through. We arrived at our venue – the Eight Locks at Ryders Green at 8.35pm. Dilly Barlow was there, recording extracts for Radio 4's *Waterlines*.

Our Friends of Mikron get-together was held this year on August 6th at the Hop Pole in Bromsgrove. About forty five people gathered on the lawn on a hot, sunny afternoon. In my speech for the occasion I mentioned that we were living in worrying times in the waterways' world. On good authority, I recounted the words spoken recently by the chairman of British Waterways. He was looking at Diglis Basin in Worcester with an eye to redevelopment, I imagine. He watched a pair of beautifully-painted old narrowboats going into the lock and, to the amazement of some of the bystanders, said "How do we set about getting rid of that sort of junk on our canals?" Progress and conservation were at odds again it seemed.

Our route was taking us towards the National Waterways Festival in Manchester. This generally involves meeting many other boats and not without incident. On the Audlem Flight on the Shroppie, I went to help a boat that was very slowly going through a lock. I raised a paddle for them and was immediately confronted by a woman who, with tense face and arms akimbo, said, "Don't you do that. It's our lock." I suggested that she must be a private boat owner. "And you must be a HIRER!" she replied, with the disdain suitable for such a word. "Oh, yes," I retorted. Fortunately, the majority of people on boats, particularly hirers, are very friendly and kind. We were well behind schedule when we reached Hack Green locks and there were fifteen boats waiting to go down. They all agreed that we could pass. Nobody was rude.

The Festival was held in the recently refurbished Castleford Basin on the Bridgewater Canal. It was a great do with bags of atmosphere. As well as the usual stalls and activities, there were buskers and street entertainers. We even watched a group of students performing a little show about the history of the canals. All was fine until they sang their first song. It was a Mikron song written by us. And so were all the rest of the songs they sang. At the end, I went up to them and asked them where they had found their songs: "Oh, they're traditional. We contacted the Boat Museum at Ellesmere Port and they sent us these old canal songs." Of course, we were very flattered to be called both traditional and old, but I did contact Tony Hirst, the curator of the Museum, and asked him to make sure that his staff gave out more accurate information in future.

Another Waterways Tour was over and, after a short break, we were soon into our local tour in the South Pennines and then, in October, we were off again to the Continent. This time we were to be touring in France as well as Belgium. We drove from Zeebrugge through flat countryside and past many of the cemeteries, where British and Commonwealth soldiers are buried, to a very quiet French border crossing. The customs officers must have been very bored as they decided to search both us and the van. They examined Clive's bedding, not an activity to be recommended to anyone. They probed our prop boxes, and examined the minutiae of the ashtray. "Have you any hashish?" they asked Billie. "Yes," she replied. "Why, do you want some?" Billie was taken to the office immediately, along with John and Kath. A detailed search revealed the following: John's false tooth, Billie's condoms and Kath's sherbet dib-dabs. So we were finally allowed into France, where we gave our first performance of *Rise and Fall* on board *Peterborough*, moored at the bottom of the boatlift at Les Fontinettes.

It was the centenary of this lift and the mayor presented us all with one of the medallions struck for the occasion. The factory which produces the world-renowned glassware, Crystal d'Arques, dominates the opposite bank. There are ten thousand employees and manufacture continues for twenty-four hours every day of the year.

We left very early the next morning and travelled along the Canal Neufosse and the Liaison Dunquerques-Escaut. We turned off the main line and tied up in the Bois de Boulogne about ten minutes from the centre of Lille. We strolled around the very pleasant city in the evening – there were people everywhere, queuing for the cinemas (there were at least sixteen screens) and sitting outside the bars and cafés, watching the world go by.

On October 22nd, we finally arrived back on the Canal du Centre in Belgium. Today was to be the climax of our visit and the realisation of one of Jean-Pierre Gailliez's dreams. We arrived at Pont Capite and were taken to Strepy-Thieu. As we approached, the lift appeared through the mist, a massive concrete structure rising 200 feet into the air. It is designed to carry 1500 tonne barges but for the moment it had no innards. All the machinery had still to be put in. We were to perform inside this monster. The echo was deafening. John declared it was going to be impossible to perform there. Without being miserable or downbeat like John, I was pretty worried myself.

When Jean-Pierre arrived, he was appalled that we were considering not performing in the lift and it was clear that the show had to go on. So, in front of an audience of dignitaries and the engineers of the lift, we performed a show about the first boatlifts in the world and the biggest boatlift in the world. It was spectacular – sometimes the echo was pervasive and our words were lost, but some of the songs were stunning, particularly *The International Anthem* which sounded like it was being performed by a choir of one thousand voices instead of a cast of four. Everyone was thrilled and delighted by the performance. The beer flowed and Jean-Pierre was in seventh heaven. It had been a unique day that we would all remember.

A footnote to this story is that the lift at Strepy-Thieu and the new link canal are due to open in 2002.

19

SUDDENLY, IT'S 1989

Was it the onset of middle age or was time really speeding up? One year was beginning to merge into another. We had no sooner finished one tour when, it appeared, we were in rehearsal for the next. What had happened to the eighties? They were almost over. We had managed to miss three World Cups and two Olympic Games.

It was suddenly 1989 and it was the time of year when a few days work would make all the difference to the outcome of the coming season – the auditions. Clive was staying on for a third year (not the wisest decision as it turned out), Kath and John went off with each other (for a while at least) and Billie just went off. I've never heard what happened to her but I still keep in contact with John and Kath. They work regularly as actors mainly for small or middle-scale touring companies.

So, three new Company members had to be found before rehearsals could begin. The first thing that happens is an ad appears in the actors' newspaper, the *Stage*. In the early days, the ad used to ask for actors who could not only sing, steer a boat and cook, but also look after a young child. Now, we merely required actors who could sing and play a musical instrument, had knowledge of or interest in the waterways and the Pennines. You would be surprised how many actors purport to possess all these qualities, as we generally received in the region of two or three hundred applications. It was Sarah's and my task to sift through these, and read between the lines and the hype. For instance, avoid auditioning people who begin their letters "Hi, Mike" or who send you photos of themselves as a child or in the bath or who tell you every detail of their brief lives ("I played fourth courtier in a musical when I was seven, entertained my granny on the mouth organ when I was eight. At nine years old I..."). There are many tips I could give to potential auditioners.

We assemble a short list of twenty or thirty people possibly to audition. Then we phone them and try to put them off by telling them how arduous the job is (it is) and how rarely you have days off (rare) when you can get away to see loved ones. If they persist in their interest in working for us, we demand that they appear in the Pennine village of Marsden (where?) on a certain date at a certain time, ready to be grilled about their habits and personality, and to play at least one musical instrument well, sing a couple of songs, perform a couple of pieces, at least one comical and at least one demonstrating their ability with accents, and to read characters from our scripts. Sometimes people just don't turn up. They flunk out at the last moment or they get another job. That is very annoying. One polite phone call would mean that another aspiring thesp would get a chance to make their name and earn their fortune with Mikron.

But most of them do arrive in Marsden, sometimes after a long journey, sometimes in the snow. We give everybody a good hour. None of this "thank you...next" for us. I've been through that myself and I know how humiliating and humbling an actor's life can be. During the hour, we ask them about their professional experience and how they feel they would fit into a company travelling the canals, where everybody lives and works very closely together for months at a time. We also ask them if they like pubs and what is their favourite tipple. From all this information and their audition itself we, hopefully, can begin to get a picture of whether they would be right for Mikron and whether Mikron would be right for them. At the end of a week of interviewing, we draw up a short list of half a dozen or more and invite them back to Marsden for what could be described as "the finals", but in actors' parlance is known as a "recall".

We spend an afternoon in a workshop session when the actors are split into groups and work with members of the current Company, in this case just Clive. After a series of improvisations using both music and drama, we all repair to our local pub. We provide the auditionees with a drink and some sandwiches, and then repair to a separate room to begin our deliberations. It may sound cruel, but we always make our decision on the day. In that way, we can then socialise with the new Company members and make sure we really like them and they like us. We are going to be working together for a long time. There are always a few tears from the unlucky ones, but they always praise our audition techniques and describe it as an enjoyable, though nerve-wracking day.

In 1989, from the auditions emerged John Spooner, Juliet Heacock and Gilly Baskeyfield (Gilly only after one actor had turned the offer down at the last minute – we were very lucky). Gilly was from the Potteries and had been a student at Hull University, and already had experience of small-scale touring. Juliet's background was Solihull and Cambridge University, where she had worked with the famous Cambridge Footlights. John actually had experience of boating, and lived on a narrowboat on the River Stort in Hertfordshire. He was from Wales, and was an excellent musician and composer as well as being a trained actor.

We were to tour *Speed Your Shuttle (and change your tune)* and *Rise and Fall* on the Waterways Tour and set off from our base in

Leigh at the junction of the Bridgewater and Leeds & Liverpool Canals on May 8th. After a short trip from Wigan to Riddlesden on board the short boat *Weaver*, we returned to *Tyseley* and began steering training for the newcomers on the easy waters of the Bridgewater Canal. One afternoon, Gilly was doing fine but, as we approached a sharp bend, I spotted a small cabin cruiser coming in the opposite direction. I immediately took over. The steerer of the cruiser must have panicked at seeing a large steel vessel bearing down on him. He was indecisive and twice changed direction. There was no avoiding hitting them, splitting the front of their bow and spilling their recently laid tea all over the cabin. They were obviously very upset but also became very angry, trying to blame us for their mistakes. They put in an insurance claim for not only the repairs to the boat but also for a lost tea and shattered nerves! Our insurance company fought strongly, and it was finally decided that there was no claim against us as, navigationally, we had behaved correctly.

One of the potential hazards of touring by water and performing at canalside pubs is a possible encounter with the police, when innocently partaking of the landlord's hospitality in allowing us to have a drink after the legally permitted hour. A kindness which we sometimes noticed he lavished on many of his customers. At one venue this year, we were drinking four minutes after the permitted drinking-up time. Perhaps slightly over-reacting to the seriousness of the crime, five policemen and a policewoman entered. Almost like magic, Gilly's and my glass were whisked away by the barmaid, but poor John was left with his, and he and many other customers were severely questioned. John had his name taken by a very nervous policewoman who confessed this was her first raid. He was only released when the landlord explained that John was his guest. We never did find out whether the landlord was charged or not

In June, we made our annual visit to one of the waterways' "jewels in the crown" – a pub on the Shroppie called the Anchor. When we first started travelling on the canals, there were many such jewels – small unspoilt hostelries divided into separate bars, perhaps serving sandwiches and a light snack but, for the most part, concentrating on being a "local" and selling good beer. Gradually the pubs have either closed or been "modernised", which means making them open-plan, removing all the character of the pub and replacing it with "stylish decor", and turning the back parlour into a restaurant. Economic necessity has demanded this in some cases, but often it is as result of a survey which has been carried out by a brewery or a pub company. This, apparently, tells them that we all want to eat in plastic palaces from an identical menu where even the number of chips and peas on a plate can be guaranteed, and we certainly don't want proper local pubs serving a good selection of real ale, hearty home-cooked food and an atmosphere conducive to live music, darts, dommies and conversation.

So, over the years, we have seen the demise of several classic canalside pubs, including the Berkeley Hunt at Purton on the Gloucester & Sharpness and the Bird in Hand at Kent Green on the Macclesfield Canal, and the modernisation and extension of other gems, such as the Holly Bush at Acton Bridge on the Trent & Mersey and the Bridge at Audlem.

But, mercifully, the Anchor is still with us and has not been vandalised. It is run by Olive and her daughter, Elaine – both non-drinkers but both aware of the needs of their customers. The beer is fetched in jugs from the cellar. You can sit talking and quaffing on the high-backed settle. There may be regulars in, there may be a few folk arriving with guitars or fiddles, there may be people who have stopped off on boats, but you'll feel relaxed sitting in front of the fire or in the large garden on balmy summer nights (yes, we have known one or two). You'll feel as if you've stepped back forty years.

We always have a good crowd turning up at the Anchor, some by boat but mostly by car. How they find it I don't know. It's down a very windy, very narrow country lane. And something always happens when we perform there. This year was no exception. Apart from the normal cold and drizzle, which seems to accompany us at this venue, there was plenty of drama after the show. One of our punters had the misfortune to have an artery burst in his leg. No-one could stop it bleeding and, as his blood began to cover the bar floor, an ambulance was called. It came quite quickly. Well, we could see its flashing light in the distance as it searched for this remote pub. Eventually, they phoned to say they were lost. A few minutes later, the man was whisked away with the ambulancemen, saying it looked much worse than it actually was.

The evening still wasn't over. The local drunk wouldn't go home. He had to be placed forcibly on to his bike. As he wobbled over the bridge, he was to be heard saying "I'll be back tomorrow morning. I'll be back."

On June 5th, we drove to Wroxham to begin our Norfolk Broads Tour. This year, we were on board the beautiful wooden wherry yacht, *Olive*. She was built as a pleasure boat in 1909 and her skipper was Barney Matthews, an ex-engineer who turned out to be a great character and great fun to be with. In stark contrast to the *Albion*, *Olive* was very comfortable below deck. We all had our own cabins with hot and cold running water. There was a sea-toilet, a compact galley and a cosy saloon complete with a five-octave piano (no G!).

We had a very poor turnout for our first performance and, after trundling all the props and costumes down a muddy track, we consoled ourselves with some wine, bread and cheese and a trip into Wroxham

Broad, which looked beautiful at night despite the rain. For the first time in my life, I spent the night not moored to the land. *Olive* bobbed gently in the middle of the broad tied to mud weights.

The next morning was idyllic as the sun shone on the water and we fed the thirty geese who had surrounded us during the night. Over the next few days we performed at Stokesby on the River Bure, Thurne on the River Thurne and Ludham Bridge on the River Ant. We had some good audiences and thoroughly enjoyed our trip away from *Tyseley*.

We travelled back to our boat. I was beginning to worry about Clive. Clive was a wonderful guy, with a great sense of fun and the ability to entertain a pubful of people with songs and games. I have seen him persuading a bunch of adults, albeit with a few beers inside them, to act out *The Grand Old Duke of York*, standing up when the men were at the top of the hill and sitting down when they were at the bottom. He was a charmer and a good actor as well. But, an occupational hazard this, he was beginning to drink too much. This particular lunchtime, he drank several pints of a strong ale called "Entire". Afterwards he was aggressive and clumsy when unloading the van. He dropped the set very heavily on to the roof of the boat and was very rude to two children who were passing. When I remonstrated with him, he swore at me and walked off. We discovered later (after he had apologised for his behaviour) that he had gone to sleep in a nearby field. Good job we had no show that night!

A few nights later, after a great show at the Bridge, Branston, a superb little Marston's pub on the Trent & Mersey Canal, we were all sitting in the pub garden having a drink. It was a hot, humid evening and everyone was feeling very relaxed. Suddenly, Clive started talking about one of the songs in the show. He was very disparaging about it and, when I tried to disagree with him, he called me a patronising c**t, and knocked all the drinks off the table. His loud shouting woke up the landlord who had gone to bed early, as he had to be up at 4.30 to run his other business – a paper shop. We all left the garden but Clive chased me up the towpath and threatened to beat me up. I heard later that he continued to rant and rave well into the night. It was all very worrying. What was wrong with him? Was it just the booze?

The next day was even hotter. All Clive said was "sorry". Was that enough? Should I have disciplined him? Tried to talk to him about his problem? I don't know. The tour continued happily enough. Clive continued to get drunk and would often not be up in the morning when the rest of us were working a flight of locks. But he did discover bread-making and he began to take a great pride in his loaves, proving them in the warmth of the engine room. We nicknamed him "Master Baker"!

Most of July was stinking hot with the temperature reaching the nineties. And August was almost as good. Going down the Thames, we stopped at one of our old venues and a particular favourite – Ye Olde

Leatherne Bottel near Goring. This was another example of a genuine pub being lost to us. The landlord was an ex-RAF man and a true eccentric. He had a microphone in the pub with speakers in the car park, and he would often address a potential arrival thus: "You can't park there. Anyway, I'm not sure I want that car here. You'd better go away." Imagine the reaction of the startled driver finding himself being berated for being in the wrong car, wanting to stop for a drink. Sometimes he would just decide to close. It may only have been nine o'clock at night. It wouldn't matter. Off you all had to go. But he was always helpful and welcoming to us. Sadly, he was no longer there and, when we tied up, we realised why we were no longer wanted. It was very smart, very yuppified and very expensive – a spritzer (wine and soda to you) was £1.35 a glass and a pint of Brakspears a staggering £1.20!

Further downstream Sarah became very worried because her mother wasn't answering the phone. After a couple of days, we contacted the police in Leeds. They went to her flat and, when there was no answer, they broke the door down. She wasn't there and everything appeared quite normal and undisturbed. I checked the hospitals but she hadn't been admitted. Where had she disappeared to? Eventually, Social Services discovered that she was in Leeds Infirmary in Ward 4 and had been admitted by ambulance with heart failure. She had somehow slipped through the admin net. It was a relief to know she was safe, if unwell, and Sarah set off for Leeds immediately.

The rest of us continued down the Thames and had another exciting trip down the tideway. We set off at 7.20am from Eel Pie Island on a flood tide and it soon became hot as we breakfasted on croissants. There was a very poignant moment as Gilly dropped flowers into the water at the spot where, a few nights before, the dredger *Bowbelle* had collided with the disco-boat, *Marchioness*, killing 57 of the young people on board. There was the usual nerve-shattering entrance into Limehouse Dock. The lock wasn't ready; so, I had to steer past the entrance and turn upstream against the strong ebbing tide. At first *Tyseley* didn't appear to move, but slowly we did creep towards the lock entrance. She bounced off the wooden bulwarks and I managed to steer her into the entrance of the lock. Once again we were all relieved to be back in *Still Waters*.

The Waterways Tour ended at Marsworth on the Grand Union on September 1st. After a short break, we left for Belgium on what was to prove our last foreign tour, and the year ended with our final performance of *Rise and Fall* on the Pennine Tour at the Railway in Marsden on December 2nd.

20

THE FIRST BOAT FOR FORTY YEARS

There is one question we are always being asked: "What do you do in the winter?" A winter spent basking in the sun on some tropical isle drinking and eating the profits, perhaps? Alas, no. First of all, *Tyseley* had to be moved back to its winter base at Leigh on the Bridgewater Canal. As we had finished the Waterways Tour at Marsworth on the Grand Union Canal, it meant we had to negotiate all the canal maintenance stoppages as well as the severely-reduced lock-opening hours. Then there was the 1990 route to plan. Although we had been visiting some venues for eighteen years, new ones were introduced every year and the actual order of the itinerary was dictated by the location of the National Waterways Festival. This year, the planning logistics were made more complicated by the fact that we had been invited to the National Trailboat Festival at Falkirk in May, Stafford Boat Club Rally in June and to the celebrations for the re-opening of the Kennet & Avon Canal in July. Many hours were spent on the phone booking the various venues.

Unlike a road touring company, who sometimes can have the misfortune of being in Carlisle one night and Penzance the next, our venues follow on logically one after the other, as long as you know the canal system like the back of your hand and the different problems you are likely to encounter on particular canals. For instance, we can just about manage two miles per hour on the South Oxford Canal, but we can dash along at a stately eight miles an hour on, say, the tidal River Thames. On a shallow, narrow canal *Tyseley*'s 24 tons feel twice as much at the tiller and she steers like a sack of coal in a crate but, once she's released on to deep water, she swims like a dolphin – poetry in motion.

At the same time, we were applying for grant-aid from local authorities and regional arts associations. We passed through the areas of as many as eight different arts associations, all of which had different types of application forms and different criteria for funding. We were also trying to raise more business and show sponsorship. We wrote literally hundreds of letters to trusts, businesses, hire firms, boat clubs and societies. Unfortunately, all too few organisations replied, even fewer gave us support.

Amidst all this welter of activity, we also had to fit in auditions and the researching and writing of a new show. This year it was to be *Free for All*, a musical taking a humorous look at the conflicts on the waterways – the almost irreconcilable clash between conservation and leisure. Sarah Parks and I spent two weeks researching the material for the show. We travelled all over the country speaking to people who had an interest in these topics including the (then) Nature Conservancy Council, Yorkshire Derwent Trust, River Derwent Appeal, Kennet & Avon Canal Trust, Surrey and Hants Canal Society, British Waterways and people involved in the town of Milton Keynes. We collected over thirty hours of taped interviews and hundreds of books, pamphlets, maps, articles and brochures. We were then joined by Jim Woodland, who was to write the music and lyrics for *Free for All* (the title emerged towards the end of the research period), and together we spent three weeks collating the material, deciding on our approach and view of it, and writing and editing the script.

A little exhausted from burning the midnight oil, I was then joined by the acting company, newcomers Jacky Hynes and Jon Keats, with Gilly and John from the previous year. John was also one of the musical directors along with Peadar Long. Together we spent six weeks rehearsing two shows, *Free for All* and *A Place to Stand*, the story of the Yorkshire Luddites which we had successfully premiered on our South Pennine Tour the previous autumn. The *Guardian* said of this show: "The writing and lyrics are fresh and original...the music is tuneful and evocative."

At the same time, we were arranging the printing of the leaflets, programmes, press releases, posters, handbills, raffle tickets, badges, pens and T-shirts, and trying to promote ourselves through local and national press, radio and television. Much of the hard slog of day-to-day administration was carried out by our associate administrator, Liz Challenger, and Sarah helped out when necessary. Many people do not realise the amount of hard work required to run a small touring company on minimal budgets, and the most under-rated person is always the one working behind the scenes to keep everything moving. Sarah was again not touring full-time with us this year. She was staying behind to support Sam. It was his A-level year and, if he did well, he had a place at Bristol University to read history.

I had given up acting in 1985 in order to administrate the Company and write and direct the shows, but I didn't feel that I was never going to tread the boards again. I thought the time might come when it would be appropriate. I never expected it to happen quite the way it did: the day before our opening performance of *Free for All*, Jacky fell ill and it became obvious she was not going to be able to perform. We do not have the luxury of understudies. The only solution was for me to play Jacky's parts.

So it was that the first-night audience at the Birchcliffe Centre at Hebden Bridge saw Mike back on stage playing women's parts. Now I didn't go as far as wearing Jacky's costumes (even if I could have got into them). I went on with the script and tried to act the characters as Jacky would have done. I didn't speak as a woman but I tried to give it a woman's twist – to emote as a woman. It seemed to work. The audience loved the show and I enjoyed showing off again (sorry, I mean acting).

I repeated my performance the following night at our home base, the Railway in Marsden. But that was it. Jacky recovered in time for our Scottish Tour. I use the words "Scottish Tour" loosely. We gave five performances in Scotland, but I don't think Scotland noticed us arrive or leave. It was meant to be six performances but we had to cancel our first show at Maryhill in Glasgow. No-one turned up, not even someone wanting to shelter from the rain. We had been publicised but, obviously, not enough. We had twelve at Milngavie and twenty at Kirkintilloch and a sprinkling of people at our three Falkirk performances. They were part of the Inland Waterways Association's National Trailboat Rally but nobody seemed to know about that either and the site was deserted. What a shame. I'm sure they'd have loved us if only they had known. Loch Lomond was lovely; so was the hospitality we received and we'd love to go back, if anybody would like to ask us.

We moved on to *Tyseley* on May 31st to begin our Waterways Tour proper. The first excitement was that Gilly announced her engagement to Christophe, a charming Frenchman she had met in London. He was working in an off-licence to practise his English. They were madly in love. He had driven all the way to Scotland from France to see her. He had a van which he had fitted out in the back as a love nest, and they spent the night on the banks of Loch Lomond. We were to see quite a lot of him during the course of the tour.

And there's another Anchor at High Offley story this year. The weather was awful as we boated towards the pub, and it wasn't looking at all hopeful for the evening. But, by seven o'clock, it had cleared a little. Fifty or so brave souls had turned out in the cold to see us (this was June 5th!). Ten minutes into the performance, it started to rain heavily again and we had to stop. After twenty minutes, there was a hole in the clouds and we started again. We only managed another ten minutes before it became obvious we would have to cancel the performance. Actors, props and costumes were all sodden. Props and costumes were draped around the cabin to dry. The coal fire was lit. The Company were warmed with a little brandy, took their instruments

118

into the pub and sang the rest of the songs from *A Place to Stand* and a couple of "tasters" from *Free for All*. Then Jon Keats, whom we had christened "Jonny Storm", launched into some rock 'n' roll with help from the audience. It was great night for us – but a financial disaster for Mikron.

The cold weather continued until June 14th. It became warmer but the sky remained resolutely grey without a sign of blue. We were travelling towards Shardlow on the Trent & Mersey Canal and it was interesting to note that, thanks to the Trent & Mersey Canal Society, all the mileposts along the whole length of the canal had been reinstated. They had all been sponsored by individuals and organisations. I had started keeping a voice log as well as a written log and, on June 17th, when we were tied up outside the Trent Navigation Inn, I observed: " We're at the junction of the Trent, the Soar, the Erewash Canal and the Cranfleet Cut. It's quite late at night and I'm looking across a wide expanse of water to Radcliffe Power Station with its cooling towers looming over us through the night sky. An Inter-City train is crossing the bridge. It looks as if it is going through the middle of the river – a flash of yellow light contrasting with the red lights of the power station. The water is very, very still. There are no other boats about. It's very lovely. It makes you realise why you travel by water. For sights such as these."

The following day we were on the Trent moving towards Nottingham. It was again very cold and very wet. A river like the Trent gives us an opportunity to see how *Tyseley* swims, that is, how she moves through deep water. She beds down and off she goes...six or even seven miles an hour. On this day, the fishermen were standing impassively in the water. I passed a bald-headed angler who wouldn't even give me a nod. Most of them were hidden under their green umbrellas like strange animals. The clouds were full of rain and it's on days like this you can feel very lonely on the back of the boat, steering. Everyone's inside...or are they? Have they jumped ship and are you really on your own? The river became very wide and there were no longer any fishermen – just a few wheeling swallows and the occasional heron. The loneliness is a good feeling. You know it's not true anyway – it's just a fantasy. Life on the boat can sometimes feel like a fantasy. It's a very real and very hard life in one way. In another, it's an escape. An escape from the real, harsh world. Being an actor is a bit like that...until the next time you're out of work.

We went down the Trent as far as Fiskerton, a few miles from Newark, and spent a very uncomfortable night there being buffeted by both heavy wind and rain and from the wash of two Whittakers oil tankers on their way to unload at Colwich. It probably didn't disturb Jacky, Jon and John, who had stayed up all night socialising with Sarah Parks, who was visiting, and Sam, who had finished his A-levels.

I'D GO BACK TOMORROW

We said goodbye to Parksy and Sam and proceeded back upstream. Sarah was steering as we approached Nottingham. Suddenly, the barge *Sobriety* appeared through the central arch of the railway bridge. At the last minute, it signalled with two blasts that we were to pass starboard to starboard. Thank goodness someone of Sarah's experience was steering. She decided that it was too late to attempt to cross the bows of *Sobriety* and just managed to steer to the right of her. We were within six inches of a major collision in which the smaller *Tyseley* would inevitably have come off worse.

We had arrived in Nottingham to perform at a rally of Community Boats. This was a gathering of boats from all over the canal system which were used for taking schoolchildren and the disabled and disadvantaged on canal holidays. We knew several of the skippers and it was a great opportunity to socialise and swap stories. The mayor had laid on a civic reception to which all the kids off the boats were invited. This was followed by a performance of *Free for All* in a marquee on the riverside and a visit to a pub where beer was only £1 a pint.

We finished the first half of the tour at Soar Boating Club on the River Soar. The weather remained persistently cold and wet.

The second half of the tour found us on the South Oxford Canal. *Tyseley* had been moved there from the River Soar by our friends, the Tupling family. While Sarah and I had been in France on the week's break, my left knee had started to play up and, travelling from Fenny Compton to Banbury, it became very painful. It was July but the weather was exactly the same as June – it was cold, it was windy and it was raining. My mood was not helped by Jacky, who was in one of her dizzy modes. She had forgotten how to start the engine. Then, just as we were setting off, she called me to the back of the boat to tell me that she couldn't reach the gear-wheel. It was too far back. I pointed out to her that she hadn't pushed the slide back!

She then proceeded to blow a few bends (which means she went up the bank, which means the boat went aground) and to blow a few straights as well. John took over and we got stuck in a couple of bridgeholes, before arriving at Claydon Locks to find thirteen boats waiting for opening time. Very kindly, they all let us go ahead after we had pointed out that we needed to be in Banbury for a show. The rain was now torrential. Just right for sticking in Banbury Lock. We had to be winched out with a Tirfor brought by Pete from the nearby boatyard. It took one hour, ten minutes.

The same Pete then took me to Banbury Hospital as my knee was throbbing badly and I was down to a hobble. Fortunately, Casualty wasn't busy and they saw me quickly. Both the doctor and the nurse were very interested in Mikron and promised to try and get to a show. Oh and my knee? They weren't sure. It could be a torn cartilage. They gave me a tubi-grip and told me to rest it. Some hope.

THE FIRST BOAT FOR FORTY YEARS

After all that activity, there were eleven members of the audience at the show that evening at the Mill. Thirty million people were watching the World Cup semi-final between England and West Germany, including me. I watched it on telly in the bar below where our poor actors were strutting their stuff. It was a great game – exciting and skilful, and it went to the wire with England missing a penalty in the shoot-out.

We entered the Thames via Dukes Cut, a deep, windy river-like connection. I always enjoy taking the bends at "full chat". This year, I was buzzed by a police helicopter for some reason. Perhaps he was trying to get me for speeding. Then it's a wonderful run into Oxford through Port Meadow, a huge piece of common land running alongside the river with hundreds of horses, cows, geese and swans. It was great to see the growth in swan numbers since the banning of lead weights for fishing. Once a year all the animals are rounded up and a check is made to see if the owners were bona fide. You know you're in Oxford. Apart from the many spires, there is the bike. People cycle everywhere – the towpath being one of the most popular routes and the many benches are used for meeting a lover, honing a thesis or eating a sandwich. The Waterman's Arms was our venue. It's situated on Osney Island with its streets of terraced houses – a backwater unknown to most tourists. And the great news was – it was hot and sunny.

Friday the thirteenth was a good day. The weather became really hot – in the eighties (you centigrade lovers will have to convert that yourselves). The Thames looked astonishingly beautiful as we moved down to Reading, particularly the steep wooded section around Goring. As you progress downstream the houses become bigger, the gardens longer and the boathouses more decorative. There is a sniff of astounding wealth in the air and you wonder what jobs these people do, and do they deserve the salaries they must receive in order to buy and maintain such palaces.

The approach to Reading has more of a sense of reality. You can see tower blocks and industrial estates. Today there were boats everywhere – hire boats, rowing boats, dinghies, inflatables. There were folk dabbling their toes in the water, lying in rubber tyres in the middle of the river and draped, with a minimal amount of clothing, across the parkland. Summer had finally arrived. After Caversham Lock, we turned right on to the River Kennet, an apology for a river at this stage after the glorious Thames. We moved up to Kennet Lock where old terraced houses used to line the river. Only two pubs survive from that era. The terraced houses have been replaced by more terraced houses. But without character, without charm.

Two days later we entered new territory – the re-opened section of the K&A to Aldermaston. We made good progress through heavy locks and several swing bridges. We awoke the following morning to find that the chains were still on Aldermaston Lock. There were fifteen boats waiting below, all wanting to get to Monkey Marsh Lock at Thatcham for tomorrow and the official opening of the lock. A few enquiries revealed that there were divers in the bridgehole at Woolhampton removing timber piles and that no boats could move until further notice. The Engineering Supervisor at Padworth was quite rude: "We own this canal. You should have dealt with us and not the Trust. I only found out about this by reading it in the paper...even when we do let you through, you'll get stuck." Terry Kemp, the Waterways Manager, was much more helpful and assured us we would get through today. At a quarter to three, we were still waiting. We would never make Thatcham for the show that night.

A historic moment: at 5.15, the lock was opened. A few boats went ahead of us, but we finally entered with *Gentle Annie* and *Sooty Seal*. There is a very bendy section of river up to Woolhampton and our mop was dragged off the boat by some trees, only to be retrieved by the boat behind. At Woolhampton Lock, I dropped the Company off. We had managed to get the van there to pick them and the gear up. Sarah and I continued on our epic journey. We stuck in several of the gaps where the swing bridges were to be, and outside Hales Lock. We were then towed along a shallow stretch to the weir below Colthrop Lock, where we found boats already stuck on a bar of silt. Eventually, with a lot of heaving and shoving and heaps of that "wartime spirit", we all got across. Next we stuck heavily in Colthrop Bridge. By the time we had struggled to the lock, it was dark. Everyone else had had enough and tied up, but we continued up the pound to Thatcham Bridge. We were the first boat to arrive there for forty years.

Sarah and I walked into the Swan, where the Company had had a great show, at a quarter to midnight. I shouted, "First boat to Thatcham for forty years." The landlord replied, " I'm opening up again. Let's have a party." And we did.

We were hoping to boat up the canal as far as Hamstead Marshall but Thatcham was destined to be the terminus for us this year. There was only two-foot-six of depth over the cill at Bull's Lock. This would be remedied later but, for now, we went by van for our performances in Newbury and Hamstead Marshall. Here we performed at the house of Robert Reid, who had written a splendid book about the Luddites called *Land of Lost Content*, which had been one of our major inspirations for *A Place to Stand*. It was a Queen Anne house with stables and acres of land. We performed in The Orangery to an audience of very rich people, many of them estate farmers. We were treated like servants. We had to shower in the groom's flat and, when we went to eat after the show, Robert said, "All the chairs are gone. You'll have to sit on the stairs." He never spoke to us except to say the show had been excellent. Now I know how medieval strolling players must have felt, when they were thrown a half-eaten leg of chicken.

THE FIRST BOAT FOR FORTY YEARS

Our journey back down the canal was relatively trouble-free. It was interesting to note the variety of locks and swing bridges on the Kennet & Avon. We passed through Sheffield Lock, a long lock with scalloped sides and Garston Lock, the only turf-sided lock remaining on the canal. I also took *Tyseley* around an amazing series of hairpin bends just before the M4 bridge. Very challenging in a full-length boat.

Sarah and I were boating alone. It was a day off and the Company had gone away to see friends and loved ones. Much as we enjoyed boating with the others, there was something very relaxing about two-handed working. We were as efficient and quick as a full crew, if not more so. We tended not to talk but to use signals. Sarah would always know the right moment to get out for the lock if I was steering and vice versa. Sarah also was an ace breakfast cook. One of the greatest pleasures on this earth is steering a narrowboat and, assuming there aren't too many hazards ahead, eating a butty stuffed full of bacon, sausage, egg and tomato, washed down with strong tea from a pint pot. For Sarah, the additional pleasure would have been that first fag of the day afterwards. The world around you. That is very nearly Paradise.

In Reading, we had the usual exciting trip through what is known as the Brewery Gut. This is where the river is channelled through a narrow section past where the brewery used to be and the large bus garage. It's bendy and tricky at the best of times. Today the river was gentle but, if there is a strong flow on, you have no real control over the boat. You just bounce from side to side and hope you can get under High Street Bridge without crashing. When Sam was little, he always used to lie on the floor until we'd passed through this section.

What a contrast as you turn out of Kennet Mouth on to the Thames. All around you are lines of boats, all charging along as fast as they can. Then they arrive at a lock and they have to queue. Some of them get into the lock (sizes vary tremendously on the Thames). They pack in, wait for the lock to fill or empty, and off they charge again, racing off along the reach to queue at the next one.

This year we again stopped off at our favourite Thames pub, the Bounty at Bourne End, and we had our best turn-out ever. The "last ferry" took the punters back across the river. But there was an even laster ferry to take the barmaid across. Landlord, Dave, was the ferryman, as usual. John, Jon and I were sitting having a chat to his wife, Sue, when she looked up. I think she was tuned to splashing noises from previous occasions. She said, "Was that Dave falling in?" I strolled out and sure enough there was Dave in the water but still holding the boat rope. He had fallen whilst stepping out of the boat, winding himself against the coping stones. Dave is a lovely man. He likes his beer, he likes his customers, and he always smiles. He was still smiling. Sue and I landed him like a beached whale. He walked into the pub, dripping and smiling. "I'm off to bed," he said. And off he went, dripping and smiling. Sue said that it was more worrying in the winter when he had fallen in with ice in the river.

The weather remained hot and sunny. But, by the beginning of August, it was getting almost unbearably hot, with the temperature in the nineties. On August 3rd, we were now on the Grand Union at Leighton Buzzard and it was 95 degrees Fahrenheit. In some parts of the country, the highest-ever temperature had been recorded – 103 degrees – hotter even than Egypt at that time of the year. Everywhere was parched. The people were parched. Everyone was desperately trying to be "continental" but failing.

We happened to pass through Milton Keynes on the day of the National Junior Angling Championships. I try to get through Milton Keynes as quickly as possible. Some people like the "new town" look – the identi-kit houses, the walkways, cycleways and the gridded road system. I don't. I also don't like the fact that the town was planned with just the car in mind, with no real thought given to a proper public transport system. There is sufficient space to have a wonderful tramway linking the residential areas to the shopping areas and the recreational areas. Yes, everything is segregated in Milton Keynes. The canal is a "linear park". Well, today I had to steer very slowly past these very young fishermen, who were all clones of their dads – no smiles, concentrated faces, fingers in maggots, pulling hooks through their teeth, as they do. The only person to smile was the sole girl angler. The competition spread for six very, very long miles; long lines of little boys all intent on catching "the biggy".

On August 11th, the weather remained constant. We were joined for part of our trip up Buckby Locks by Margaret Brooks, who had featured in our show *Still Carrying* along with her husband Alan. Alan had died and Margaret was now seventy-one years old and had last steered *Tyseley* in 1954. Today she took the tiller again and steered up and through the locks as only a person born to the job can. I shall never forget the look of delight on her face.

We woke up on the morning of the 15th August to find out that it had rained in the night and that it was a cold, windy day. It was ironic because it was the first rain we had had for weeks and it was the day that we first suffered from the canal being low due to lack of water. We dragged ourselves along the bottom of the Bascote pound and through Leamington and Warwick. The canal through both places is rubbish-strewn and grotty and they both neglect their canal frontages. What a shame, because they are lovely places with much to delight the visitor.

The following day, we were going up Lapworth Locks on the North Stratford Canal when Sam phoned to give us his A-level results – two A's in History and Sociology, a B in English, an E in the General paper plus an S-level in History. That's our boy. The delights of Bristol now awaited him.

124

THE FIRST BOAT FOR FORTY YEARS

Later in August, we were on the Gloucester & Sharpness Canal, a deep, wide ship canal with superb views across the Severn Estuary. The day was very humid, with little wind and no sun and the canal was very busy with boats. Sadly, they were not ships and barges on their way to Gloucester Docks or up the Severn, but modern narrowboats who were all booked into the National Waterways Festival at Gloucester at the weekend, and were taking the opportunity to explore the G & S. This canal should be a major freight corridor linking with the motorways of the Midlands but it is normally deserted. If Gloucester Docks were in Europe, they would be a major inland port. Here, they are a tourist attraction. The eighteenth century buildings have been beautifully restored but they are just a romantic image of yesteryear.

Our last moving day of the tour ended in dramatic fashion. As *Tyseley* was approaching Wolverley Lock on the Staffs & Worcs Canal, I noticed that there was a fair amount of water coming through the top gate. I warned Jacky to clear our foredeck, so clothes and books didn't get wet, and told Gilly to get the paddles up quickly, but *Tyseley* stuck coming through the bottom gates and we couldn't shut them. In the meantime, water was pouring into the foredeck. When the gates were finally shut and I dashed up to the other end, I realised the boat was in danger of sinking – the water had now filled the foredeck and was halfway up the front door of the cabin.

I shouted for John, who was sleeping through all this, to put on the bilge pump. He dashed to the front door and tried to open it. I screamed "No!", knowing that the water would have poured into the cabin. He switched the bilge pump on and Jacky also appeared in the cabin, holding up saucepans and towels to stop the water coming through the door. The boat, fortunately, did rise in the lock but listing heavily. As soon as I could, I jumped into the water in the foredeck and started bailing. Jon joined me. We pulled the boat out of the lock and opened up the storage locker under the foredeck. All the props and electrical equipment were floating about. With the bilge pump and buckets we managed to empty it. We also had the bilge pump on further down the boat as the water had travelled right down the cabin under the floorboards. Gilly's cooking (lamb for dinner that night) had gone all over the floor. We decided to give it a quick wash and put it back in the oven.

We were all shaken. I knew that was the closest that *Tyseley* had ever been to sinking. A quick nip of Portuguese brandy helped to restore the spirits. We dried out the electrics and props with a hair dryer, and the packed audience never realised the traumas we had been through as the Company gave their last performance of the tour. The next day, we packed all the gear and everyone's belongings back into the van and returned to Yorkshire.

The South Pennine Tour finished on November 3rd. Both shows

had gone well and press reviews had been excellent. One character anyone who saw *Free for All* will always remember was John Spooner's stuttering bat. John was leaving the acting company but he was going to be the musical director for the second production of *Free for All*. Gilly also left the Company to spend more time with Christophe. They settled in Marsden, didn't get married, and now have two children, Luc and Annie. More of Gilly later. She was, however, a sad loss to the acting company. She has immense talent, and that enviable ability when performing of making you laugh one minute and cry the next.

Jon and Jacky left us after just one year. They both wanted to try other types of acting and singing work. We keep in touch from time to time.

21

HOUSEMAID'S KNEE AND WEEPING RIVETS

So, we had a completely new Company to find. We were looking for four actors who could play instruments and sing, and have sufficient range to play 58 characters between them. The auditions produced Clare Fairley from London, who had travelled and lived on a Broads Cruiser before training as an actress, and whose proudest achievement was her ability to play two recorders simultaneously through her nostrils; Neil Gore from Brum, fresh from a season with Solent Young People's Theatre; Janet Hughes, a native Yorkshire lass, who, as well as being a stand-up comedienne, had just finished a tour with the Medieval Players; and, completing the team, Rodney Matthew from Dundee. Rod had auditioned in 1990 but didn't make it into the Company. But he came to see us when we were on tour in Nottingham where he was working and insisted he was excellent Mikron material. Not only had he been to the same drama school, Webber Douglas, as myself but, unwittingly, Sarah and I had walked past the bar in Limnos on the Greek island of Rhodes where Rod was playing and singing. We were on holiday; Rod was on a summer residency. Now was the time to make amends for missing him that night by employing him.

Between writing a new show and rehearsals, I had an exciting new project to deal with. As a recognition of our knowledge of local history and the local waterways, Kirklees Countryside Service commissioned me to write and direct a video using Mikron actors. It was to be shown at the Countryside Centre, which was based at the old tunnel-keeper's cottage just outside the Marsden end of Standedge Tunnel. The twelve minute video, entitled *Pennine Passage* was to tell the story of Standedge Hill and its tunnels, including the longest canal tunnel in the country at $3\frac{1}{4}$ miles.

My intention was to produce something a little different from the run-of-the-mill documentaries you sometimes see at museums and visitor centres – pretty pictures with a sonorous voice-over. I used the actors both to portray navvies, boatpeople, and millowners and, using voice-over, to let the people talk for themselves, be it a woman telling the story of her navvy husband's death while building the tunnel, or the boatman describing the journey of the last loaded boat to pass through the tunnel. We filmed packhorses crossing the moors, navvies and leggers inside the tunnel, the opening of the canal and, using archive photos, the demise of the canal and the rise of the railway.

You should be able to see for yourself whether I have succeeded if you visit the new Visitors' Centre, which will be based in the old warehouse at Tunnel End in Marsden, when the Huddersfield Narrow Canal re-opens in 2001. Hopefully, it will be on show there.

Music for the film was written by Jim Woodland and sung by Janet Russell. Jim was again involved in writing the music and lyrics for our new show, with myself and Parksy as the researchers and writers. *Spirit of the Age* was the third in our productions about the Yorkshire woollen industry and it received a great review in the *Guardian*, after the traditional first night at the Railway: "...banged out with rollicking energy and banner headline style to an enthusiastic audience...The play chronicles a loose thirty-year period, moves from the horrors of the Peterloo massacre to the half-hearted concessions of the Factory Act on to the self-congratulation of the Great Exhibition at Crystal Palace. We are taken on a whistle stop tour of weavers – their livelihoods threatened by the new machinery, Luddites despatched by the noose at York, children pinioned by a fourteen-hour mill day and manufacturers seeing their mills as a corner of thrusting little England, counting profit and crushing dissent in a policy of free market self-interest, quite breathtaking in its self-righteousness. Social ironies are pounced upon by a musically gifted and energetic cast of four, who move with dexterity from portraying kids to mill owners, curates, Luddites and new women. Janet Hughes is particularly affecting as a weaving woman who has a radical and threatening vision – the elusive one, the glimmer of social consciousness."

Two days later, we were packing to go on the boat. My left knee had become very painful and I could only walk with crutches. Our new administrator, Janet Armstrong, took me to the Huddersfield Infirmary where they diagnosed a severe case of bursitis, more commonly known as "Housemaid's Knee". This was inflammation of the knee due to a build-up of fluid. Remedy: a tubi-grip, nurofen and rest (what?).

Despite everything, we arrived on the boat which was tied up at Dutton at the northern end of the Trent & Mersey Canal at 5.30pm. Sarah had to take the brunt of organising which props and costumes went where on the boat, and of finding spaces for all the Company's personal belongings. No-one else, all being new, knew what the hell was going on. I did still manage to cook a meal for everyone – some sparkling wine helped to ease the pain.

Two days later my knee had improved sufficiently to enable me to enjoy my 50th birthday and even the weather tried to be sunny and warm. We moved to the Stanley Arms above the still-defunct Anderton Boatlift and our designer, Kim Reuter, arrived with the magnificent back-drop for *Spirit of the Age* – the Crystal Palace, held up by children, bedecked with Union Jacks. More sparkling wine was consumed and I had some wonderful presents from Sarah and the Company. It was a cold evening for our first outdoor performance, but it went well and was much appreciated by the audience.

The leg continued to improve and the crutches were abandoned. We made our way to the Shroppie in weather cold enough to warrant lighting the coal fire on the boat. On the evening of June 3rd, we had sleet! And on June 6th, we had to perform inside Angus and Midge's house at Wild Hollow in Gnosall. It was raining heavily. The Mayor and Mayoress of Stafford sat on the front row about one foot from the actors, whilst some of the unlucky ones watched from outside through the windows.

By June 14th, we were back on the Trent & Mersey heading towards Shardlow. The night before we had performed at the Rising Sun at Willington, a proper local pub. Landlords, Carol and Alan, were always very hospitable but, this year, thanks to my big 50, even more so. After the show, we ate chilli and chips washed down with a bottle of 1953 Taylor's Port, now worth £250. What a present!

The weather was the worst we had ever encountered in all our years of touring. It had been consistently cold, wet and windy with the very odd burst of sunshine to remind us that it was midsummer. It was a familiar sight to see smoke pouring out of *Tyseley*'s front chimney. It was bleak. Just like the feeling in the country at this time. We were in the middle of a recession. Everyone was suffering but, as usual in times like these, it was the Arts that had been clobbered first. We, like many arts organisations, were in receipt of stand-still grants from local authorities and Yorkshire Arts. We had told Yorkshire Arts that we realistically needed £28,000 this year; they had given us the usual £4,000. It was to be another year of struggling to survive.

But the Company were great. They loved the boat and they loved boating. It had taken Sarah and me a week or two to train them in the skills of steering a 72-foot narrowboat. Now they were all competent, and Sarah and I were able to relax a little.

We continued on our way with the weather stuck on very drear. The approach to Nottingham is always fascinating, first along the Beeston Canal and then along the Nottingham Canal right into the centre of the city. First you travel for at least a mile alongside the landscaped lawns of the enormous Boots factory. I noticed that through the windows of some of the offices could be spotted rows of men in white shirts, their suit jackets removed, working at desks. I decided that I was happy being me looking at them, rather than them beavering away and looking up for a second to see a quaint old boat passing.

I'D GO BACK TOMORROW

There was a person jogging along the towpath. Did the pain on his face mean that the pleasure was intense? Strange pursuit – jogging. On the opposite bank, many old cars were piled perilously one on top of the other looking as if, at any moment, they would all plunge into the canal. And at the bridge ahead, a freight train lumbered across. The driver may have noticed the broken windows (air rifles?) of Eric Salford's sheet metal works.

Then it was under the bridge with the murals desecrated by graffitti and past the House with The Garden – there's a man in some stocks, a dog and cat made out of plaster, an old mangle, a ship's mast, canoes and signs of all kinds, including one saying "Slow Down Or Else". Past the wonderful nineteenth century boatyard of Trevithick's with its wooden and sea-going boats.

Suddenly, you are going alongside the tree-lined Lenton Boulevard, past the huge new marina stuffed full of boats. (I wouldn't like to be around if they all decided to come out for the day). Past the Baltimore Exchange Diner, Sainsbury's Homebase and Sainsbury's itself. Past ever more new buildings and restored warehouses, with the rather stolid castle dominating the upper part of the city. The canal may remain the same (sadly, without any commercial traffic) but the surroundings change every year. That's what makes travelling through "Back Door Britain" (to quote my mate, Tony Burton's brilliant book title) so exciting.

The longest day came and went. The nights started drawing in but summer still refused to begin. There were good days and bad days on the canals. Some were so smooth, my log reveals nothing about them. Others...well, take June 26th. We were on a long haul from Barrow on the River Soar to Kilby Bridge on the Leicester section of the Grand Union. The first incident of the day only had significance for me: the bag for my monocular, containing the cap and sunfilter, blew off the back of the boat. Next, Clare drove us aground on a bend on the river going through the middle of Leicester. Shortly afterwards, she didn't notice Freeman's Lock and headed for the bottom of the weir. We stuck front and back on a very weedy, unnavigable section of the river. Rod leapt in and swam to the bank taking a rope with him. He managed, with the help of a few passers-by, to pull us off but had lost his slip-ons while crossing the river and banged his toe-nail.

We then stuck in the bridgehole approaching Aylestone Lock, managed to rock through but, immediately afterwards, Rod was hit on the head by an overhanging branch while steering. The branch also knocked the back chimney off (fortunately chained) and, in the confusion, the painted water can was crushed by the bridge. The water from the can spilled into the back cabin and soaked the Vodaphone, which ceased to function. It took twenty-four hours to dry out before it worked again, but we did manage to bash the Buckby can back into some sort of shape.

HOUSEMAID'S KNEE AND WEEPING RIVETS

The day hadn't finished yet. We stuck badly in Bridge 93 and it took a quarter of an hour to rope and rock ourselves off. And, to cap it all, when we arrived at the Navigation, Kilby Bridge, our venue for the night, the landlord informed us that the local council had heard about our performance on Radio Leicester and had sent fire-officers to the pub, who had decreed that we could not perform inside. So, we did the show outside in the cold, accompanied by the enthusiastic shouts from an adjoining boules match. We never saw the landlord again; he had gone out for the evening, so there was no hospitality and no landlord donation.

The Leicester section always seemed badly maintained, with non-functioning paddle gear and missing steps and safety handles – and as for the state of the cut itself... This year, we were passing through Yelvertoft and had to slow down for a dredging team. Me to them: "It'll be good up ahead then – well-dredged?." BWB in reply: "Oh, no. We're dredging out a private mooring." Me: "But it's terrible along this stretch." Them (as they wave goodbye): "The whole of the Leicester section's terrible."

Another great day for me on the tour was July 27th. It was, remarkably for this year, a hot sunny day as we travelled down the Thames Tideway from Eel Pie Island to Brentford. Then Sarah and I went off to Kentish Town where Sue Prickett was having a house-warming party. It was also my 50th birthday party (delayed). Sue had invited lots of my old friends from drama school and the early Mikron days. It was a hot evening and night and we danced in the garden until 4 am. Well, I did; Sarah had to retire to bed with a very sore back. We had been rock 'n' rolling brilliantly (or so it appeared to us after a glass or three)when, on one of our extravagant twirls, we missed each other and Sarah fell backwards against a wall. Very painful.

After three or four hours sleep, I had to drag myself up and get back to the boat, from where we were going by van to do a lunchtime show at the Ruskin House Trade Union and Labour Club in Croydon. Sarah rejoined us on the boat later that night – hobbling and still in pain. She had suffered bad bruising. It took several days before she could walk properly again.

On the run up the Grand Union, one very frequently has to slow down for linear moorings, lines of boats tied up on the off-side of the canal. It can be frustrating having to chug along very slowly but you can relieve your pent-up emotions by looking at the vast variety of boats that have been assembled in one place. Who owns them? Why do they want to own a boat, particularly that one, and how often do these boats get used? It helps to read the names out loud as you pass. They gain a rhythm as you progress: *Muthega, Guildford Griffin, Sulcartus, Kotor, Bermondsey Rowes, Hannah Seer, Kiskadee, Clayton, Prudence, Stella Maris, Tilly, Kitty, Eridamus, Umea, Nimrod, Isobel Marie, White Heather, Baltic, Constance, Jaguar,*

131

Lorella Strasse 6 Dusseldorf(!), *Nutcracker Suite, Poppy, Water Chestnut, Emmalisa, Galadriel, Cleopatra the Second, Gail the Ninth*(!), *Eleanor, Balmoral Castle, Vulcan* and *Chieftain*. My favourite names, of those spotted over the years, are still *Slop Along Placidly* and *Cirrhosis of the River*.

The second half continued to go very well; even the weather improved. Morale was good and the days went racing past. The canals have a feeling of timelessness, and you can often think you are living in your own linear village away from the tensions of everyday life and the world in general. Not for too long though. Reality intrudes in the form of the mobile phone. Our administrator, Janet, had an uncanny habit of phoning at an inappropriate moment. The Vodaphone was fixed just inside the back cabin and was charged up when the engine was running. This meant that the person steering had to answer the phone, and the phone never rang when you were tootling along a nice straight bit of water. Oh, no, Janet seemed to know. As soon as you were going into a lock or negotiating a particularly difficult bend or junction, *ring-ring, ring-ring*. I suspected that she was watching us via some hidden camera. She would watch...and choose her moment.

On the larger global scene, we were made aware of the attempted coup by the army over Gorbachev. On the August 21st, it was defeated and the army moved out of Moscow. On the 22nd, we were moving smoothly up the Staffs & Worcs Canal, although the boat did bang over a lot of rubbish deposited in the canal in Kidderminster – cars, shopping trollies and all the other detritus of twentieth century civilisation. We were about to enter Wolverley Court Lock, when Neil called me urgently. Water and oil were spraying out of the engine room. Thinking that one of the copper pipes in the water-cooling system had vibrated loose, I took off my shirt, jumped into the engine-room and switched off the engine. I then noticed that the water was pouring through the limber holes from the back cabin – we were sinking. All hands to the pumps – the hand pump in the engine room, two stirrup pumps and a bucket in the back cabin. After an hour of pumping, we were only just keeping up with the flow. We got ahead a bit by also using the electric pump from the back bedroom.

I phoned Paul Lorenz, our boat supervisor. He said that we had to empty as much water out as we could and then start clearing out the ballast until we found the leak. He also gave us advice on how to stop it once we'd found it. Neil did most of the lifting of the ballast – really heavy 1936 tram track and chairs. After a quick break for a bite to eat, Rod took over and started searching the bilges with a torch. Eureka! He spotted three rivets which had moved and were weeping heavily. Following Paul's advice, we stuffed the holes with tea-towels liberally soaked with thick grease. On top of them went some heavy weights. After a couple of attempts at this, the water did seem to be coming in less quickly. We replaced the ballast and set off again after six hours of hard labour. And this was on our day off. Mind you, it was a good job there wasn't a show that night. We were all knackered. We arrived in Kinver, checked the bilges (the water was now down to a slow trickle) and then walked into the village for a welcome pint of delicious Bathams' Bitter and an Indian at the International.

I woke up in the middle of the night and checked the bilges. We seemed to have cracked it – the water was still coming in but very slowly indeed. Over the next few days the grease in the tea-towels stopped the flow completely and the tour finished safely at the National Waterways Festival at Netherton on the Dudley No 1 Canal.

On the South Pennine Tour, we introduced a third production, *A View from the Hills*, a re-working of our show about hill-top farmers, originally entitled *From Where I Stand*, but now renamed to avoid confusion with *A Place to Stand*. But the highlight of the tour was our return to the Marsden Mechanics, newly re-opened after a massive refurbishment programme and once again our home base. We had been there for ten years before the renovation work started and we had to move lock, stock and rehearsals to Slaithwaite Civic Hall. We had already been involved in a series of events at the Mechanics to celebrate its re-opening and to help the Community Association raise money for the building.

22

IDLE WOMEN

Fortunately, Rod and Neil decided to stay with us for another year. Janet was now engaged to John Spooner and they were setting up house together in Todmorden, and Clare went off to have babies, I think. We knew we needed to find two highly talented women, as in 1992 we intended to write a show about women as part of our 21st celebrations. The women we chose were "the trainees" who worked and crewed narrowboats during the Second World War. Two books were written about their experiences immediately after the war by Emma Smith and Susan Woolfitt and, much later, books followed by Eily (Kit) Gayford and Margaret Cornish. I already knew Margaret from the days when she had lived on her boat *Alphons* and it was this connection, and the fact that one of the trainers, Kit Gayford, had recently died, that made me realise what perfect material for Mikron this story was. Many of the women were now in their eighties. They would all have their own personal views of this period in their lives. We needed to talk to them and not just read the books.

It was a wonderful research period. Parksy, Sarah and I had only just over two weeks in which to locate and interview these remarkable women. Margaret was superb. She had kept her own diary, had written a book and was still brimming with sharp and witty reminiscences of that short period in the war when women were recruited to work on narrowboats operated by the Grand Union Canal Carrying Company. Advertisements called for women of robust constitution – a vital quality. A typical journey involved picking up cargo, anything from tins of corned beef to aluminium ingots, from Limehouse Docks, delivering it to Birmingham, then going on to Coventry to collect coal for delivery to factories and mills in the south. The round trip took three weeks with the women getting a week off on their return. They were paid a weekly wage of £3. The women trainers got £5.

The women who, on the whole, took to the life the best were middle-class, well-educated women. So it was that Margaret was able to put us in touch with Helen Skyrme, Virginia Strauss and Daphne French, her boating companions, with whom she had remained friends with and kept contact over the years. Helen was eighty-five, living in

Salisbury, feisty, fit and full of tales. Virginia was very young when she joined the boats and was now still in her sixties. A stripling. Daphne was a trainer, along with Kit. She lived in Southern Ireland. She was now eighty-six and was amazed when we phoned her and said we wanted to talk to her: "You're coming all the way here to just see me?" It was worth all the effort of missed ferries and only a few hours spare to visit some of Dublin's fantastic bars. She was delightful – modest and with a gentle humour.

We also found time to visit and talk to Sonia Rolt (now one of our patrons). She had, unusually, married a boatman and had carried on boating after the war. Later, she was to marry Tom Rolt who stimulated so much interest in the post-war waterways with his book, *Narrow Boat*. We visited Averil Scott-Moncrieff, a wonderfully eccentric lady living in the Churnet Valley, near to the Caldon Canal, and Olga Kevelos, a youngster of sixty-eight, now a pub landlady in Kings Sutton, near to the South Oxford and full of scurrilous stories of her fellow trainees.

We also talked to boatpeople like Arthur Bray, Ernie Kendall, Margaret Brooks, George and Gladys Carter, Laura Carter, Ron Hough, John and Phyl Saxon, and Rose and Bill Whitlock and asked them how they had reacted to these all-women crews.

From the richness of this material, Parksy, Jim and I wrote a show which, we hoped, would do justice to these wonderful women. We called it *Imogen's War* after the logo "IW" on the women's badges. It stood for "Inland Waterways" but the boatpeople jokingly referred to them as "Idle Women". Our Imogen was fictional (or was she?). From auditioning, we found a wonderful Imogen. Beccy Hall has real natural qualities as an actress. Her own endearing, bubbly personality shines through when she is performing, and she was able to capture both the eagerness and naivety of Imogen's first days on the boats, as well as her growth into a mature woman, much more aware of the world around her and of the different people that inhabit that world. She was ably assisted by Judith French playing her trainer. Neil and Rod were kept busy playing lock-keepers and boatmen.

The good news on the grant front was that we had managed to secure £4,000 from West Yorkshire Grants, the organisation run by the five West Yorkshire Metropolitan Councils. This was in addition to the grant-aid from Kirklees and Yorkshire Arts.

Sarah and I set off in good spirits for our 21st tour. Sam was enjoying university life in Bristol; both *Imogen's War* and *Spirit of the Age* had gone well on their respective land-based first nights; *Tyseley* was in good nick; and it looked like being an immensely enjoyable tour.

And so it proved to be. We had no dramas either from the Company or from boating. The tour was punctuated by many good moments, and I even found time to take a closer look at some of the areas we passed through on the canal. Take Handsacre, near Rugeley on the T&M...(yes, please, as far away as you like, I hear some people crying). Handsacre, from the canal, appears to be a mile or so of suburbia. It's always fascinating to look at the back of people's gardens: there's a huge aviary with hundreds of tropical birds twittering away; there's a woman sunbathing, scantily clad and with scant regard for the susceptibilities of us uninvited passers-by; there's a garden with washing on the line; one so unkempt it's doubtful the owner has been in it for months; one so suburban, so neat and tidy – immaculate flower beds, grass cut with a razor blade; there's a patio at the canal edge for that after-work glass of wine; there's dogs and cats, chickens and ducks and even sheep and goats; there's a kestrel on the roof (real, not like the stone swan on the boat just passing); there's an increasing number of satellite dishes on the roofs with Sky and BSB trying to lure us into watching non-terrestrial football.

We had another Mikron first – our first visit to prison. We were picked up from Berkhamsted on the Grand Union and taken in a large yellow van to Mount Prison at Bovingdon. We weren't strip searched or showered, but instead taken to a recreation room and asked to perform *Imogen's War*. The prison had been built four years previously to house young offenders but it was now home for Category C adults, serving anything from six months to ten years. Thirty-five of them watched the performance and loved it. They shouted for an encore and chatted to us afterwards: "Are you coming back here?" "Probably next year but I don't know how long you're in for." "Oh, I'll definitely see you next year." It was the first of several enjoyable visits we made over the next few years.

Imogen's War had been tremendously well received at all our venues but the one we were all looking forward to, and the one that would mean the most to us, was our performance at the Perrier Building alongside the River Colne at Rickmansworth. This was to be the reunion for the trainees and where they would see the show for the first time.

I thought of them all as we came down the Grand Union, and wondered what they would make of the canals today and particularly some of the canalside buildings. At Apsley, for instance, the old paper mills, where they would have delivered coal, had recently been pulled down to be replaced by a huge monolith of a building – grey and with no windows facing the canal. Happily, a little further down the canal, Wander's Ovaltine factory still remained unchanged. The trainees would have remembered the Ovaltine fleet of narrowboats with their colourful signwriting.

The day of the reunion arrived. It was hot and sunny and a little humid. There was a tremendous sense of anticipation in the air as the women began to arrive. Daphne had come over from Ireland. Her hair was beautifully waved and she was full of gusto. She spotted Olga: "Come and sit down here, dear. It's been 45 years. I wouldn't miss you anywhere. You haven't changed a bit." Helen had braved British Rail and arrived with Margaret. Virginia was with her husband, Peter, and Averil with Edward and a supply of gin and tonic. Sadly, Sonia couldn't make it, but John and Phyl Saxon were there with Aunt Nell and Mrs Best. It was a very emotional performance both for us and them. I watched them watching their young selves in the shape of Beccy and Judith. I watched the handkerchiefs appearing and I was so moved by the thunderous applause at the end. Some of them shouted, "Hooray! Marvellous! Absolutely wonderful!" Daphne, Margaret, Sarah, Parksy, Beccy and Judith were interviewed for *Woman's Hour*, and I think my favourite sight of all was Helen and Virginia walking along the gunwhales of *Tyseley* to look at the back cabin. I was worried for them but Helen shouted, "If I want to fall in, I will." A totally memorable day.

A few days later, on July 1st, I thought of Margaret, Daphne and the rest as we crossed Limehouse Basin to go out on to the tidal Thames. It was changing out of all recognition. No longer were narrowboats being loaded from coasters, as the women would have remembered. The area was being completely "yuppified" – smart new housing was going up and moorings for sea-going yachts being erected. Even the ship lock had been reduced in size; only recently, coasters had been loading scrap metal for Spain. No more.

It was an overcast day as we pulled out on to the wide river and a bit choppy as we punched the tide before it turned and swept us up to Teddington. London's riverside was changing all the time. The old pub, the Prospect of Whitby, was still there but Surrey Docks had been filled in and much of the warehousing was being turned into housing. There were many trip boats charging about as we approached Tower Bridge. I let Neil off with a windlass to lift the bascules (no, I didn't). We passed HMS *Belfast* (yes, we did – it has permanent moorings just above Tower Bridge) and the old Billingsgate Fish Market, now vying with modern buildings built of green and black glass, all with their own trendy atriums. Past a new pub, appropriately called the Banker (or near to that spelling anyway!), and the new old Globe Theatre, now near to completion after years of painstaking effort by Sam Wanamaker, and Bankside Power Station before it became an art gallery. We had several friends on board, as was traditional for this trip, and we pulled the cork on some sparkling wine as we passed Big Ben (11.37am) and the Houses of Parliament to celebrate another five years of Conservative government. (I am joking, of course; the May election had seen John Major surprisingly re-elected).

It was good to see the rubbish barges being loaded at Wandsworth, but that was the only sign of commercial traffic. We consoled ourselves by timing our trip along the Boat Race course from Putney to Mortlake. Neil encouraged us with a megaphone. We managed nine miles an hour but we would still have been minutes behind Oxford and Cambridge. But we had come up the river so fast on the flood tide that we had to go through the half-tidal lock at Richmond (cost then: £3.50) and shortly afterwards, we went through Teddington Lock and we were back on non-tidal water.

At Shepperton, we left the Thames to go up the Wey Navigation. We were on our way to the Independence Rally on the Basingstoke Canal. A very large, very jobsworth lock-keeper at the first lock said he had been ordered to charge us as a commercial craft (£70). We refused and said we had been told that we would be able to pay the rally price of £5. The boss was phoned. We told him we were a charity. He told us he was a charity and that the waterway had to be self-financing with no extra cash from its owners, the National Trust. Eventually and very reluctantly, he agreed to charge us the weekly rate less 20% (don't ask me why, but it was £23.20). The whole of this trip was a bit annoying: the bureaucracy of the Wey, the poor turnout at the rally and the closure of the Basingstoke throughout its length due to lack of water – this a *restored* waterway! We had to go by road to our other Basingstoke Canal venues.

Restored by a week's holiday in Portugal visiting our ex-Mikron friend, Sarah Wilson, who was teaching in Cascais, the second half of the tour took us up the Thames and on to the South Oxford. At Thrupp, we were thrilled when three hundred people turned out for *Imogen's War*. We took the best ever after-show collection of over £700.

By August, we thought Beccy and Judith had had enough experience to be given a little test to see how much they had learnt from playing the trainees. We were getting towards the top of the Hatton 21 Flight of locks. At a given signal, Rod, Neil, Sarah and myself disappeared behind a hedge, leaving just Judith and Beccy to complete the last couple of locks. For a minute they looked bemused at our disappearance; then they realised, and proceeded to bring *Tyseley* up the rest of the locks with all the aplomb of their wartime predecessors.

Another emotional day was the Friends of Mikron get-together which celebrated Mikron's 21st year. Nearly ninety people turned out at the Hop Pole in Bromsgrove, including ex-Mikrons Mark Steeves, Hilary Rikof, Juliet Heacock, Gilly Baskeyfield, Katherine Dow-Blyton, John Elkington, Clive Lucas, Sarah Wilson and Alan Bridger. The buffet was excellent and the cabaret brilliant (especially Rod's hilarious history of Mikron) as were the cricket and boules matches. Our Council of Management presented Sarah and me with a plate, jug and cups specially made by Wisbech potter, Liz Mathews, and Janet Armstrong had made a superb birthday cake – a very accurate replica

Sam Lucas working his passage on the South Oxford, 1979.
(Waterways World)

A youthful audience for I'd Go Back Tomorrow at Wild Hollow, Gnosall 1981. Mark Strickson, Thea Bennet, Mike Lucas and Sarah Wilson.   (John H. Denton)

Sarah Lucas and Sarah Wilson at Dukinfield on the Peak Forest Canal in 1981.

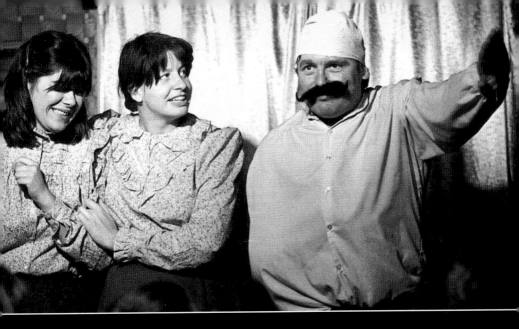

Over The Top from 1982. Eluned Owen, Sarah Wilson and Mike as Captain Webb, complete with broken shoulder.

Mealtime on Lune, the ex-Leeds & Liverpool wide boat in 1984. Sue Dyde, Caron Pascoe, Mark Williams, Mike Lucas and Geoff Wheat.

The Company, 1985.: Maria Murtagh, Kathryn Brierley, Glynis Davies, Jane Mansel, Mike Lucas, Mark Williams, Louise Waddington, Sarah Lucas, Steve Connolley, Stuart Moreton, Geoff Wheat and Paul Lorenz.

Mike at the tiller, South Oxford, 1984.

of *Tyseley*. Sam was there, of course, saying how proud of us he was and that he wanted to get a really good degree so that we would be proud of him. The whole evening was rounded off dramatically with a violent storm.

The heavy rain caused us problems when we arrived at the River Severn and I had to sign an indemnity form absolving British Waterways of any responsibility. We travelled at ten miles per hour downstream to Upton on a swollen river and knocked two hours off our normal time to Gloucester! All this happened shortly after we heard that West Midlands Arts had axed the grant which we had received from them since 1973. Although it was only £2,500, it formed a vital part of our expenditure budget. The *Birmingham Post* picked up on this and wrote a tremendous review of *Imogen's War*: "The first bouquet goes to this company for sheer endurance and the ability to create theatrical excitement wherever they perform." The article finished with: "Axing Mikron's grant is a sad decision." We were getting used to grant-giving bodies withdrawing funding from us. It didn't make it any easier to accept, particularly at a time when we were continuing to raise our artistic standards.

The Waterways Tour ended at the National Waterways Festival at Wakefield. We had left *Tyseley* at Audlem on the Shroppie, and moved on to the Leeds & Liverpool short boat *Weaver* for our trip from Riddlesden on the Leeds & Liverpool Canal to Wakefield on the Aire & Calder, with performances in Riddlesden, Rodley, Leeds and at the festival itself, which had the distinction of being one of the wettest, muddiest festivals there had ever been.

The year finally finished on November 28th, after an eight-and-a-half week South Pennine Tour. In October, I had taken part in a special week on the Grand Union. I was one of the co-ordinators of a Euro-Canal Project which involved taking three boatloads of young people from all over Europe from Stockton to Stoke Bruerne and back. During the week, they worked on producing a newspaper, linking with other countries via e-mail, making a video and improvising some short plays about the canals. It was a very exciting week, exhausting but totally rewarding. The culmination was a performance at Warwick University. No-one was allowed to speak their own language; so, an Italian would be speaking English, a German speaking Italian, the British speaking French, and so on. It was a very successful attempt at making us all feel more European.

23

"IT WON'T HAPPEN TO ME"

1993 began normally enough. It was not to remain so but, for the time being, Sarah and I were planning for the new season blissfully unaware of the trouble lying ahead. We lost Judith and Neil from the Company. Neil had done splendid work for us over two years and we missed his talents and his warm personality. We've never lost touch and see him frequently. He now has his own narrowboat and has written a one-man show based on *The Flower of Gloster* by E. Temple Thurston, who in 1911 hired a canal boat and travelled the waterways of central England. Judith went on to write and perform about Jane Austen and is now married to Roger Parks, who was Sarah Parks' husband. Life is never simple!

Rod not only rejoined the Company for a third year but had settled in Marsden, was running the drama workshops for young people with Gilly Baskeyfield, and written a one-man show which he toured locally in the early part of 1993. This was called *Another '45* which told the extraordinary story of the Jacobite Rebellion of 1745. Rod's writing was excellent and, when Parksy became unavailable to write with me, I had no hesitation in asking Rod to join me as co-author of the new show.

We approached British Waterways and they agreed to provide £2,000 sponsorship over two years as part of their Canals 200 celebrations to mark the bi-centenary of the canal building mania of 1793. We were to research and write a show about that frenzied period in canal history. In that year alone, sixty-two canals were being built, a third of the entire navigable waterway system in Britain.

Apart from reading books like Anthony Burton's *The Canal Builders* and *Canal Mania*, we did most of our research for this production at the Public Records Office at Kew examining the reports and records of several canal companies that were formed around that time. With Jim again writing the songs, Rod and I wrote *The Threads of Revolution* about a canal and characters that never existed but could well have done. Our canal was the Slackley & Pitbrook Canal, built between 1793 and 1798, in a period when the French king had lost his head (guillotined in the Revolution) and George the Third had lost his (he had been officially declared mad) and many people had lost theirs. Gripped by entrepreneurial fever, rich men and poor men alike rushed headlong to invest in projects that would rapidly transform the world they knew. There were parallels to be drawn with the speculation brought about by privatisation in the 1980s.

The show was premièred at the Marsden Mechanics on May 20th and the next evening performed at the Rickmansworth Canal Festival. British Waterways' *Update* reported that the show was "a poignant reminder of a bygone age as seen from the push-button comforts of 1993. Excellently directed, it maintains the high standards that have kept Mikron a canalside winner in live entertainment for over two decades."

So, when we boarded *Tyseley* to begin our Waterways Tour on May 25th, everyone was in great spirits. Beccy had stayed on and was again performing brilliantly in the new production of *Imogen's War*, and she and Rod were joined by newcomers Lucy McAra, another import from Dundee, and Richard Povall (much more of him later).

The tour began on the Peak Forest Canal, and Lucy and Richard soon showed that they were going to like the boating life and settled into steering and cooking rotas quite quickly. The weather wasn't going to be kind to us this year. Rain and wind were regular features of our boating days and those balmy nights when you could sit out on the foredeck into the wee hours sipping a whisky, gazing at the stars and listening to cows chewing the cud in the field opposite, were few and far between.

Just over a week into the tour and we were again at our old favourite, the Anchor at High Offley. Everything is the same – a great atmosphere, large crowd and singing and playing in the packed pub afterwards, but Sarah and I sit watching, worrying whether all this and everything else is ever going to be the same again. The reason for this deep unease is, that afternoon, we have discovered that Sarah has a large lump in the upper part of her left breast. Neither of us had noticed it before but there it now was. We both knew that you mustn't ignore a lump like this; so we tell Janet, our administrator, who has come from Marsden to see us and the show, and she offers to drive us to Eccleshall, the nearest town, the next morning to see a doctor. In the meantime, we try singing along with everyone else.

I shall never forget Sarah's face when she came out of the surgery in Eccleshall. She was smiling: "The doctor says that it's most unlikely to be cancerous. It'll almost certainly be hormonal. He says that it'll have disappeared in a week or so." What a relief. Now let's just get on with our lives and the tour.

The weather continued to be awful and, as we approached the Severn at Stourport, I began to worry about the state of the river. When we arrived in the basin, we discovered that Holt Lock had been closed since the previous day for repair to a broken paddle and was not due to re-open until 4pm. We had a show that night at Grimley ten miles down the river.

We locked out from the basin but, when we arrived at the first river lock, Lincombe, there were already eight boats waiting. The lock-keeper wouldn't let them through until he had news from Holt as there were other boats further down the river. We spent several hours chatting up the lock-keeper and he eventually let us through with the first lockful at 5pm. The river was running very fast and within thirty minutes we were at Holt, only to discover that the paddle had again broken and no boats would now be allowed through for at least two days. So, again we started the chat-up, explaining the seriousness of our position to the foreman. Eventually, he decided to try and lock us through with one other boat. Amazingly enough, one of the passengers on this boat was Amanda Murray, an actress who had worked for Mikron in our very early days, in the production of *Sitting Pretty* at the Kings Head, Islington, whom I had not met since until now.

The lock worked and we set off for Bevere. We had great difficulty tying up at the Camp House. The river was running very fast and still rising. By now it was 7.15, and we were due on at 8pm. We set up very fast under a long shed in the garden and performed to thirty brave souls with the rain pouring down outside. We felt we had deserved our post-performance scrumpy that night.

The rain was intense for the rest of our journey downstream the next day. After a shopping stop at Upton, there were a few hairy moments setting off again. After we had untied, *Tyseley* was carried sideways down the river. I managed to turn her while passing under the bridge, and then had to work the tiller like mad in order to avoid a tree and three moored boats. We arrived at the Coal House at Apperley only to discover that the landing stage was under water. We had to wait while a temporary landing place was built with scaffold poles. In the evening, the rain eased, the river stopped rising and the scaffolding poles held.

A few days later we were on the Worcester & Birmingham Canal. It had been nearly two weeks since Sarah had seen the doctor in Eccleshall, but the lump in her breast was still very much there. We decided to seek a second opinion and went to see a doctor in Worcester. He said that, even though 90% of breast lumps were benign, it was always best to have them investigated by a specialist. We phoned our own doctor in Marsden. He acted very quickly and fixed an appointment for Sarah at the specialist breast unit at Huddersfield Infirmary the following week. On this same day, Sam arrived to say that he and his girlfriend had broken up and that he was getting his final results at about the same time as Sarah was due at the hospital.

I remember nothing of the following week, except I know we gave performances in Bromsgrove, Birmingham, Fazeley and Branston. We were now on the Trent & Mersey and, while the Company moved the boat the short distance to Willington, Sarah and I went by van to Huddersfield. We were only at the hospital for a couple of hours. It all happens very fast: an examination, an X-ray and the verdict – some of the cells are abnormal. Sarah is going to have to have a lumpectomy (to remove the lump) and some lymph glands under the arm removed to check if any are infected. We decided to cancel our holiday in Portugal and go for the op the following week, which happened to be a break in the tour. All being well, Sarah would receive radiotherapy treatment about six to eight weeks after that, every day for four weeks at Cookridge Hospital in Leeds. Neither of us was really taking all of this in. We returned to the boat to the support of the others.

Two days later, we were in Nottingham and the weather was hot and sunny. Sarah was due to go up to Huddersfield the following morning. At least we'd had some good news from Sam; he had got a 2:1 for his history degree. It helped to divert us from brooding too much about Sarah's op. Music is another great way of forgetting one's troubles and that night, after the show, in the warmth of a summer's evening, Rod and Richard played their guitars on the foredeck of the boat, and Sarah and I danced under the old Fellows, Clayton & Morton transit shed. We danced our socks off, and now I never hear *Little Sheila* being played without remembering that evening.

Sarah caught the train the next morning and we moved to Newark. She had the operation the following day and the message came through that she was okay. We missed her terribly that evening. The Old King's Arms at Newark was one of her favourite pubs and we always, traditionally, had a late night there (quite often until five or six o'clock in the morning). Of course we only managed until 2am this year, but we did have a good time with Captain Pete and his friend, Merrick, from the narrowboat *Azteca*, who had travelled some of the way down the Trent with us. Pete was a captain of a container ship and worked at sea for six months and then spent six months touring around on his narrowboat. He'd never seen Mikron before but had loved the show and, despite his hangover the next morning, he turned up at *Tyseley* with a cheque for £200 and a box of very large cigars. He has followed and supported us ever since.

I left the others to move to Fiskerton and drove up to see Sarah. She was feeling fine physically but was anxious to find out the results of all the tests. We would know in two days time. I drove back to Fiskerton for the last performance of the first half of the tour. I was exhausted and worried, but the show went a storm. At least now we had an eight day break and I could concentrate on making sure Sarah was all right.

Friday July 2nd was one of the worst days of my life. Sarah and I were told that, although she had had a lumpectomy and some lymph glands removed, she still had signs of pervasive cells in her breast and that two of her lymph nodes were cancerous. This meant she would have to have a mastectomy, followed by chemotherapy treatment to try and catch and kill any cancerous cells that might have got into her system. We went for a walk to try and absorb the full impact of this shocking news. The consultant at Huddersfield Infirmary happened to be one of the top breast cancer specialists in the country. He had written the definitive textbook on the subject. We needed to find out more and, very kindly, he offered to meet us in his office on the Saturday morning.

We asked him if there would be any problem in delaying the mastectomy until September, when the Waterways Tour had finished and we would be back in Marsden. He saw nothing wrong with that. It was not normal practice but, if the pre-invasive cells in the breast became cancerous, they ought to be caught by the chemotherapy. It was a gamble but the whole process was a bit of a lottery anyway. So, that decision was made. I phoned a pub in the Peak District to book a room and, a few hours later, we were eating lunch in Lathkil Dale. We spent a delightful four days together, trying to forget that the next few months were not going to be fun.

Sarah started on her course of chemotherapy on July 8th. Sadly, this coincided with Sam's degree ceremony in Bristol. We were choked to have to miss this, but there was nothing to be done. Sue Prickett went in our stead, took the photos, paid for the lunch, and did everything in the style of a loving aunt.

The rest of the tour was punctuated by visits to hospitals near to a canal or river for blood tests and trips back to Huddersfield for more chemo. Sarah stood up to all this very well and continued to help crew the boat and look after *Tyseley*. It was all a bit of a blur really. I remember the odd day like a journey from Aynho to Thrupp on the South Oxford, always a delightful six or seven hour trip, rain or shine. This year it was a cool, windy day as we locked through Somerton Deep, a beautiful, tranquil spot. The lock is reputedly the deepest (at 12 feet) on the narrow system, although it does vie with Tardebigge Top Lock and Eturia Top Lock amongst others. The M40 is no longer in sight; nor is the railway and there is no road access to the simply-built but aesthetically pleasing lock-house. You either walk along the towpath to it or arrive by boat. The meadowlands of the Cherwell stretch away from the lock and there always seem to be great masses of sky there, today with thick fluffy clouds scudding by. A place to forget one's troubles and just enjoy being alive.

Mind you, one has to remember to remain alert at all times, as I discovered a short while later. Beccy put a cup of coffee and a biscuit down on the side of Lower Heyford swing bridge for me to pick up as I steered through. Unfortunately, the biscuit landed under the bridge itself and, as I reached down to pick it up, the bridge came down on two of my fingers. Luckily, it immediately swung back up again and I was

144

able to retrieve them, still attached to my hand, I'm glad to say. They were just badly bruised, but I only managed to get half the biscuit.

The trips up to Huddersfield were always long and tedious. On one occasion, we were at the hospital for nine-and-a-half hours. It was always good to get back to *Tyseley* and rejoin the tour.

The Waterways Tour ended with our annual visit to the National Waterways Festival. This year, it involved a journey down the River Nene to Peterborough, a trip we had only made twice before. After queuing to get down the locks on the Northampton Arm, our first performance was in Northampton at the Britannia Inn. The locks on the Nene can be very hard work, not made easier this year by the amount of queuing involved. Many boats were on their way to the festival. Most people were very relaxed and friendly, but Sarah and Richard did have an altercation with the crew of a pair of boats. Sarah accused them of being selfish by going so slowly through the locks but not letting us pass. They screamed at her and said that she was unhinged!

We had the river mostly to ourselves after Wellingborough, as the majority of the boats had tied up for Tesco's. We met one poor boatowner (sporting many badges on his hat) who had stopped to take his daughter to hospital. She had tripped on the lockside and broken her ankle. He said sadly, "Oh dear, I hoped this year would be incident-free. Last year I ended up in Wolverhampton Hospital... I was shot. They had to dig the pellet out of my back." Oh, the joys of boating.

We continued down the Nene, which gets increasingly more scenic and interesting the further towards Peterborough you get, performing in Wadenhoe, Barnwell and Wansford-in-England. The weather was excellent for the festival and we had good attendances at our three performances. Sarah and I then spent a week at a *gîte* in Normandy and a few days in Beccy's parent's caravan perched high on the hills looking down on Harlech, with Snowdon in the distance and Portmeirion across the estuary.

During the course of the South Pennine Tour which ran from September 17th (Sarah's birthday) until November 13th, Sarah had four weeks of radiotherapy at Cookridge Hospital. Although the treatment only lasted a few minutes, your whole day was taken up travelling and waiting...and waiting. Sometimes (no, quite often), the machine would break down or would need maintenance; so, the four weeks of daily treatment took nearly seven weeks. I went with Sarah as often as I could and, although she was tired, she came through it all marvellously and without any of the side-effects connected with this lethal treatment.

This bizarre year drew to a close with a decision by Sarah not to have a mastectomy. The chemo and radiotherapy should have zapped the pre-invasive cells and the hospital would be checking her breasts regularly.

24

BACK TO NORMAL

1994 turned out to be a much better year. We said farewell to Lucy and to Beccy, and welcomed Sandra Osborn and Joanne McGowan. Sandra had studied drama at Hull University and had had a fair amount of professional experience with companies like Theatre of the Gorge and Forest Forge. Joanne was from Oswaldtwistle and had trained at the Birmingham School of Speech and Drama. Her main claim to fame was that she had clog danced for the Pope at the Vatican.

Way before our two new recruits arrived, we had managed to secure a grant from the Foundation for Sport and the Arts to help pay for a repaint of *Tyseley* and to help fund a winter tour of Rod's one-man shows. Rod was about to go into his fourth season as an actor with the Company, was now co-writing Mikron's shows with me, running the drama workshops with Gilly and, in addition, had written two shows, which he now toured locally during January and February, *Another '45* and *The Lyon Still Mourns*, the epic story of Bonnie Prince Charlie's escape after the Battle of Culloden. As one reviewer said: "Rod's wry humour does much to underline the human side of one nation's very personal tragedy. And his warmth ensured that the audience was captivated from start to finish."

Rod was also working closely with a local community organisation. He ran a series of drama workshops with children, aged twelve to eighteen, resulting in a production which explained the origins and workings of credit unions. A rural credit union was about to be set up in the area, and Mikron Youth Theatre's show was performed at public meetings in the region to demonstrate the benefits of saving and borrowing through a credit union. Today, there is a flourishing credit union in the Colne Valley. Another example of how drama can be used to highlight and explain current issues.

Help for Mikron came from another source this year – Alan Bridger, who featured so prominently in our tours of 1974 and 1975. Bridger had left Mikron after his second tour and, indeed, he left the acting profession – only to join another profession which relies on acting skills, the law. I had studied law and given it up to become an actor. Bridger took the other way round. He was now a successful defence solicitor in Bradford with his own firm, but he had not forgotten his poor thespian mates. He was sponsoring Mikron for the second year, this time with a substantial amount which enabled us to claim money from the government scheme, the Association for Business Sponsorship of the Arts.

I had set Rod and myself a daunting task this year. For a long time, I had wanted to write a show about pubs and beer. Many of our venues are pubs, and we had watched the changes take place over the years; we had seen the continuing demise of the "local" pub and the growth of eating houses and themed establishments, but we had also witnessed the fight back against that gross 1960's invention, keg beer, and the re-emergence of real ale. There was a story to be told here and somebody had to do it. So Rod and I were faced with the research for this project. We had to visit pubs and breweries, talking to landlords, brewers and customers and, of course, occasionally sampling the products in the interests of accuracy. From all this came *Beer Street*, which told the tale of beer itself, featuring monks, hop pickers, maltsters, brewsters, coopers, hops, barley, yeast and water, and then the story of pubs and the efforts of a young couple to run a proper local with proper beer, and to stave off the predatory breweries, who wanted to knock down the dividing walls and generally cash in on its success.

The production opened at the Marsden Mechanics on May 20th. For me, the first few minutes were horrifying. In one of the first scenes, Jo and Sandra played two hop pickers in Kent at the end of the nineteenth century. The women used to pick the hops wearing stilts to get at the high vines. Jo and Sandra were on short stilts to illustrate this – or rather Jo was on stilts. Sandra was mainly off hers. Twice she crashed to the ground, twice she got back up. Both times I thought she must have seriously damaged some part of her body. But, no, she was intact. Game girl. Whether it was first- night nerves or what, it never happened again, although lots of other things happened to Sandra on the tour. *Beer Street* was a resounding success. Jim had written some wonderful songs, not least *Happy Hour*, which had 120 words for being drunk. As the *Oxford Times* said: "...the cast of four are simply terrific."

Jo and Sandra must have been a little bemused by the start of the Waterways Tour. They had been warned of the difficulties of steering a 72-foot boat around the system of narrow canals with scary bends and shallow channels, but here they were on their first day on the Manchester Ship Canal, a very wide waterway, 30 feet deep in places, and with immense locks. We were tied up at Trafford Wharf in Manchester. *Tyseley* looked great, sparkling with her new paint, but very small in the vast empty waters of Salford Docks (now renamed Salford Quays). Only one glitch – the signwriter had made a mistake and one of our funders had been acknowledged as "West Yorksire Grants".

147

After Jo and Sandra had done their nest-building and settled on board, the next morning we left for our trip down the canal to Ellesmere Port. It was cold enough to have the coal fire going. We saw our first ship at the grain terminal and a Russian ship at Irwell Wharf, but very little else until we reached Runcorn. We were passed by a dredger and then, as we approached Stanlow Oil Terminal, a huge tanker, *Esso Clyde*, appeared in the distance with tugs fore and aft. As we drew nearer, we heard a disembodied voice, emanating from a bankside tannoy: "Stay this side of the ship. Stay this side of the ship." At first, we thought they meant we could pass on the right-hand side of the ship but, as we proceeded, they screamed at us again and we realised what they were really trying to say was: "Keep out of the bloody way." We did, until the ship was safely moored and the tugs had moved away.

We arrived at Ellesmere Port to find the entrance blocked by a tug called *Vanguard* from Liverpool. We were delayed for nearly an hour while we waited for the skipper to come from Eastham. We made our way up the badly maintained locks to the Waterways Museum, where we were performing that night in the LTC Rolt Centre. The following night, we performed in Chester at Telford's Warehouse, which was a warehouse designed by Thomas Telford and is now a pub and restaurant. Rod was suffering from very sore ribs. A few nights before, he had been riding his bike home from the pub, in the dark, when he hit a sheep which walked into the road. He was catapulted over the handlebars. The next day was a day off; so, Rod went to the Huddersfield Infirmary. He was told that he had broken a rib. It would take six weeks to mend properly. For the next few weeks, Rod bravely carried on performing, but he was not allowed to steer or work the locks nor do much carrying of props and set.

Sarah, however, was in ebullient mood. She was feeling well and was so delighted to be back on the canals. We both felt confident that the cancer had been cracked. Although the weather in early June was cool and very hazy, it was a great time to be back on the water. Everywhere was burgeoning – the grass was that bright green colour you only get at this time of the year, the gorse was a beautiful yellow, as was the rape, which is so out of place in our countryside, causing havoc to the wildlife wherever it's grown. Then there was the May blossom, the cow parsley, the irises and the stunning rhododendron bushes. Sarah particularly was appreciating all this with great relish.

The weather improved as we moved down to Stourport and on to the River Severn. By June 15th, we were moving up the Worcester & Birmingham Canal towards Brum. We had performed in Kings Norton and Jo was on her way back to the boat, when she found an old lady lying on the towpath, who told her she was trying to commit suicide. It was clear she had already had a go at slashing her neck and wrists but not very effectively. Rod's girlfriend, Tue, drove her home. Her husband did not appear to be very surprised or shocked. "She's disappearing all the time," he said, "She should be in a hospital but, of course, the Tories have closed them all down."

The Birmingham area provided us with several other incidents. A few days later, we were on our way out of the city making for the North Stratford Canal. Just after Edgebaston Tunnel, Jo was steering and we felt the boat land on a large object. I maintained that Jo was slightly out of the channel and that we would have been all right if she had been steering along the middle of the canal, but Jo and Sandra both disagreed. Sandra even added an addendum to my log: "In my opinion, Joanne was not out of the channel at any point in the manoeuvre. Mike Lucas is a stubborn old git when he wants to be." Who am I to disagree with two such experienced hands?

We tried rocking the boat and prising with shafts but to no avail. Jo's boyfriend, Mark, was with us. He went into the water and discovered there was a large piece of concrete lodged under the boat. We called for help from British Waterways; two hours later there was still no sign of the cavalry. Shortly afterwards, the first boat to arrive managed to pull us backwards off the obstacle and we were on our way.

An hour later, we were passing through Bourneville. A boy was lying on the towpath, obviously in a bad way. We discovered that he had been fishing and somehow had fallen into the canal. He couldn't swim and was quickly in trouble. One of his mates had run off for help, the other (about ten years old) had jumped in to rescue him. He was joined by a passer-by. Together, they managed to pull him on to the bank and, when we arrived, they were trying to get the water out of him. I rang 999 on the mobile while Jo and Sandra jumped off to help.

After about ten minutes, the ambulancemen arrived running down the towpath. Using *Tyseley*, we transferred everybody to the other side of the canal which was where the ambulance could get access. The boy was pale and shaken but alive. We left them to it and hurried on to our venue, the Wharf at Hockley Heath – except hurry is not a word you can use in the context of the North Stratford Canal. We stuck in the guillotine lock and bumped our way there.

In mid-July, Sarah and I had to leave from Banbury to go to the Huddersfield Infirmary. The van wouldn't start and we had to call out National Breakdown. As a result, we were late getting there but, when Sarah was finally seen, the news was good. Everything was fine, and she wouldn't need another mammeograph for two months. So, it was a dash back to Banbury for a great show in the Mill Theatre.

The next day was beautifully hot and sunny for our move to Aynho. It was our Friends of Mikron afternoon with the usual speeches, cabaret and boules match. Our mate and Chair of our Council of Management, Tony Burton, danced enthusiastically and, at one point, even frantically when he appeared to be literally hopping. It turned out he was in agony and it was only two days later, when he was back in Bristol, that he was told he had torn a ligament in his foot and was immediately put in plaster (well, his foot at least).

Amazingly, we had warm sunshine for four weeks. Quite a relief after some of the previous years. It was great to get up every day, put on just shorts and sandals and know you were going to be performing outside that night.

Sandra's escapades with the stilts were perhaps a foretaste of things to come. Sandra is a lovely person with a warm, engaging personality. She is also a damned good actress. But – and here I do have sympathy with her, because I have been known to suffer in this department – she is also accident-prone, and it was the Kennet & Avon Canal where she demonstrated this best. She hit trouble at Theale Swing Bridge. It was not fully open, but Sandra was taking *Tyseley* through too fast and at the wrong angle. She hit the bridge, denting the side of the boat and smashing the bathroom window.

We continued up the K&A. For the first time, we were going as far as Devizes. We performed at the Barge at Honeystreet, a charming pub but quite often, as today, invaded by crop circle aficionados, mainly Germans and Americans. This part of Wiltshire is famous for its wide variety of crop circles. These people were all more interested in looking at the videos they had taken than in watching a touring theatre company. But, after the show, we all watched a fantastic storm circle round the pub. It never passed overhead and it never rained; so, we were able to listen to the great crashes of thunder and watch the lightning flashes, both sheet and forked, vertical and horizontal.

From All Cannings to Devizes, we struggled though a thick carpet of weed. Several times we had to stop and clear out the mud hatch. But we made Devizes Wharf and gave a performance in the skittle alley of the Old Crown.

It was on the way back down the K&A to the Thames that Sandra came into her own again. While tying up at Great Bedwyn, she fell off the front of the boat, much to the cruel delight of passing walkers and other boaters, when they realised the only thing hurt was her pride. Mind you, a day later, Sarah also fell in. She was ahead of the boat setting the lock. When we arrived, she was standing on the canalside soaking wet. On this canal, there are some ground paddles that are heavy to operate and lean out over the canal. Sarah had given one push too far. She had lost her sunglasses but, in true boating tradition, was still holding her windlass.

Sandra was not to be outdone though. The following day, she took over steering from Jo and immediately hit the wooden step on one of the gates of Burghfield Lock, leaving a give-away stain of red paint. She then proceeded to sit us on the cill. Prompt action from the rest of the crew saved *Tyseley* from tipping and the rudder from bending. To alleviate shock, we stopped for a drink at the Cunning Man, only to find it closed for refurbishment. Instead, Jo baked a couple of cakes which we ate on the way to Henley.

The tour continued on its way. The performances were excellent and the Company was fine. It all ended on the August 29th at the National Waterways Festival at Waltham Abbey on the River Lea.

For the Autumn Tour (as the South Pennine Tour was now called), we introduced a third production into our repertoire. With support from the Foundation for Sport and the Arts and the Manchester Ship Canal Company, we updated and revised *Manchester-Super-Mare* to coincide with the centenary of the opening of that great canal. The *Huddersfield Examiner* described it thus: "Sometimes witty, sometimes poignant, but always entertaining and informative, the story chronicles the birth of the great ship canal, from the original Act of Parliament in 1884, through to its construction ten years later...a thoroughly enjoyable tale expertly told by four richly-talented actors. For those people who have never experienced pub theatre before, I would certainly recommend a visit to see this talented outfit. You don't know what you're missing."

The last night of the season was again held at the Marsden Mechanics, where we gave our very last performance of *Threads of Revolution*. This is the night when I am able to thank not only the Company who are seen and applauded every night, but all the other members of Mikron who work behind the scenes to make our tours successful – Sarah, of course; but also Jim, our song writer; Janet Russell, our musical director; Dean Meacham, who in 1994 was designing all our publicity material (leaflets, programmes, posters, T-shirts); Jez Dolan, who was designing and making our costumes, props and set; our associate administrator, Janet Armstrong, and our boat supervisor, Paul Lorenz.

25

ALARUMS AND
EXCURSIONS

In February 1995, I had an opportunity to tread the boards again – well, not so much the boards as the streets and towpaths of Stone in Staffordshire on the Trent & Mersey Canal. The Trent & Mersey Canal Society was celebrating its 21st birthday and the committee asked me if I would like to play James Brindley for the weekend. Brindley had been the engineer of the T&M and many of the other early canals as well. I had played him several times for Mikron; so I readily accepted. I kitted myself out in suitable eighteenth century gear and off I went to Stone (well, I changed at the Crown Hotel when I got there; I'm not that much of an exhibitionist).

I had to visit the statue they had erected for me at the junction of the Caldon Canal, and even got the job of cleaning all the pigeon shit off myself. I visited the refurbished dry and wet docks and, in the evening, gave an after-dinner speech. There was a considerable British Waterways presence at the do and, speaking as James Brindley, I was able to criticise certain modern day aspects of "my" canal that would not have been proper if I had been Mike Lucas. I was also able to express my pleasant surprise at the number of leisure boats using the canal: "But what a strange collection of craft, eh – traditional narrowboats – it's funny, I never saw a narrowboat with windows and buckets of flowers all along the roof, and people in brightly coloured raincoats with the words "Captain" or "Cook" on their 'ats. And all the canalside pubs that used to have stables have pulled them down or turned them into "Family Rooms" or "Stable Bar Bistros" or whatever. It's a damned good job I didn't have to come by horse tonight. It's a funny world...and then there's dumpy boats and noddy boats and houseboats (ah, say no more about that one)...what struck me as a visitor is that there's lots of these boats tied up in long lines on the canal itself. It must be a bit galling, just as you've got up a nice steady speed with these new-fangled motors, having to slow down again for a long line of boats. I've an idea...it's only a suggestion, mind...but how about little arms going off the main canal where you could store all these funny craft. Not my job, I know, but I can't stop thinking. Just as I can't stop thinking that, when I was alive, there were many people who used me without really knowing who I was, and today there are boats and pubs called "James Brindley" run by people who don't really know anything about me."

Another winter activity was getting a sixth recording under our belt at Beaumont Street Studios in Huddersfield. Jim Woodland and I produced it, and it featured the 1994 Company singing songs from *Beer Street* and *Threads of Revolution*.

Meanwhile, a new production had to be researched and written to join *Beer Street* and *Manchester-Super-Mare* on this year's Autumn Tour. Rod had decided not to tour again this year but he was going to continue writing with me. This time, an all-male team of Rod, Jim and myself was going to write a show about the women's suffrage movement. Obviously, we felt a particular sense of responsibility towards the material. Rod and I researched carefully using archive material from the British Museum Library and Newspaper Library, and the London Museum. We read lots of books including *One Hand Tied Behind Us* by Jill Liddington and Jill Norris and *Queen Christabel* by David Mitchell. We were very interested in women from the North of England and researched the archives of all the local libraries, reading *The Life and Times of a Respectable Rebel* by Jill Liddington and *A Brave and Beautiful Spirit* by Les Garner. Les was particularly helpful. He came from Oldham but lectured at the University of Greenwich, specialising in the women's suffrage movement. It was he who informed us that many men supported the suffrage campaign and that the whole women's movement began in the North.

So, we were inspired to write *A Woman's Place*, from the perspective of a working-class woman and her family. She was part of the grass-roots support for women's suffrage which started in the Lancashire mills. She becomes captivated by the Pankhursts but, eventually, grows resentful of the violence which the aristocratic leaders felt was essential to secure votes for women.

Sandra was leaving the acting company as well as Rod. She has kept in touch with us over the years and continues to tour regularly with companies like Forest Forge and Alive and Kicking. Our newcomers were Vashti Mclachlan and Edmund Harcourt. Ed had trained at the Mountview Theatre School and appeared in a national tour of the musical *West Side Story*. Vashti had studied drama at Manchester University and worked with local groups like Red Ladder and Proper Job. She was living in Slaithwaite, the next village down the valley and knew Mikron's work. We also had another part-time administrator, Andrea Walker. Andrea had joined us for a week's work experience from her computer course and had never gone away...I'm glad to say. She took over from Janet Armstrong, when she left in 1997 for the wilds of Scotland (or rather the lowlands), and is still with us today as a vital part of the Mikron team.

The tour began on the Trent & Mersey at Church Lawton on the 22nd May. We had a potential problem with the Company in that, during the rehearsal period, Vashti and Richard had rather taken a shine to each other or, to put it another way, they had fallen madly in love. They were sharing the double cabin on the boat; so we had two couples travelling aboard (Vashti and Richard, Sarah and me) and two single people, or rather two people whose boy/girl-friend was not on the boat. The delicate balance of the Company could have been upset by this arrangement, but it was apparent from the first week of the tour that everyone was mucking in together and, more importantly, they all liked each other a lot.

On the 26th we had our first day off. Richard and Jo went off, leaving the rest of us to move *Tyseley* the twenty miles to the next venue. We stopped the night at Alrewas, where Richard rejoined us. We didn't meet up with Jo until the next day. When we arrived at the Bridge Inn at Branston to find Jo sitting there waiting for us, she had a Hardyesque story to tell. She had gone to see a friend in Birmingham on her day off, but her friend had gone away on holiday. She then tried to phone the mobile on the boat. Without success, as it wasn't operational. She had no idea where we were stopping for the night but decided to try and find us anyway. She had missed the last train to Burton; so she caught a train to Lichfield and thence by bus to Rugeley. The driver kindly diverted off his route to drop her at the Plum Pudding, close to the Armitage Tunnel on the T&M. No-one had seen *Tyseley*, but Jo set off down the towpath in the direction we would have gone. It was now 7.30 in the evening. She walked to Fradley. Again, no-one had seen us pass by (amazing, really, considering we are such a conspicuous craft). She plodded on to the Navigation at Alrewas and decided to call it a day. She had walked seven miles and it was dark, and she was beginning to get scared. The landlady of the pub fixed her up with a local bed and breakfast. What Jo didn't know was that, if she had walked another quarter of a mile, she would have found *Tyseley* round the bend. She even phoned the George & Dragon in the village to see if we were there. We were having a very pleasant drink and meal in the King William, thank you very much.

The next morning, Jo decided to walk on to the venue at Branston, another five miles down the canal. The landlady of the B&B told her she could cut a corner off the canal walk by going along the A38 for a short distance. So, she managed to miss us again. We were having a lie-in and she arrived at the Bridge way ahead of us. She wasn't a very happy bunny when we did finally pull in.

The weather in early June was dreadful. I had never before worn a woolly hat and gloves at this time of the year. We performed outside at the Napton Bridge Inn to one of the bravest audiences I have ever met. How they managed to unfreeze their fingers to applaud remains a mystery. By mid-June, it began to warm up and, by the 22nd, it was warm enough to swim in the Thames at Bablock Hythe. Were we going to get a proper summer?

The Kennet & Avon is a tricky navigation. It is partly river and partly canal and has an immense variety of locks, paddle gear and swing bridges. We usually have an incident or three and this year was no exception. It started at Aldermaston when I couldn't start the engine. I was convinced the starter motor was knackered, until Sarah made the sensible suggestion that there might be a loose wire. There was. At Woolhampton, we hit a bar of silt across the river. It pushed *Tyseley* sideways across the river, with the current pushing us against the bank. Richard managed to scramble ashore but, as fast as he pulled the boat round, the current pushed us back. We scrabbled amongst the paint tins, the anchor and the bags of coal in the forepeak and pulled out a hundred foot line. Eventually, with this rope off the stern and with the pulling power of Richard, Ed and six canoeists, who happened to be firemen, we managed to get off and into the lock. Just as I was going into the lock, Janet, in her own inimitable way, phoned but with good news – Kirklees had given the jazz festival a grant. (We had helped to get the Marsden Jazz Festival going in 1992 and it was now growing apace). While on the phone, the boat banged in the lock and some glasses broke. Stupidly, I then left the back counter to continue with cooking Ed's breakfast, which I had been in the middle of doing an hour before, when we got stuck. It's amazing how often one is about to serve food when disaster strikes. Anyway, in my absence, the tiller-bar caught in the hydraulic tube of the lock. Although we managed to release the boat by dropping the paddles, the rudder-post was quite badly bent. Thank goodness, we were going to Bill Fisher's boatyard in Newbury. We could get it sorted there. Finally, at another lock, Ed and I flooded the foredeck. The gate paddles on some of the locks are lethal. One notch too far and...it's a soaking for the props stored under the deck.

The K&A had another "delight" in store after we returned to the canal from our first half break. Sarah and I spent an absolutely stunning week on, would you believe, a boat holiday, travelling between Aswan and Luxor on the River Nile and visiting all the famous tombs and temples. Our first lunch-time stop on our return to the boat was quite a contrast. May I recommend you all stop and visit the Cunning Man at Burghfield. I recommend it in the same way I would recommend everyone to read *The Sun* occasionally... to see how life is really lived. The Cunning Man is a Harvester, which is a symbol which guarantees that when you go into one of their pubs, you will immediately feel at home. The ambience will be exactly the same as in the last Harvester pub you visited and, as for the food, you are promised the same number of chips and peas on your plate at every establishment. You will marvel at the extravagance of their cheese and ham sandwich, on this occasion served on hard, stale bread with Vitalite, tasteless coleslaw and lattice chips. Shortly after leaving the Cunning Man, you go past a weir which has this intriguing sign: "Danger. Drowning Black Spot. Many People Have Died Here". One is tempted to contemplate how many of those have been suicides after savouring a meal at the Cunning Man.

Apart from Harvesters and their ilk, over the last few years more and more canalside supermarkets have been springing up. They are, of course, very convenient for boaters, but what has tended to happen is that holidaymakers stop to shop and then move on, without sampling the delights of canal towns and villages and without using the local shops, which before had helped to bring prosperity back to these places. I was shocked this year to arrive at Bull's Bridge, the junction where the main line of the Grand Union continues down to Brentford and the Paddington Branch goes off under a little, classic, white canal bridge. The British Waterways Depot had gone, where, in the past, you would have seen much activity with boats being fitted out and repaired. Now there was one small shed left with the sign "Bull's Bridge Wet and Dry Dock". The rest of the site was occupied by a lego-style Tesco, with a car park running alongside the canal. Admittedly, there were lots of bollards tempting boaters to tie up and shop until they drop. But the saddest thing, apart from the canal bridge being diminished by a huge motorway bridge, was a dry-dock which had been retained as part of Tesco. A sign read: "This is a non-working example of a canalside dry-dock. This is not operational."

The weather stayed hot and sunny throughout July. One very humid day, Sarah and I had to travel up to Huddersfield. At the hospital, she was told everything was fine. Sarah was worried, however, by a painful, swollen mosquito bite on her left hand. She had no lymph nodes on that side; so had very little protection against infection. The consultant lanced it for her and prescribed antibiotics.

The weather at the end of July and beginning of August was very hot indeed. Every day, the temperature rose up to the high 80s Fahrenheit, and the evenings were pleasantly warm and an escape from the mosquitoes and horse-flies which had been out in force during the day. The words "Global Warming" were being bandied about; pollution in the cities was diabolical and the advice went out to not drive your car. People were dying of asthma and lack of air-conditioning. Twenty people had drowned, throwing themselves into lakes, rivers and canals to cool off, without realising the dangers.

We were slowly being affected by lock restrictions. For instance, the locks on the South Oxford were only open for an hour a day. We were also being affected by a plague of flies on the boat, which were breeding at about the rate of a million a day. We, eventually, had to fumigate the inside of the boat completely to get rid of them.

In these tropical conditions, we were a motley crew: me dressed in just a pair of baggy, black shorts; Sarah with her black bikini top and rolled up shorts and Greek sandals; Richard, covered by a white tropical hat and sporting striped swimming trunks; Vashti in a blue hat, with a loose shift hanging from her; Ed, hiding from the heat, and Jo looking like an eccentric female pirate.

The heat does funny things to people. The running gag between me and Jo during the tour was that, whenever I was steering and she bought me a cup of tea or a sandwich, I used to say to her: "Come on, Jo, show us your breasts." This had been going on for months but, on August 1st, she brought me a cup of tea, I repeated my usual mantra, she returned to the other end of the boat, dropped her bikini top and showed me her breasts. Albeit a satirical gesture on her part, despite what you may have heard of the acting profession, it's not every day that an artistic director gets to see the breasts of one his company. I put it all down to the heat.

The next shock was arriving in the centre of Birmingham. It was suddenly the new Venice. The sad little canal, which almost apologised for being there as it passed through the city, had been transformed. Brindley Place ("there's my name being used again") was full of canalside pubs, restaurants and *cafés*. It was the first Sunday all-day drinking was legal (August 6th) and the place was heaving. The sun was shining and the canalside seemed stylish and full of life. Birmingham was never going to be the same again.

Most of the boaters we meet on the canals are great. It's very occasionally that we meet someone who is obstinate or rude. Fishermen can be tiresome and I have threatened to throw one or two of them in in my time. We have friends throughout the system, many of them being the landlords of the pubs we have visited. Once in a while, though, we have a bummer like this year with George and Moira at the Boat & Railway, Stoke Works. We had an excellent turn-out on August 9th in the function room of the pub where we had been performing for many years under different landlords. At the end of the evening, I asked for our usual landlord donation, which we had arranged beforehand. George denied any knowledge of having to pay and said we were lucky to get the room free as he usually charged £100. I went and fetched the letter which I had written to Moira in the February confirming the donation. He then proceeded to heap us with abuse. He called us "New Age Hippies", said the audience were the "pleat-skirted brigade", and that he had only taken £30 at the upstairs bar (arrant nonsense). He tried to stuff £35 into my file and told us to "piss off" and take our boat with us. I returned the money to him and said to Moira, "You did agree to pay a donation, didn't you?" She replied, without looking me in the eyes, "I cannot disagree, but I don't remember." We walked out, shocked and in total disbelief at this behaviour.

The heatwave lasted for six weeks and it was again in disbelief that I woke up in the middle of the night on the 23rd August to hear it pouring with rain. Sarah, enterprising as ever, leapt up and ran naked around the boat shutting all the windows including Richard and Vashti's hatch which was wide open. They would have had a very soaked bed; they remained oblivious until told the next morning.

The last few days of the tour took us towards the National Waterways Festival at Chester on the Shroppie. This is where we met our first real water problems. We were about to stop for lunch at Calveley, when we ground to a halt on a long straight and right in the middle of the channel. There appeared to be a bar of mud right across the canal. Sod's Law dictated that no boat appeared for over half-an-hour. Eventually, two private boats arrived and tried to pull us off but, when our rope broke, they just left us. They were able to get through with their shallower-draughted boats. We were finally rescued by three elderly Germans on a Dartline hireboat. Once the language difficulties had been sorted out, they set about the task with a will. With the help of another boat, they pulled us over the mud. They then offered to tow us to the top of Bunbury Locks. We were very grateful to them, as we had been stuck for over three hours. Even more so, after BWB told us on the mobile that there was nothing they could do. All their boats were at Chester. There might be some more water down in a couple of days! So, full marks to the hirers, zero points to the private boats (all bearing IWA stickers).

We plodded steadily on under our own steam, without any major mishaps, into the evening. We tied up for the night at Crow's Nest Bridge, having noticed in the Nicholson's Guide there was a little local pub down the road. When we arrived, exhausted and ravenously hungry, we discovered it had been turned into a Banks' Poacher's Pocket, a horrendous "theme" pub, whose claim to fame was that no-one had ever eaten all the chips they gave per plateful. True, nobody could possibly have eaten the obscene number of chips piled high on the plate, burying any food underneath. Sarah, without ceremony, pushed her chips on to the table in order to get at the sad piece of fish underneath.

Leaving everyone to sleep on, I set off the next morning at 7.30 in order to get to Chester in time for the show. All went well for about an hour-and-a-half, when I arrived at a bridgehole to find a wideboat stuck just the other side. It had been there a day and had held up twenty boats. They had all eventually managed to squeeze past but we had a three foot draught, like the wideboat. We weren't going to fail at this late stage and, with the help of the boat behind and with many strong people pulling on ropes, we inched *Tyseley* through. Slowly, we approached Chester. It was very shallow but we kept going, and arrived in time for our performance – just.

Another tour was over. We opened *A Woman's Place* on the Autumn Tour and it was tremendously well received: "A powerful and emotive piece of theatre... the four-strong company are in fine form as they recreate for us (with tremendous versatility) a maze of colourful characters. Do see it, if you get the chance." (*Huddersfield Examiner*). In September, Sarah and I celebrated our thirtieth wedding anniversary with a trip to Scotland. The tours had been great, the Company superb – all was well with the world...

On Friday December 1st, Sarah and I went to the Huddersfield Infirmary. At a routine examination the week before, Sarah had complained of a pain in her side and in her back. The doctor had sent her for a bone scan. We weren't too worried, since, over the last few days, the pain had gone and Sarah felt confident that it was something muscular. She had had a susceptible neck and spine for several years. But my heart sank when Valerie, the breast cancer counsellor, came into the consulting room with us. The counsellor only comes in when it's bad news. We knew this from our previous experience two-and-a-half years ago.

We were told that the bone scan was positive. There were four "hot spots", two on her ribs and two on her spine. There was a long silence. No-one spoke. We all knew the implications of this news. Finally, the doctor said that he was putting Sarah on a drug which was good at halting the progress of tumours – of stopping them in their tracks. Sarah asked him how long they were effective. He wasn't very forthcoming, but did say the longest he had known anyone survive using the drug was five years, but that was exceptional. Sarah swore vociferously. She cried. She asked questions. She was magnificent. Valerie said nothing. I asked what the side-effects of the drug were. "Ladies get very hungry and put on weight – most of them don't like that." Sarah asked," Will the hot flushes stop?" "Oh, yes." "Whooh, a benefit!" You can only talk for so long. Sarah gave the doctor and Valerie a big hug. The doctor was in tears. Valerie had her Christian beliefs to see her through. She'd better not try any of that on Sarah. "What God? Oh, that cruel bastard. Oh, I see."

We went down to X-ray and Pathology. Everyone was so kind – offering us cups of tea everywhere we went. They must know. And then I drove home in the van in disbelief. It can't be Sarah. Why her? Why is she so unlucky? Why didn't they examine her earlier? Why didn't she or I find the lump earlier? What is the use of chemotherapy and radiotherapy? For what? Questions, questions, so many questions. Sarah said to me, "Oh, my poor love. You poor thing." and "I'll never see my grandchild or how Sam manages in life."

We went and spent the weekend with friends. We told them the news but they didn't seem able to talk about it. On Monday, I worked in the office, organising our 25th tour but my heart was heavy and dull. Mikron seemed very insignificant. A few days later, we both caught colds. Sarah threw hers off in a day. Mine went to my chest and I was coughing badly. Sarah said, "See, I'm so fit... yet, they tell me I'm dying."

We went to see our own consultant. He had been away when we got the news. The blood test and chest X-ray were fine, but he wanted to do a liver and chest scan. Ironically, the mammeograph is fine. Just as well Sarah fought to save her breast. What a bastard it would have been to have been sitting there with only one breast and being told your illness was terminal anyway. We asked him how long Sarah could expect to live. He replied that statistics were pretty useless because they never apply to you. He did admit that the median level was eighteen to twenty-two months. He was very helpful and gave us an hour of his time but we knew we had to do some research, keep asking questions, and saying, "You must not let this woman become another breast cancer statistic."

While waiting to hear the results of the scans, we tried to think about Christmas. We were planning to have it on the boat with Sam. We'd join up with friends on their boats in Middlewich. But Christmas seems a tawdry affair – the shops full of people buying unwanted and unneeded presents for their loved ones, the remorseless churning out of the totally commercialised carols, the dashing, the rushing, the panic. For what? For life, of course. The one thing we are all determined to hold on to. It'll never happen to us. Oh, poor thing, and at Christmas as well.

We got the results. There were signs of secondaries in the liver but it was Sarah's lungs that were more immediately worrying. The consultant thought there were various options. Firstly, do nothing, in which case Sarah would probably only have a few months to live. Not an option. Secondly, the moderate approach: chemotherapy treatment as an outpatient with the minimum effect on leading a normal life and with a 70% chance of some remission. Thirdly, a much more radical approach using a drug called Taxol, which would give a 75% chance of remission but 30% of the patients died of the treatment. This would be done as an in-patient at Leeds and last six weeks. Finally, there was the option of HDC, High Dose Chemotherapy. There was a doctor in London who would decide if Sarah was a suitable case for treatment. The last quoted price was £60,000! Sarah decided she would like to see Dr Perrin in Leeds, who used option three for some treatments. She thanked the doctor and gave him a huge hug. The following day, we went off to *Tyseley* and had a wonderful Christmas, iced in outside the Big Lock at Middlewich. All our friends were marvellously supportive. It was a time of pause for us – a lull before the storm. Sarah said she had never felt happier. I have a feeling of infinite sadness.

26

HOPES AND FEARS

In early January, we went to see Tim Perrin at "Jimmy's" in Leeds. We were with him for nearly one-and-a-half hours and both Sarah and I came out afterwards feeling elated – a strange reaction when one is talking about terminal illness; but we felt here was a man who would do his utmost to prolong your life and to maintain the quality of your life, who was concerned and interested in extending the range of treatments, and who had an open mind as to how effective new treatments could be. At the end of our time with him, we felt that we more clearly understood the options available to Sarah. He told us to go away and think about it. In the meantime, he would look at all Sarah's scans and confirm or not Huddersfield's analysis.

After more scans, we went back to "Jimmy's" in early February. Perrin told us that the scans had revealed that there were, in fact, no cancerous cells in Sarah's lungs. But that piece of good news was soon overshadowed by the liver scan results – there were a number of metastases (rogue cells) scattered throughout all segments of the liver with the biggest being 2.5 centimetres wide. After further discussion, we told Perrin that Sarah was going to go for the option of having an induction course of conventional chemotherapy followed by the high dose treatment, if all went well. We both now knew that this year was going to be very hard. Our wonderful day was summed up by three road incidents on the way home: a driver pulled out in front of me when I was going eighty miles an hour on the M62; we skated on black ice on one of the back roads; and I had to do an emergency stop on the Manchester Road to avoid a sheep.

At the beginning of March, Sarah's treatment began. From now on, our year was to be punctuated by visits to hospitals for blood tests, scans and the injection of various lethal cocktails into Sarah's body. We tried to live as normal a life as possible. It was going to be Mikron's 25th Waterways Tour and that involved a revival of one our most popular shows *Still Carrying*, in repertoire with *A Woman's Place*, and we were planning an extra special Friends of Mikron do to celebrate this anniversary.

The year would have been even more difficult to cope with if we had had to recruit new Company members. But Ed, Vashti, Jo and Richard had all decided to stay on. Richard was also going to take over from me as tour supervisor, which meant that he would be responsible for the day-to-day running of the tour, leaving me free to come and go with Sarah. This would be the first time that the same Company had stayed together for two seasons and it couldn't have happened at a better time.

Just before rehearsals started at the beginning of April, Sarah and I decided to have a few days away in Shropshire. On the day of departure, we were, as often happened, delayed at the hospital while they took blood and replenished the bag of chemicals. We managed to get away in the early afternoon and all went until we arrived at the Wenlock Edge Inn. Sarah began to feel very troubled. She had severe neck and arm ache, which, by the morning, had become almost unbearable. I phoned the hospital and they advised us to return as soon as possible. But, before we left, an amazing incident took place. The family who ran the pub were Christians and the son, Stephen, claimed to have healing powers. So, I watched as Stephen knelt behind Sarah and waved his hands over and around her to release his "healing energy". His mum and sister stood behind him praying. After half- an-hour, we were given breakfast. I would like to be able to record here that Sarah leapt up from the chair completely free of pain but, alas, the pain was, if anything, worse. But it hadn't harmed her and they were very genuine and kind people. Apparently, Stephen had had many successes in healing.

On the first sunny day for weeks, we drove away from Wenlock Edge without ever seeing it. Back in Huddersfield, Sarah was kept in overnight. They were not certain what was causing the pain; it could be the Hickman Line which was inserted in her or the chemicals themselves. After a couple of days of painkillers, X-rays, an ECG and oxygen and blood tests, Sarah came home. She was feeling much better. She was obviously feeling livelier, as she was complaining about how much she was being messed about. She had never been ill with the cancer, only from the treatments. She wanted to get on with her life without the disease and the treatment becoming an obsession. That was the tricky bit.

On April 10th, we went to the hospital to get the result of the recent scan. This was vital. There had to be some sign of reduction in the size of the cancer cells, or Sarah would not be allowed to continue with the same chemotherapy regime, and her route to the High Dose treatment might be barred. We had, obviously, talked about this and the consequences but, on the way to the hospital, we were both too nervous to talk. Unusually, it was not raining – it was drizzling instead. The Breast Ward seemed overburdened. There were patients waiting to leave beds, patients waiting for beds and patients waiting for chemo treatment. The day room was packed and muggy. After about an hour's waiting, a woman started screaming – her husband had collapsed. We were all ushered out of the room and, within seconds, a'"crash team" had arrived and were working on him. They pulled him round, but he then lay on the day room floor for an hour or so while the hospital tried to find him a bed! People were feeling faint, shocked and sick as a result of this incident. For us, the tension of waiting was almost unbearable.

Eventually, just before 1pm (we had arrived at 9.30), we were taken into a side room and told by a junior doctor that there had been no real improvement. Some lesions had healed but there had been more spread. We were both dumbstruck. We knew this could be the outcome. We knew the statistics said that there was only a 50% chance of some success, but I think we both thought that Sarah was due a little bit of luck and she could be one of the 50%. It was not to be. We went home and sat in almost silent, mutual compatibility, neither of us being able to accept that Sarah could die sooner than even our worse fears had anticipated. We must be able to do something. Today, unusually, we are able to complete the main *Guardian* crossword – Rufus No 20,623. Time passes.

A few days later, we met with Dr Joffe, who was looking after Sarah. We suggested (yes us, not him; we'd been doing our research) a new drug, Taxol, from the yew tree. He agreed that was a possibility but wasn't sure the hospital could afford it! What has the government done to us? Later, we discovered that there was a random trial of Taxol commencing at the hospital soon, which Sarah might be eligible for.

While we waited to hear further about this, we tried to get on with life – shopping, going to the cinema, eating out and meeting friends. For a few hours, one can almost forget it's happening; then all the problems flood back in great waves and you are overcome by a feeling of utmost depression.

The Company arriving for the start of rehearsals was a great help. It was wonderful to be with younger people who were our friends and very supportive. A week later, we heard that Sarah would be allowed on the random trial. This would be paid for by the American drug company, Baker Norton, who were trying to get the NHS to buy their drug, Paclitaxol, distilled from the American yew tree. Three hundred women would be on trial across Europe and Australia, but Sarah would be the only person from Huddersfield. If the first treatment was successful, Sarah would be able to have further treatments and, if these were successful, she would be eligible for High Dose Chemotherapy. The harsh reality is that there is only a 25% chance of some remission. Sarah has no hesitation in going for it. It's a slim chance, but it's a chance. And it's an American drug company offering her the chance, and not the NHS.

While we waited for the trial to begin, I finished directing the two shows, the first night of *Still Carrying* went well at the Mechanics, and we all moved on to *Tyseley* to start the Waterways Tour. Thus began the to-ing and fro-ing between the boat and Marsden which was to be the pattern for the whole tour. My view of this tour is completely affected by this, and Richard would have a different tale to tell if he were writing this book. But I do know that the tour went well and was hugely enjoyed by the Company, who were used to each other and worked so well together. Richard coped brilliantly with his new role of tour supervisor.

It was only three days into the tour before we had our first incident. We were all up at 7.30 for our trip through Harecastle Tunnel at the start of a long day's run to Denford on the Caldon Canal. Probably because we had only run the engine for an hour-and-a-half the day before, and probably because everyone had had a shower, we had no power in the battery to start the engine. (We've learnt our lesson and now have a separate battery for this purpose). The bulb had also gone in the headlight and we had no spare. Richard went to the other boats tied up to see whether anyone had jump leads or, alternatively, would tow us through the tunnel. They hadn't and they wouldn't. The tunnel-keeper went off to borrow his mate's jump leads, Richard went off to fetch our van (which, fortunately was still not far away) and Ed went off...just to find help. He found the local vicarage and returned with the vicar's wife, complete with jump leads. The vicar's wife was such an archetypically vicar's wife that I was convinced she was being played by an actress from the local am-dram. The tunnel-keeper also returned with jump leads and, with the aid of our van's engine, we started up *Tyseley*. Meanwhile, Ed had rigged up a temporary headlight using one of the lamps from the show and a twelve volt plug. As a precaution, I rang Mike Carter, our boat supervisor, to check if that was okay: "No way. You'll blow the whole system." So, I steered through Harecastle, a distance of 2897 yards, with the aid of a torch! Later, we discovered a spare bulb in the engine room.

The weather was extremely wet and cold as we proceeded up the Caldon Canal. The wonderful Ethel had left the Black Lion at Consall Forge and, although the pub had not yet been ruined, changes had been made. There were outside lights and signs with friendly notices ("No Dogs", "No Dirty Boots"). This is a pub in the middle of wonderful walking country.

The Red Lion at Cheddleton was even more worrying. The landlady maintained she wasn't expecting us, even though we had sent her a confirmation letter and posters and leaflets. Although it was very cold, it looked as if we would have to perform outside, as there was a function booked in the main room. A while later, the landlady informed us that we could have the room at 7.20 as the function would be over. A while later, she returned to tell us that she had moved the function downstairs and that we could have the room whenever we liked. We never saw anyone come to this "function". Obviously, we had a very small audience that night. When we asked the landlady if we could have a drink after time (not an unusual occurrence), she said she couldn't as the police were very hot in the area. As we left, we looked through the window of the other bar, to see all the locals settling down for more drinks and a Chinese takeaway. Strange place, Cheddleton.

A few days later, the others had a day off and Sarah and I took the boat to the Lime Kilns on the Ashby Canal. Apart from one dip in the canal for me to retrieve a whole traffic island cone (complete with "Keep Left" sign) which had jammed in our prop, it was a pleasant day with just the two of us. Well, that's what I thought. Sarah said I had been difficult and we had not worked together very efficiently. She wondered whether I was finding everything – Mikron, her – too much. I thought I was coping well. Maybe I was deceiving myself.

We emerged from the coldest May since 1740 into the relative warmth of early June. The day before we were to drive up to Huddersfield for more treatment, I slipped getting off the back counter of *Tyseley*. Only my right foot went in the water but, when I stood up, I saw blood seeping out of my trousers. The trousers were untorn, but I had caught my knee on the rough concrete piling and the blood was pouring from a three-inch cut. Dave, the landlord of the Great Western Arms at Aynho, kindly drove Sarah and me to Banbury Hospital. I hoped it wasn't too serious as I had to get Sarah to Huddersfield. Chaos reigned in Casualty. There were queues of people – broken limbs, heart attacks, nose bleeds – and I had to wait two-and-a-half hours, with my leg still bleeding, to be seen. Eight stitches later and I was back on the boat. The next morning my leg was very sore, but I was able to drive.

Sarah was determined to make the most of the times when she was not at the hospital having treatment. Despite problems all the time with blood counts, aching muscles and bruised veins, Sarah was still physically fit and we were able to boat and also to take extra holidays. We spent a few glorious days in early July in a tiny caravan perched on the hills overlooking Harlech Castle. We returned knowing that we were about to find out if the treatment had worked. The latest scan would reveal the truth. We were supposed to be told on the morning of July 9th, but they had various crises on in the hospital. They would try to let us know in the afternoon.

We went back to the boat for the start of the second half of the tour. We boated down the "Maffers" Flight on the Grand Union. I had never felt so tense in my life. It wasn't until late in the afternoon that the hospital rang. The scan showed that the liver was stable. Sarah would be allowed to continue with the trial. What relief! It wasn't a lot. There had been no reduction, but it did mean there was still hope. In nine weeks time, we would have to go through all this again. The next stage of treatment would begin immediately.

The second half of the tour happened and all went well, but my life seemed to be more connected to hospitals and scans and tests and drugs. Sarah and I got away from all the angst in late July and spent a week going to the opera in Verona and visiting the wonderful villas and gardens on Lake Como. After the tour was over, we spent a week with our son, Sam and friend, Josh, boating on the Canal du Nivernais. We forgot about Mikron and cancer, and just enjoyed the relaxation of being on a canal and not having to reach a venue at a particular time on a particular day. Just as well, because a few days after we were back, and the day before Sarah's fifty-third birthday, we were to get the results of the latest scan.

On the morning of September 16th, we both woke up with the knowledge that, if the results weren't good, Sarah would be off the trial and what then? We didn't talk much but we were both making our own lists – is HDC at all a possibility; what about the new forms of cancer treatment, which include sponges and maggots? There has to be something, especially when Sarah is feeling so well. After another agonising wait, we were told by a passing nurse that all must be well as she had been asked to order the next batch of chemo. When we got to see the doctor, we were shaking with relief. He said that the scan showed that the lesions had definitely lessened, not just stabilised – lessened. What a magnificent birthday present for Sarah.

Next day, the sun slowly came out as we lay in bed drinking champagne and eating nectarines and Marmite butties. Happy Birthday. When we returned from the hospital, we were inundated with flowers. Sarah was back to her normal acerbic form: "Why can't people be more imaginative – a plant, anything, but not another bunch of flowers, grown and picked by underpaid women in Columbia. People are so kind but..."

The day after, we heard that there had also been a reduction in the number of tumours in the bone. This was a great week in our lives, rounded off on the Saturday with Mikron's 25th Anniversary Party. One hundred and forty people turned up at the Mechanics, including former Company members – Richard and Thirzie Robinson, Alan Bridger, Anna Bentinck, Caron Pascoe, Sue Dyde, Juliet Heacock, Cliff Barry and John and Janet Spooner. A group of us cooked food for everyone. The courses just went on and on: *paté*, chicken, cheese, *tarte tatin* and savoury sausages, made by our local butcher and served at 11pm. Two bands played, we rock 'n' rolled, and Sarah and I both made emotional speeches. Sarah urged all the women to check their breasts regularly. It was vital.

Life seemed good. Sarah continued having the treatments, we went to France for a week, and we helped to organise another successful jazz festival. We also heard that our application for an Arts Council Lottery Grant had been successful; we were to receive £26,000 to buy a new van and computer and office equipment. The Autumn Tour finished. Sadly, Sarah missed the last night at the Mechanics – a staggering night, with an audience of over two hundred giving the Company a rapturous reception. She had contracted an infection and was advised to stay away from crowds.

Ironically, Sarah's ebullient mood and resilience began to change at about the same time as *Waterways World* printed a lovely article by Dennis Needham in his "Waterway of Life" series. He interviewed us while we were performing at Milton Keynes earlier in the year. He concluded his article thus: "Those meeting her for the first time can scarcely credit that she is so stricken. Her hair is growing again, the mischievous grin is still in place and the occasional volley of invective as strong and pointed as ever... 'I've always been a bolshie bastard, now I've got a bolshie cancer as well. They expect me to say I've got aches and pain in my ribs, but I haven't. Good, I'm not giving up my steering.' So life goes on for this happily married couple... Our conversation dwindled to generalisations and warm reminiscences. By coincidence, the show that had been taking place a few yards away drew to a close amid tumultuous applause. The couple looked at each other and grinned. True showpeople, there is no greater reward for Mike and Sarah Lucas than a satisfied audience. Another successful performance played canalside to an audience who arrived on foot, bicycle and boat, bringing picnic suppers. OK, so there was no champagne, but for honesty of production, Move Over Glyndbourne."

Sarah had been fine physically, but she had become very low in morale. She knew she had the next scan hanging over her and nothing seemed to cheer her. She was not connecting with anything or anybody – even me.

On Friday November 15th, we were told the result of the scans. All of the 50% reduction that was achieved by the earlier treatment had disappeared over the last nine weeks. The liver scan showed that there were as many, if not more, tumours than in January. In other words, we were back to square one. Sarah would be taken off the trial, another failure for the statistics.

There was the usual stunned silence. We hadn't expected this, or I hadn't, at least. We thought that the rate of reduction might have slowed down, not that those bastard cancer cells had found a way to defeat the drug and come back even more virulently than before. Helplessness, numbness. No feelings. Feelings would be too difficult at this stage. We recovered sufficiently to ask the doctor how long it would be before Sarah started having symptoms. He was very cagey, saying it could be weeks, it could be months. We are both staggered by the possibility of "weeks".

We went home. We ate. We watched television. We watched a whole evening of television without noticing anything that was on. We went to bed. Mercifully, we both managed to sleep.

November passed. We managed to get through a very difficult Mikron annual general meeting discussing the plans for Mikron's future. Sarah was low-key but she spoke during the meeting, knowing full well that this was her last AGM. We began to notice how much of daily conversation is about planning and anticipating the future.

By early December, Sarah had uncomfortable symptoms in her stomach and pains in her back and neck. She had acupuncture but, when we went for Sarah's next appointment at the hospital, the doctor told her that her liver was enlarging. We had a short discussion about possible other treatments but there was very little to cheer us or give us hope. A terrible feeling of hopelessness pervaded us. What should we be doing for the best? We had been trying to live normal lives but that was gradually getting more and more difficult. We nevertheless decided that we would spend Christmas on *Tyseley* with Sam at the usual gathering of boats.

For the first few days on the boat, Sarah coped well. Although her stomach and back were bothering her a lot, she still managed to lockwheel. The weather was wonderful – sunny all day long but bitingly cold with a raw wind. There were heavy frosts at night and ice on the cut in the mornings. I steered the boat, sometimes for seven hours at a stretch. I felt happy that we were together on *Tyseley* for Christmas and that Sam was joining us, but I could not stop thoughts racing around my head. One moment, I'd recall moments of happiness we had had together; the next, I was simply overcome by sheer fear, panic and desperation.

Christmas Day and Boxing day were spent tied up at Gnosall on the Shroppie. Sarah ate little and was too uncomfortable to sleep properly or really enjoy the presence of her son. She was now saying quite often, "I wish this was all over. There seems no point." She seemed to be losing the will to live. I kept thinking that, if only she could get some relief from her pain and discomfort, she might be able to be more positive and connected. In the pub, Sam told me that he was able to bear the thought of his mother's death only because he expected to outlive his parents and because, unlike many of his friends, his parents were still together and had given him a great upbringing, allowing him to talk to us as friends as well as his mum and dad and to be completely open about his life and lifestyle.

One of our friends on another boat gave Sarah some sleeping tablets and she slept soundly for the first time for many days. We continued to boat, with Sam and me taking turns at locking and steering. The ice was getting thicker and, by the time we had made it to Stone for New Year's Eve, it was snowing heavily as well, and it was becoming apparent that the sensible course of action would be to leave the boat and go back to Marsden.

New Year's Eve! Now, that was an ordeal. We joined the others for the celebrations in the Rising Sun. It was very painful. Sarah sat and cuddled the five-month-old son of one of our friends, but I could only remember the scene just a year ago. Sarah had been told she had secondary cancer, but the treatment was all ahead of her. She was vibrant and happy. Now she was forlorn. The moment of New Year itself was desolate. We were offered champagne and best wishes. Everyone was very supportive, but all Sarah and I could share was despair. We left as soon as we could and, two days later, we went back to Marsden. Sarah was leaving *Tyseley* for the last time.

27

ANOTHER YEAR

We managed to make two more trips in early January, one to a friend's fortieth birthday party in London, and one to my Dad's eighty-third birthday (Sarah: "I envy him"). We even managed a few more games in the local pub quiz league, but most of the time Sarah was in pain. I still could not accept that Sarah was dying, although I saw that she was losing weight and looking grievously ill. It had all been very sudden. One minute she was fine, declaring war on the world and his wife, now she was hardly able to hold a conversation, she was in such discomfort. I made an effort at diversion with work, shopping, cooking and washing, but I was not really able to fool myself.

The latest scan showed that the liver had worsened a little. For the first time, Dr Joffe prescribed morphine in case Sarah needed it. We had a long session with Rosaleen, a Macmillan nurse. Sarah talked about how she felt and about how we had dealt with cancer over the last three years. She explained how she was not afraid of death – she had had a good life – but the long process of dying, of gradual deterioration and increased pain.

Over the next couple of weeks, Sarah was on an increasing amount of medication of all types and she seemed to improve a little and take a little more interest in the outside world. Over the weekend of January 18th and 19th, we even went for a walk together along our beloved Huddersfield Narrow. We had drinks, laughs and nostalgic chats with friends. Later our doctor, Dr Deacon, told me that Sarah had made one last supreme effort that weekend. It would have totally exhausted her. A week later she was dead.

Death for some, apparently, comes easy. Not for Sarah. Hers was a hard, ugly death. But I was with her all the time, and she died at home. Black humour has a habit of creeping in even in the most desolate of times. So it was on this Sunday morning. The nurses who had come to see Sarah were also attending a sick person across the road. No sooner had I got them to come and look at Sarah, Sarah died and there was a knock on the door downstairs. "Would the nurses come – my father's just died." "So has my wife." It was 10.15am and the sun was pouring into the bedroom. I shouted. It was sadness for her, anger on her behalf, and self-pity. She had left me behind.

Friends soon started arriving and we stood in the garden in the winter sunshine, drinking wine and beer, talking about Sarah and hugging each other. Over the next few days, Sam and I were kept very busy making arrangements, and crying over the wonderful words hundreds of people had sent us in letters and cards. Sarah had, many months before, told me exactly where she wanted her funeral and, although we hadn't spoken about it recently, I knew what had to be done.

On Friday January 31st, the weather was dry and still and, as the morning progressed, the sun came out and Marsden looked beautiful. By noon, over seventy of our special friends were standing outside our house. We progressed through the village, helped across the Manchester Road by the lollipop lady, and up on to the hillside. For some it was an easy stroll, but for others it was a big effort ("Make the bastards walk," Sarah had said). The line of people snaked out across the hill. They were not quiet and funereal but talking, looking and listening. We approached the three trees which stand looking down over Marsden. Sarah's and my favourite spot. As everyone gathered beneath the trees, they suddenly formed a small, intimate, cohesive group at one with the surroundings which were calm, tranquil and welcoming. The three trees, which from a distance look so small and vulnerable, bending from the force of the wind, here looked solid and forceful. It was a haven. It was where we scattered Sarah's ashes. A few words were said by myself, Sam and friends. There was no religion. It was short but stunningly moving. Afterwards everyone lingered, not wanting to rush away from such a place. Someone put some of Sarah's ashes on her face, someone planted daffodil bulbs, children scattered seeds.

Obituaries for Sarah appeared in the *Guardian*, the *Yorkshire Post*, the waterways press and in our local papers. In one of them, Richard Povall was quoted. He said of Sarah: "She never made a secret of her cancer. She railed against the disease and selflessly urged other women to screen themselves... I will always remember her attitude to children. She obviously felt an enormous responsibility towards them – guiding, coaxing and attempting to inspire them. She never seemed to think of them as equals, never talking them down. She would not take anything for granted and I would often see her taking the time to explain things to people carefully. This is not to say she treated everyone the same – small-minded bigots got short shrift and any hint of sexism would meet a wave of abuse. In these situations she did not temper her language!... It would not be an exaggeration to say that every day I measure my own actions against what she would have done and hear her commonsense informing me. In this sense she will always be there."

So it was with me. She was still with me. For anyone who has not suffered it, it is very difficult to describe bereavement. Every day, for weeks, months afterwards, I would be feeling fine and then I would be suddenly stopped dead in my tracks. It could be anywhere, walking along a road, standing cooking. It was like being kicked in the stomach. I would groan out loud. Sarah was dead. I was living on my own for the first time in my life. My memories of her, which were many and profound, were all I had left. No-one to hug, no-one to cuddle, no-one to talk intimately to. It was a totally new experience. People would stop me in the street and ask if I was getting over it. You never get over the loss. You learn to live with it.

Thank goodness for Richard. He had taken over from me the responsibility of organising the Waterways Tour. This took a considerable strain off me and I was able to concentrate on planning the productions. We had also been joined the previous year by Shelly Frape, who had taken over the job of fundraising and grant applications. Shelly's husband had died from cancer only a year or so before. Her advice and support were invaluable.

Sarah had asked that we should have a celebration of her life at the Mechanics. I organised this for March. It was an incredibly moving day. Over 120 people came to Marsden just because of Sarah, because they loved and respected her and missed her deeply. I think we all expected her to turn up to drink, dance and laugh with us all. 120 people from all over the country – from her school and university days, from her early work days, from Mikron and Marsden. They came to celebrate her life. There was joy and sadness, much laughter and reminiscence. There were many highlights: I played ten of Sarah's and my favourite records; I read out poems from people who couldn't be there; Jim and Janet had written a song about Sarah (everyone wept openly at this); people spoke about Sarah or read out poems they had written about her; and Sam read his favourite children's story for her and spoke eloquently about his mother. There was a beautiful 24-foot long frieze of photos of Sarah's life, integrated with all the words spoken on the day the ashes were scattered. More and more photos were added as the day progressed. Then there was Jeff Button's crazy idea – to blow up a picture of Sarah, cut it up into 49 sections and to give these to different people to draw with crayons. The result: a magnificent six foot by four foot picture of Sarah, which captured her perfectly. Then there was the "faith food" – everyone was asked to bring a dish. It could be savoury or sweet, hot or cold. What a spread. What choice. Then there was the money raised for the Huddersfield Breast Clinic. In all, £2,500 was raised by friends – £500 just on this one day.

Life, of course, had to go on. Kirklees Cultural Services chose this year, when our co-founder had died, to defer a decision about our grant, a vital part of our income, even though it was only £6,800. One of the officers was concerned that "the quality, quantity and subject matter of Mikron's output had been falling over recent years." We found this decision staggering, considering that most people – audiences and press alike – felt our work was getting better and better. We appealed and had a meeting with the Head of Cultural Services, who apologised unreservedly for these remarks and said the officer should not have issued such a press release. She was then quoted as saying: "We are very pleased to give Mikron a grant to help them carry on taking live theatre to a wide range of venues." Very strange!

We were delighted to receive a Guinness Pub Theatre Award of £2,000, and raised a glass of the black stuff to toast our success. We also received a bequest from the will of Charles Hadfield, the doyen of waterways writers, who had been our patron until his death in 1996.

Our new production this year was to be something very different. Alan Bridger, who was now on our Council of Management, came from Newbury and his sisters and mum still lived there. They reported back to him that he ought to go and look at what was happening down there. Hundreds of people were occupying the trees along the route of the proposed Newbury bypass. Alan, initially, went down as an observer, but discovered that the protestors were being very badly represented, if at all, when they were arrested. So he stayed on and, when the evictions began in earnest under the leadership of Nicholas Blandy, the Under-Sheriff of Berkshire, he worked for many weeks as a defence solicitor.

Alan returned to Yorkshire full of praise for the commitment, resourcefulness and adaptability of the protestors, and suggested that the whole subject might make a brilliant Mikron show. So, in the spring of 1997, Rod Matthew and I went down to Newbury to see for ourselves. By this time, most of the camps had been evicted – there were just a few left. We spoke to protestors, security guards, the police, the sheriff himself and to the local citizens, who were split almost 50/50 in favour of the bypass and against. We also went to see the new camps being erected at the Manchester Airport second runway protest. We watched tree-houses and tunnels being built and, yes, we did speak to Swampy, the most famous of the new breed of campaigners. We heard that they were being supported by many local people – a baker delivered to the site every day and a mobile chip shop went once a week. Both Rod and I were swept along with the feeling. I went and sat among the trees, and thought that everyone ought to visit such camps to see for themselves how much of our countryside was being destroyed in the name of progress.

It was impossible, having done the research, to remain impartial, but we tried to represent all viewpoints in the new show, which was called *If You Go Down to the Woods...tales from the Newbury bypass*. Jim wrote some brilliant songs, Janet Armstrong designed an evocative backdrop and the show opened at the Marsden Mechanics on Friday June 13th.

We needn't have worried. The show went a storm. The *Colne Valley Chronicle* said: "The play's sympathies are always with the protestors, but it never crosses the line between partiality and propaganda. Its honesty was its best feature but humour was present in abundance." The *Oxford Mail* said: "You cannot fail to admire the even-handed approach of Mikron's new play about the shameful events in Newbury last winter... A first class show. Don't miss it." Some of the Manchester Airport protestors came to the show, including Merrick, a wonderful, saint of a man, who had been at Newbury, and whose book about his experiences, *Battle for the Trees*, had been such an inspiration to us when we were writing our show. They loved it and were surprised that Rod and I hadn't been there at the evictions. We had captured the atmosphere so well – the humour and the fear. Merrick was quoted as saying: "We all still find it hard to talk about Newbury, because the memory's so fresh. It's great that the story of Newbury is going to be told in a truthful way."

So the Newbury show joined a revival of *Just the Job* as the two productions of 1997. The Waterways Tour began at Aynho on the South Oxford Canal. I had moved *Tyseley* down there, from her winter base at Sandbach on the T&M, with a little help from friends but mainly by myself. Single boating a craft as large as *Tyseley* can be quite daunting, but it can be very satisfying as well, working out the best methods of going up and down locks and being prepared to work carefully and steadily, waiting, for instance, at a liftbridge until another boat arrives, if you cannot raise it on your own.

Richard, Vashti and Ed were still with us. We were very sorry to lose Jo, who is such a talented actor. She still lives in Marsden with her (now) husband, Ian, and their (now) daughter, Libby. She keeps very much in touch with the Company.

The other three were joined by Janet George, who was back with the Company after her stint with us in 1991. It was very strange climbing on to the boat in Aynho without Sarah being there. She was always the organiser on these occasions. This year, we had to work out where the curtains and cushions went and where everything, including all the props and costumes, was best stored. For a lot of the tour, I left Richard in charge. I visited occasionally to check out the shows, give notes, get a feel of the Company morale and to have a bit of a boat. I missed the steering and lockwheeling and the camaraderie. Richard coped admirably with the day-to-day problems of running a canal touring company, including floods on the Rivers Soar and Trent in July.

Sarah and I had always intended to do less touring after the 25th year. One of the projects we were planning to do together was to write a book about our years with Mikron. This I now decided to do on my own, and I made a start in late June. It wasn't easy as, of course, I was constantly being reminded of Sarah and our life together. I missed her deeply. I missed her friendship, her sexuality, her practicality and her sheer bolshieness, which she used to show towards me as often as the world outside.

The summer passed. At the end of August, we gave our last performance of the Waterways Tour at the Waterside Centre in Newbury. Many protestors and locals came to see the show and gave us a standing ovation at the end. The following morning (August 31st), the others all left early to go on their three-week break. They left me a cryptic note: "Switch on the radio. Shocking news." It certainly was. Princess Diana and Dodi Fayed had been killed in a car crash in a Paris underpass. This sensation was to dominate the news and, apparently, the thoughts of the nation right up to her funeral on September 6th. On that day, I had the bizarre experience of driving through the empty roads of rural France on my way to Saumur, listening to the commentary on Radio 4. The sound of the horses, of people sobbing, of Diana's brother's remarkable oration, all came over with a dramatic starkness on radio. I stopped for some diesel, and the woman who served me (they still do in France) asked me why I was in France and not at the funeral!

The Autumn Tour came and went. Mikron had had a good year. 1997 was almost over.

28

A NEW STAGE

In the afternoon of January 26th 1998, I walked up to the three trees. It was the anniversary of Sarah's death. Despite the cold, it was still on the hills, just as it had been the day we scattered the ashes. In a strange way, it was peaceful and reassuring. I always feel calm when I go up there. Appropriately, it was quiz night (Sarah was our best player). We were soon twenty points behind. I knew the whole team wanted to win for Sarah, although it was never mentioned. Miraculously, we pulled back the points and stormed to victory. 1998 was going to be a good year.

Reality struck the next day, when, at a meeting with the Yorkshire & Humberside Arts Board, we were informed that our funding was going to be withdrawn. There were question marks about our "sustainability" and even, apparently, "the quality of our work". The arts body could not afford to give us extra funding and did not feel we could manage with a stand-still grant. This decision was made with the knowledge that, at the end of the 1998 season, Mikron would be compelled to close down and without the knowledge perhaps that, with it, would go all our "additional" work – the exhibitions, music and theatre at the Mechanics, the Mikron Youth & Community Theatre and the Marsden Jazz Festival.

Praise be to the FAX! We contacted people who we knew would be horrified by this decision and would certainly question the doubts about our "sustainability" and "quality". Faxes poured into the Yorkshire & Humberside Arts office from our MP, our Council of Management, British Waterways, patrons and local representatives and, thankfully, the decision of the officers was reversed at the board meeting. Once more, we lived to fight another day. The response from our supporters had been tremendous. Just to quote from one fax: "What!! No Mikron! I don't believe it!! They can survive on standstill, if that's the best you can do. Twenty six years of creativity, service and commitment. New work, creating new audiences and, as is sadly not always the case with some companies, bringing some fun into our lives. Please reconsider." Obviously, more work had to be done to convince the arts boards and local authorities that we deserved a good deal more funding than we were currently receiving.

Another, although not unexpected, disappointment was the failure of the Arts For Everyone Lottery bid for our *Traveller's Fare Project* – a three-year plan to produce a series of shows looking at the arrival of a new century, the future of transport and the environmental consequences. It was a good bid, but only 10% of those applying were successful. We had also been turned down the previous year by the Arts Council for a project grant towards our Newbury show. The reason given was bizarre: they could not envisage how a company of four could portray an event which involved such large numbers. Had they never seen a Mikron show? As one newspaper said of the production: "It is hard to believe four actors could produce such a multitude of characters. Rarely have I seen a production dealing with contemporary issues performed with such fierce commitment."

Thus, sponsorship remained vital to our survival. We created a new level of sponsorship – Mikron into the Millennium. A person or organisation could become a Millennium Sponsor by pledging a minimum donation of £250 per year for at least three years. We had an excellent response. We also had two business sponsors for this year – CWA Creative Communications of Leicester and Tynemill Ltd. As a result of their sponsorship, we received £1,000 from the Pairing Scheme of the Association for Business Sponsorship of the Arts.

Despite all this, we were still under severe economic constraints. We couldn't afford to research and write a new show but were delighted to revive *Imogen's War*, which had been such a success in 1992 and 1993. This would be seen in repertoire with the Newbury show. Ed and Janet were not returning (not that we'd seen the end of Ed, thank goodness). So, Richard and Vashti were joined by Charley Moon and Liz Eves. We also welcomed Annie Dearman and Michael Camden as our costumes, set and props team.

The April showers arrived in large bucketfuls. The rivers and canals joined and merged with the countryside. It all happened very fast and, when the waters finally began to subside, many boats were left high and dry in fields and up trees, stuck on the towpath or completely sunk. *Tyseley* stayed steadfastly afloat and we were able to reach moorings on the River Soar in readiness for our first performance of the season at Loughborough.

But, by the time we went down to join the boat in June, the rain returned. We were only able to make it to the flood gates at Zouch. The river was impassable, and Liz and Charley had the indignity of doing their first canal gig by road. We were able to get moving the next day and had an exciting, fast run down the Soar and Trent to Nottingham. It started to rain heavily as Nottingham Castle came into view and continued to rain for several days. Audience turnouts were poor, probably due to the weather and the dreaded World Cup. It was not what we needed, when we were trying to boost our finances.

I'D GO BACK TOMORROW

The weather did improve, the World Cup ended, and audiences began to appear from out of the woodwork. The Company worked well together and I visited them every so often. But my life was changing. I had begun to emerge from bereavement slowly, as time passed. Gradually, I had begun to take stock of my life. One thing I decided I was not very good at was being on my own. I had managed over the last year or so; in fact, had become used to my own company and deciding when I wanted to do something without consultations with other parties. But I knew it wasn't really me. Sarah used to say that, when she died, there would be women flocking around me from all directions. Very kind of her. But I must have kept looking the wrong way, as I was never able to spot these flocks or herds or even a lone predator.

I can recommend to anyone my next course of action. I advertised in a lonely hearts column, actually it was "Soul Mates" in the *Guardian* and the *Observer*. I won't reveal all the details of the experience (it's a book or a play in its own right) – only to say that, although I received many replies to my ad, I only spoke to one person. She had said on her message that she thought she knew who I was. I was immediately curious and rang her. "Yes, you are Mike Lucas of Mikron and I claim my £5." No, it wasn't quite like that but Lynne, for that was her name, knew me from her days at Yorkshire Arts and we had possibly even met, though neither of us remembered if we had.

I liked the sound of her voice, and we immediately discovered that we had many things in common and decided to meet. Lynne and I never stopped talking for days and, I hope she wouldn't disagree with me, we quickly fell in love. Yes, it's possible at any age, you cynics.

We spent the summer seeing each other as often as possible, getting to know each other and Lynne's eleven-year-old son, who was fifteen years younger than Sam and quite a personality in his own right; sometimes in Leeds, where Lynne lived, sometimes in Marsden, and sometimes together on the boat.

Lynne and Chris had their first trip down the Thames tideway, which was even more exciting than usual. As I approached Limehouse Lock, I noticed that the wooden fenders, which were usually in place to help one's entrance into the lock, were missing. There was work being done and, in their place, stood a steel structure with nasty pieces of iron sticking out of it. I tried to avoid it but, as usual, I was pushed against it as I turned into the lock. I thought at first that one of our windows had been broken, but *Tyseley* escaped (or so we thought at the time) with one small scrape on her side and some broken glasses and plates. It was a relief to be on the still water of the Grand Union again.

Six days later, I was back in Marsden, when Richard rang to say the boat was letting in a lot of water. They had woken early to find the boat was listing heavily and there was water in the back bedroom. The bang at Limehouse must have shifted a rivet or split the chine. We urgently needed to find out. The next day, Richard found the leak under the kitchen area. I gave him the "rags and much grease" advice. This did the trick, and they managed like that until the end of the tour.

The return of *Imogen's War* was very popular, helped by a tremendous performance as the eponymous heroine by Liz. She was delightful. One of the most moving performances of the tour I witnessed was at the Anchor at High Offley. A terrific downpour forced us inside at the interval and the second half was performed as a "radio version with facials", with the audience crammed into the tiny bar, the actors sitting in the window seat and me sitting next to them and narrating. The closeness and intimacy of this was stunning. The other performance was at the Marsden Mechanics with Margaret Cornish present. She loved it again, of course, but stood up at the end and made an impromptu speech saying that the all-female crews had never been as frivolous as our play suggested. Sadly, her ex-trainer, Daphne French had died earlier in the year.

In September, Lynne and her son, Chris, moved to Warehouse Hill. The commitment had been made. We intended to live with each other for the rest of our lives and I was to go through an "action replay" of the transition of a boy to teenager to adult. Lynne was now having to commute by train from Marsden to her job at Leeds College of Art & Design. This experience was to come in very handy for my research for one of our transport shows.

In a short time, my circumstances had changed completely. I never thought I would feel this way about a person again, but it had happened and I was grateful. There were not many days when I did not think of Sarah, but now it was not painful thoughts but passing recollections and memories. Thirty-one years would never be wiped out. This was a new stage of my life.

29

REFURBISHMENT

It became obvious, as soon as *Tyseley* was back at her winter base and on dry-dock, that the bottom plate of our 63-year-old boat was so paper-thin in places, the only option was complete replacement. Also, much of the interior of the boat would have to be removed to facilitate the repairs and would probably disintegrate in the process. So we needed to raise money for an extensive refit of the inside cabins as well as for a new bottom. If we were also to renew the original back cabin and engine room, which were rusting badly, we would need to launch an appeal for somewhere in the region of £50,000.

Applications were sent to trusts, and appeals went out to our Friends of Mikron and to the general public. At the time we held our AGM, we were not sure whether we would be able to raise such a large sum. We had to have a minimum of work carried out on *Tyseley*, which we might still have had to pay for out of our ever-decreasing reserves. It was, wisely, decided that in 1999 we would play safe. We would mount one production and reduce the size of our acting company, for the first time, from four to three.

The new show was to be the first of our *Traveller's Fare Project*, in which we would be looking at transport and the environment as we approached the new millennium. In the first part, we had decided to look at the movement of goods in this country, particularly in relation to the gross underuse of the waterways for this purpose. This sounds a very dry subject but, as one barge owner said after the first night of what was eventually called *Just in Time*, "The play wasn't at all how I expected it to be. You managed to portray the barge business in a very positive light, and to dramatise the play so convincingly. The acting was as good as I have seen anywhere and the script was constantly engaging. The waterway navigation situations were delightful, and even the completely uninitiated amongst the audience were enjoying them."

First, the show had to be researched. Rod had joined Dundee Rep on a three-year contract; so, for the first time, Jim Woodland was joining me on research and co-writing the script, as well as the music and lyrics. We had a great two weeks or so travelling on barges on the Aire & Calder. This waterway has been constantly modernised over

180

the years, and still sees sand and oil traffic. Not nearly enough, but how many people know, when they're crossing Leeds Bridge on their way to work and cursing the number of heavy lorries, that a few hundred yards downstream, there are sand barges being unloaded, each one carrying the equivalent of fifteen lorry loads? Already four million tons of freight is carried annually by water. Imagine the reduction in pollution and noise, if more freight were taken off the roads and moved by rail and water.

We also spoke to bargemen, bargeowners and lorry drivers and did our research on the latest statistics. The whole subject had become very topical. The Government had issued a White Paper, *A New Deal for Transport*; lorry drivers were protesting that their livelihoods were at stake because of the rises in diesel prices and road tax; our motorways were grinding to a halt every day; and a government grant had been given towards the cost of reinstating barge-handling facilities at Rothwell, near Leeds, on the Aire & Calder, which would enable 200,000 tons of distillate oil to be moved by water over the next five years, saving over 16,000 lorry trips.

We wrote a show in which, for the first time, the actors only played one role each. It was a tale of three misfits thrown together on a canal barge, battling to find their place in a rapidly-changing world. It had a darker, less comic and more dramatic edge. It certainly reflected my own emergence from bereavement and was described as "thoughtfully-written and thought-provoking". Jim and I were pleased with the piece; many people enjoyed it, some felt it was "untypical" of Mikron.

Charley and Liz went off to ventures new, and Richard and Vashti were joined by Sophie Russell. Sophie was only twenty-four but, since graduating from Middlesex University, had already worked for Box Clever Theatre Company, Tiebreak Touring Theatre and English Teaching Theatre. She was to prove to be a highly-skilled actress with a great sense of comic timing. She also really enjoyed the boating. It was to be particularly arduous this year as, for most of the time, there was only a crew of three. Richard had planned some "good" boating days – for instance, Lapworth to Warwick (42 locks) followed by a performance. Sophie did admit to feeling "quite tired" at the end of that day.

In the meantime, the money was coming in from our appeal. The response had been amazing. The general public contributed over £14,000, with donations from £3 to a £1,000. We had a large anonymous donation and a grant from Yorkshire Forward, the Yorkshire and Humber Regional Development Agency. Later, we were to be awarded a large grant from the Foundation for Sport and the Arts, run by the football pools companies. All this meant that, over a two-year period, we would be able to refurbish *Tyseley* completely and keep her going for another sixty years.

I'D GO BACK TOMORROW

The start of the National Waterways Tour was definitely different. We began, appropriately, with a week of performances on the Aire & Calder, travelling on board the barge *Sobriety*, which is run by the Waterways Museum in Goole. Despite an appearance on BBC's *Look North*, our audiences were sadly small, although many of the men and women involved with commercial carrying on the canal came and loved the show. But it did give the Company the opportunity to see commercial traffic on the move by water, and to steer in the comfort of a wheelhouse, before being exposed to life at the tiller. Richard became so enamoured with the way of life that, in the winter of 1999/2000, he went boating on the River Trent, working for Geoff Wheat on *Selby Linda*. He has some horrifying tales to tell (about the boating, not Geoff!).

We arrived at Dutton, adjacent to the Preston Brook Tunnel, on June 8th to collect *Tyseley* and start the main part of our Waterways Tour. It soon became clear that we were not going to be able to leave that afternoon as planned. There was still a lot of painting, screwing and hammering going on. *Tyseley* was not ready. Also, there was an engine problem; it needed a new fuel pump. It was all very frustrating, but there was nothing to be done. Canal engineers cannot be rushed. Richard, Sophie and Vashti went off by van to their performance in Anderton. Lynne, Chris and I stayed and tried to make some semblance of order of the inside of the boat. When the others returned, we finally opened the bottle of sparkly intended for the celebration of the start of the tour and *Tyseley*'s refurbishment.

The next day a fuel pump was fitted, all the little jobs were finished, and we left by boat in the afternoon for our next venue at Marston. *Tyseley* really did look splendid, and the interior of the boat was a pleasure to live in.

One of the sections of the trip, when I was aboard this year, was new territory for *Tyseley* – from Bristol to Devizes on the Kennet & Avon, a beautiful waterway with the highly impressive Caen Hill Flight of locks.

I was, of course, also there for our usual incident on the Thames tideway. It was six o'clock in the morning on Saturday July 31st when we passed through Teddington Lock. We moved very fast downstream on an ebbing spring tide. As we moved through Richmond, there was a mist hanging over the river, but very soon the sun burnt through and the day became very hot. We travelled under all the famous London bridges and past the ever-changing riverfront, and Big Ben struck 8.30 as we passed the Houses of Parliament. We met no other traffic, not even the usual complement of early morning rowers, except for a fire-tender which circled us, causing *Tyseley* to pitch and toss for a few minutes and frightening poor old Sophie on her first trip.

The approach into Limehouse depends on the state of the tide.

REFURBISHMENT

Today, the lock was ready for us and all seemed well as we turned to cross the river. Richard put his thumb up and I began the final turn into the lock. It was then I realised that, try as hard as I could to push the tiller over, the stern of the boat was being pulled by the strong ebbing tide, and the bow of the boat was heading inexorably towards the concrete buttress which jutted out from the side of the lock. With a glance off the side wall, we hit head-on with a mighty crash. We were now in calm water and I was able to reverse and steer into the lock. The only word from the lock-keeper was: "What happened there then?" No-one spoke. We were all too shocked. But I think we were all quietly thanking the people who had donated money towards *Tyseley*'s refurbishment, particularly her new bottom. She survived the crash with only a split fender, a few broken glasses and plates, and some spilt oil to show for it. The "old" *Tyseley* would, I fear, not have fared so well – some of her rivets would have sheared, her ceiling would probably have collapsed and she may even have sunk. It's a frightening thought. So, if anyone out there has any thoughts on how you gain entrance to Limehouse without endangering both craft and crew, please let me have them.

At the end of June, Shelly our fundraising administrator, had left to live in France. Lynne had all the right experience, particularly in marketing, to fill her place. She decided to give up commuting to Leeds and join the Mikron team. Shelly had been with us for two-and-a-half years and had worked with great enthusiasm and skill, committed to the quality of our work and its value to the communities we serve. Lynne had the daunting task of looking at our marketing brief, as well as continuing the search for further funding and sponsorship.

At the November AGM, it was agreed by our Council of Management that we should go for broke – mount two productions and restore the Company size back to four. The second part of our *Traveller's Fare Project* would examine the problems of people-moving – private and public transport, rural and urban. We would also revive our vastly popular show, *Beer Street*, which would be revised and updated to reflect the latest crises in the pub trade and the brewing industry. We were able to plan all this because of a sizeable donation from the Esmée Fairbairn Charitable Trust. Only 16% of our income was now coming from funding – an intolerable situation, when we have to rely so much on the generosity of our sponsors and on trusts. One of Lynne's tasks was to persuade the funding bodies of our worth. Some ammunition had been provided by the audience survey we had carried out this year. For instance, 40% of our audiences on the Waterways Tour and over 30% on the Autumn Tour were new to Mikron. Although we had many very loyal regulars, more and more people of all ages were being introduced to us every year.

30

LOOKING FORWARD

The world seemed to survive the entry into the twenty-first century and the predicted collapse of our computer systems, our videos, fridges and pets did not occur. After the universal hangover, life went on pretty much as before. Mikron has moved into its twenty-ninth year and we are all looking forward to celebrating the thirtieth birthday.

The refurbishment of *Tyseley* was completed in the spring by Tim Leech and his team. The final flourish was the superb lettering and decorations by Tony Lewery. We have had yet another Thames tideway incident; this time, the engine failed when we were travelling upstream on a flood tide, and we had to be rescued by the Port of London Harbour Master's launch. The repair cost £2,000 and again we have had to put out an appeal for funds.

The second part of our *Traveller's Fare Project*, *Don't Start From Here*, has touched a nerve with the public. Everyone, it seems, has a "travel disaster" story to tell, and our show features the nightmare journeys of two people trying to meet. *Beer Street* is also going down very well, and our audience figures and collections are both well up. It's also great to have Ed Harcourt and Liz Eves back with us this year. Their experience of boating and their acting skills have proved a tremendous asset. We have also welcomed Anna Winslet, who is married to Ed and proving to be very popular with our audiences. Vashti has taken some time out from Mikron. Her work for the Company has grown in confidence over the years, and we very much hope that sooner or later she will perform with us again.

Show sponsorship is staying very buoyant but our funding problems remain. The right noises are being made about small-scale and community theatre but, for the time being, they remain mere noises. It is, I think, being recognised that live theatre in small, intimate surroundings has an important part to play in the world of the arts and leisure. There is nothing like a live performance to stir the soul. Although it may appear that, by surfing the net, you are part of a wonderful global village, in essence it is a lonely and solitary experience. You are never alone at a Mikron show (even though, on odd occasions you have been one of six!). I may sound like a Luddite

LOOKING FORWARD

(I may even be a Luddite – after all, they were a group of hardworking people trying to protect their skilled jobs and their livelihood), but all I am saying is that there is a place for everything – books, theatre, cinema, television, the internet. Don't let's abandon one thing in preference to anything else. This is what has happened to our transport systems – one form replacing another. Out went packhorses, in came canals. Out went canals, in came railways. In came roads, out (mostly thanks to Dr Beeching) went railways. The realisation is finally dawning that we need all methods of transport, and we need them to be integrated. Some passenger and freight traffic needs to be transferred to rail and water, and the systems need to be linked. Will it happen? I would like to think so, but it will take time and commitment.

It is pleasing to note that, in the Government's White Paper, *Waterways for Tomorrow*, the commitment to give Freight Facilities Grants for both capital and non-capital costs is clearly stated, and that new road developments are to take proper account of waterway restoration. These proposals, alongside ideas for water transfer and the building of new canals (like the link between the Bedfordshire Ouse and the Grand Union), are encouraging. We have been induced to be hopeful in the past about the proper care of our waterways but, this time perhaps, we will see the right actions taken to preserve and develop one of our most important national assets. So Mikron looks forward optimistically to the future. We have proved our staying power. We have proved we are not a "gimmick". The range and standard of our work continues to grow and, as long as there is an audience out there wanting to see us, we shall continue to service that need.

What about myself? I am sitting writing this in the garden of my canalside cottage. It is peaceful. Soon, it will be busier. The Huddersfield Narrow Canal, the 'impossible restoration', is due to re-open throughout its length in May 2001. Back in 1979, when we first moved to Marsden, the locals used to scoff at the idea of the canal ever being used again. "Best fill it in, lad, and use it as an extra road." We joined the Huddersfield Canal Society, who believed it could be done. Sooner than any of us ever hoped, thanks to the involvement of the local authorities and British Waterways and funding from the Millennium Commission and English Partnerships, the dream is to become a reality. Boats will be toiling up the 42 locks from Huddersfield, (controversially) being towed through Standedge Tunnel, and then descending to Ashton to join the present system at the junction of the Ashton and Peak Forest Canals. It's a great canal with wonderful Pennine scenery and fascinating industrial archaeology. I'm tempted to set up a little tea garden here, and regale the passing boaters with stories of the good old days on the waterways, while they sip their Earl Grey tea and eat a freshly baked scone, generously doused in cream and jam. Tempting, but not that tempting...

I'D GO BACK TOMORROW

I've enjoyed my years with Mikron. I honestly cannot think of anything else I would rather have done (paucity of imagination, maybe) and I hope to be able to contribute to the work of Mikron for several years yet. It's reassuring having Richard as a long-term member of the Company. He is a person of great integrity, who believes in the values I have tried to maintain for Mikron over all these years. He has developed out of all recognition as an actor and has a quirky style of his own, which still remains consistently honest. As tour organiser and leader, he has had to develop the diplomatic skills which Sarah and I learnt, sometimes painfully, in the early years. He is a vital cog in the Mikron wheel. Long may he be with us.

They say that boating and love of the waterways can become obsessive. Trying to keep a small theatre company afloat can sometimes verge on madness. Okay, I confess – I am an obsessive madman. But I've always remembered not to let the bastards grind me down.